Trenches & Camels

Oliver Hogue

Trenches & Camels
Australian Recollections of Gallipoli and the Imperial Camel Corps During the First World War

Trooper Bluegum at the Dardanelles

and

The Cameliers

Oliver Hogue
(Bluegum)

LEONAUR

Trenches & Camels
Australian Recollections of Gallipoli and the Imperial Camel Corps During the First World War
Trooper Bluegum at the Dardanelles
and
The Cameliers
By Oliver Hogue (Bluegum)

FIRST EDITION

First published under the titles
Trooper Bluegum at the Dardanelles
and
The Cameliers

Leonaur is an imprint
of Oakpast Ltd

Copyright in this form © 2014 Oakpast Ltd

ISBN: 978-1-78282-381-0 (hardcover)
ISBN: 978-1-78282-382-7 (softcover)

http://www.leonaur.com

Publisher's Notes

The views expressed in this book are not necessarily those of the publisher.

Contents

Trooper Bluegum at the Dardanelles   7
The Cameliers   163

Trooper Bluegum at the Dardanelles

Contents

Preface	13
A Soldier of the King	17
We Sail Away	23
The First Fight	28
In Egypt Still	34
Heroes of April 25	38
Light-Hearted Australians	46
At the Dardanelles	51
Anzac	59
Stories That Will Never Die	65
To Drive Back the Turk	71
War Vignettes	76
"George"	80
"Robbo"	85
"Come and Die"	90
The Bombs	96
Aeroplanes	100
"Padre"	105

"Stunts"	108
Lonesome Pine	113
Lucky Escapes	122
The Church Militant	126
Sergeants Three	131
Mail Day	135
Reinforcements	139
Shell Green	142
The Anzac V.C.'s	147
The Final Phase	152

Dedicated
To
All the Braves
Who fought for Australia and the Empire in the Great War; The Dead who yet live, And the Living who bear their Battle scars upon them, or, scatheless, thank God for His Mercy.

*When cannons are roaring and bullets are flying,
The lad that seeks honour must never fear dying.*

Preface

Among the legacies, good and evil, tragic and inspiring, which the Great War of Nations is destined to hand down to posterity, one of the most valuable and permanent in its influence will be the literature which this Armageddon will have brought forth. In that fountain of knowledge the world will have command of vast stores of intellectual treasure—History, Poetry, the Drama, Philosophy, Fiction—which will continue to fascinate, to appal, to instruct, so long as books are read and the crimes, the virtues, the calamities and follies of mankind are subjects of human interest.

Such a literature, sanctified by the blood of millions of heroes—the world's best manhood—and by sacrifices and sufferings that have literally staggered humanity, will comprehend and crystallize events, compared with which all former world-cataclysms will seem but passing ripples on the ocean of life.

While in its inception and progress this greatest breach of the world's peace has exhibited a section of mankind as hardly at all removed from fiends incarnate, it has also shown men inspired by the highest virtues and striving for the loftiest ideals; and it has produced women only a little lower than the angels. Thus we seem to see, in all its naked deformities as well as in its beauty and majesty, the very soul of nations.

Not to "the future historian," but to whole battalions of historians will it fall to relate the tragic story of this mighty conflict, to pass judgment on the guilty authors of it, while giving to valour and the champions of right their due. They will have ample material to work upon, and they should have little difficulty in sifting out from the mass of evidence before them that which is true from that which is false, certainly as to the real instigators of the rupture.

As to the conduct and prosecution of this war of big battles, the fighting over (and under) thousands of miles of land and ocean, and in the air, the work of the armies of war correspondents has been, on the whole, worthy of the highest traditions of that dangerous class of literary work. In many respects it has even surpassed that of the great war chroniclers of the past, from Russell and Forbes onwards, who have shed lustre on British and foreign journalism. The old race of war correspondents has passed away, but their spirit survives. A new school has been founded. They who graduate in it must accommodate themselves to new conditions of warfare, wherein the Censor plays his part.

To the work of these writers the historians of the war will be largely indebted for their material in relating the operations of the opposing hosts. The private letters of soldiers throw a clear light on minor phases of the engagements in which they took part. These provide intensely interesting reading, too often of a painfully absorbing kind, their authors the eyewitnesses of and actors in the scenes they describe.

The *Trooper Bluegum* contributions to the literature of the war were written for and have appeared in the *Sydney Morning Herald*. They are the work of a Sydney native, a trained journalist, who for the time gave up a responsible position on the literary staff of that journal to enlist as a trooper and serve at the front. As a military writer his reputation had been well on in the making when General Sir Ian Hamilton, a few years ago, came to Australia to inspect the Commonwealth Forces. Here came his chance as a military critic and descriptive writer on training operations. For his insight into the manoeuvres and sham fight engagements of our troops, and his descriptions in the *Sydney Morning Herald* of the important movements under Sir Ian Hamilton's observation, the future "Trooper Bluegum" earned the special commendation of that distinguished British general. From the rank of trooper the author of these sketches speedily rose in the service, obtained a commission, and, as second lieutenant, was chosen orderly to colonel (afterwards brigadier-general) Ryrie, commander of the Second Light Horse Brigade. Soon after landing at the scene of operations at Gallipoli, he was promoted to first lieutenant.

It was just before Christmas, close on five months after war was declared, that the Expeditionary Force which included General Ryrie's brigade sailed from Sydney. Nearly the whole of Trooper Bluegum's descriptions of the operations in the Anzac sphere were written in dugouts between intervals of the fighting, often with shells screaming overhead, shrapnel bursting, and bullets flying about him.

A feature of the descriptions in this book is the clear light thrown on the rollicking yet unconquerable spirit of the Australian soldier in action, on his never-failing good humour and love of fun even in the face of death in any form, his amenableness to discipline, his cheerful, patient endurance of hardship, and his fine contempt of danger whenever and wherever confronting him. Here is seen the Australian (his New Zealand brother in all respects his exact prototype) in the full integrity of his young manhood.

Whence came these qualities in a branch of an immortal race bred to peaceful pursuits? The analytical psychologist may not unprofitably try his hand at explaining. The root principle is that the fighting spirit which to the astonishment of the whole world, flashed out on Gaba Tepe heights, was in the blood of the race, fostered in the schools, on the playgrounds, and sustained by undying attachment to the great Empire whose flag is the symbol for all that free men hold dear.

This book is a narrative, with sidelights and commentary, of the operations of the Australian Imperial Expeditionary Forces, from the training encampment at Holdsworthy to the time when, chastened but still unconquered, the heroic band of Australians, or rather the remnant that was left of them, returned from Anzac after the most glorious failure in the annals of war.

J. A. Hogue.

Sydney,
December, 1915.

Anzac Cove Gallipoli

Chapter 1

A Soldier of the King

"Trooper Bluegum, you're next."

I stepped forward. A hundred volunteers had been marched down from Victoria Barracks, Sydney, and were undergoing the riding test prior to being drafted into the Australian Light Horse.

"Mount and ride," said the sergeant.

I leaped on the bare back of a hog-maned colt. Three other candidates were already mounted waiting for the signal. One was a Sydney "bushman" and was obviously nervous. The other two were bushmen from Riverina and the Hunter River and they grinned confidently.

"Cross this flat," continued the sergeant; "leap the bog, jump the sod wall, gallop to that marker, and return."

Some fool orderly gave my mount a crack over the back with a rope and away we galloped. The flat was easy, though I had not ridden bare-backed for some time. The bog offered no resistance and we leaped the sod wall neck and neck. Then the horses wanted to bolt and they took some stopping. Anyhow, the first half of the test was safely through.

The Sydney bushman was looking more at ease. The others grinned expansively. "That's dead easy," said the man from Narrandera. "Call that a riding test?"

The return signal was given, and the quartet started off. All went well till the water jump loomed ahead. Here half a dozen yelling orderlies were posted to spur on the chargers to the leap. The three bushmen cleared the obstacle with hardly a splash, but disaster was in store for the City bushman. Right on the brink the horse stopped dead and the hapless rider was shot with catapultic force head first into the bog, amid roars of merriment from the assembled army. We three countrymen "passed," were promptly marshalled with the horsemen, and marched to the doctor's for medical examination. The City bushman was sent to "the gravel-crushers."

In a huge marquee in Rosebery Park were a score of virile young Australians stripped for the fray. Sun-tanned bushmen they were for the most part, lean and wiry, with muscles rippling over their naked shoulders. Splendid specimens—strong but not too heavy, rarely topping thirteen stone, for all the heavier men had been sent to the infantry. But these were ideal Light Horsemen.

"Bluegum forward."

I stood, and the sergeant ran the tape over me: Weight, 11 stone; height, 5 feet ten; chest, 37, expanded 41; age 34; beauty spots and identification marks, none; eyes, brown; hair, brown; religion, Presbyterian.

Then the doctor got busy; tapping here, sounding there, finally with a word of approval sending me over to the sight specialist. There was a jumble of letters of various sizes set before me, and finally, with a score of others satisfactory in wind and limb, I was sent on to the adjutant. My name, age, occupation, next-of-kin, and other essential details were recorded. Then we were lined up to swear allegiance.

On the flat the volunteers were still doing the riding test, with hundreds of onlookers keenly enjoying it. Each time some luckless aspirant for fame and glory was precipitated into the bog the crowd roared with delight, and when he emerged, mud-bespattered and crestfallen, the hilarity of the bushmen knew no bounds. Pointed advice was hurled at the failures, and they were urged to join the "gravel-crushers," which most of them did.

For a couple of hours the fun continued, and with the end of the day another hundred rough-riders were drawn up, passed and enlisted ready for anything and everything. One by one we went forward and took the oath.

The sun was just setting over the western rim of dear old Sydney town when my turn came. The clouds were all gold and rose and amethyst, and the whole scene was as peaceful as could be. The First Light Horse Regiment—in fine fettle, ready at a moment's notice to sail for Europe—cantering gaily back to camp, reminded us that the nation was in a state of war, that the empire was engaged in a life and death struggle, and that on the issue of the great conflict depended the fate of Australia. And we of the Sixth Regiment were to make good the "wastage of war."

So, solemnly, I kissed the Book and swore this oath:

I, James Bluegum, swear that I will well and truly serve our Sovereign Lord the King in the Australian Imperial Force from September 1914 until the end of the war, and a further period of four months thereafter, unless sooner lawfully discharged, dismissed, or removed therefrom; and that I will resist His Majesty's enemies and cause His Majesty's peace to be kept and maintained; and that I will in all matters appertaining to my service faithfully discharge my duty according to law. So help me God.

I was a Soldier of the King!

Once more we were lined up and marched away to the quartermaster. Each man was given a waterproof sheet, a pair of blankets, a knife, fork, spoon, tin plate, and pannikin. We were to form part of the Second Light Horse Brigade, and being minus tents we were relegated to the stables. We raided the straw store, made beds, and lay upon them.

It was not ours to go with the first lot of heroes to take part in the Great War. Most of us had waited till the Germans got within cannon shot of Paris. Then we "butted in." We were selected to supply the wastage—that was all. If we could not be the first in the firing-line, it was something to know that we would take the place of the men who were killed or wounded—all of us, the man from Narrandera, in Riverina, the man from Hunter River, the men from outback everywhere, Trooper Bluegum among them, all whistling merrily "Soldiers of the King, my Boys!"

We of the Light Horse started with many things in our favour. We reckoned we could ride as well as, if not better than, any body of men in the world, for we could ride almost as soon as we could walk. Also, we were pretty good shots. Many were Rifle Club men. All had done a bit of shooting in the bush, for dingoes and kangaroos and wallabies are not yet extinct in Australia. So half of our lesson was learned before we started. The drill and the discipline only remained. We did not mind the drill, but the discipline was irksome.

It is a recognized flaw in our military make-up, this want of discipline. Sir Ian Hamilton, when he visited Australia in 1914, found the colonial compulsory trainees much more amenable to discipline than he expected. But the militia are caught young. We of the Expeditionary Force were a little bit too old to rid ourselves readily of the habits of the bush, and adapt ourselves to the rigid routine of military life.

But perhaps it would come in time.

It is a strange world, my masters! I have before me as I write a copy of a Sydney newspaper, dated May 21, 1914, giving the report and recommendations made by General Sir Ian Hamilton in Australia, and it is headed "If War Came." And there I read of the Australian infantry:

> I have now seen the greater portion of the Australian Infantry, and I wish very much I could transplant 10,000 of these young soldiers to Salisbury Plain. They would do the croakers good and make them less frightened of other nations, who have no overseas children getting ready to lend them a hand. The majority of the non-commissioned officers and men are still very young, but they are full of intelligence and grit. On at least two occasions I have seen brigades tested severely, once by heat and heavy marching, the other time by floods and mud. In each case the men made light of their trying experiences, treating them as an excellent joke.

It was of the same men that the same man was to write but a few short months afterwards:

> They have created for themselves an imperishable record of military virtue.

But it is a long, long way to ———. Day after day we performed the tiresome evolutions of troop and squadron drill on foot, for the horses were not yet ready. We mastered the mysteries of sections right, form troop, form squadron column; then day after day we engaged in rifle drill—"stand at ease," "attention," "slope arms," "present arms," till our arms ached. Then we fixed our bayonets, and in fancy bayoneted thousands of *"kultured"* Germans.

But it was not till the horses came that we really felt like Light Horsemen.

> *Let the sailor tell of the roaring gale,*
> *Or the blue waves' rippling laughter;*
> *Let the soldier sing of the sabre swing*
> *And the laurels of glory after;*
> *There's a melody in the changeful sea,*
> *A charm in the battle's thunder,*
> *But sweeter than those the bushman knows*
> *Is the bound of a good horse under.*

It was not child's play tackling those horses. Some of the kind-hearted station folk in the backblocks had sent down some wild warrigals of the West; bucking brumbies that beat the band; old outlaws off the grass that the station hands could never master. But Colonel Cox ("Fighting Charlie" we called him) had in his command some of the crack rough-riders of Australia. And it was a joy to see these men tackle the outlaws. There were Crouch of Wagga, McDonald of Barrington, Whiteley of Wellington, Bullock of Melbourne, Sievewright of Gunnedah, Kennedy of Gloucester, Rex Moffatt of Goulburn, Harry Heath of Moree, and a score of others. Nearly every man in the regiment could sit a buck, or puff nonchalantly at his pipe while his mount pig-rooted merrily. So when the wild horses were led forth there were hundreds volunteering for the honour of riding the rebels. One after another the horses were saddled up, and while the regiment cheered itself hoarse, there was enacted again and again the old-time struggle for mastery. There were plunging and reefing and rooting and sidling and rearing and bucking, as the panting chargers swung this way and that in vain endeavour to dislodge the riders. But the bush boys stuck to the saddles as the Old Man of the Sea stuck to Sinbad the Sailor, and one after another the bucking brumbies were broken and led away.

Then came the first mounted parade. A squadron of Scots Greys or Life Guards might have kept better line; they might probably have wheeled with more order and precision for each troop here had a few half-broken colts prancing and dancing all over the shop, but—well, somebody said that these troops would compare favourably with any body of mounted infantry in the world. Certain it is that when, one fine day, the officer commanding, Colonel Cox, accompanied by the Brigadier, Colonel Ryrie, made a careful inspection of the whole regiment, every one from the officer commanding down was satisfied. And certain it is that we sang the Australian Light Horse war song with unusual enthusiasm—

Sound the good old bugle, boys,
Let's sing another song,
Sing it with a spirit
That will send the troops along;
Sing it as we'll sing it
When we're twenty thousand strong,
When we go marching through Germany!

Hurrah! Hurrah! We're off to Germany!
Hurrah! Hurrah! the A.L.H. are we!
We're rounding up the bushmen from the
Darling to the sea
And we'll go marching through Germany!

How the bushmen shouted
When they heard the joyful sound,
"'Fighting Charlie's' going to lead,
So pass the word around;
Australia wants another batch
Of bushmen to astound
Poor old Kaiser Bill of Germany!"

Chapter 2

We Sail Away

"Who's the Jonah?" That was mild.

"Curse our luck!" That was moderate.

But when Trooper Newman said, "To hell with the ship!" most of us felt that he showed a proper appreciation of the position.

For days and days we had ploughed our way across the Indian Ocean, and, as the long leagues in front joined their comrades behind, we felt that we were getting farther and farther from sunny New South Wales. But we were steering straight for Ceylon, and looking forward with keen anticipation to a few days of the picturesque Orient. Some of the impressionable young subalterns were singing "Cingalee, Cingalee, I have lost my heart to a Cingalee." All of us for the last day or two had been taking station on the forecastle-head, shading our eyes and gazing into the misty horizon for the first glimpse of the enchanted isle.

But alas for hopes unfulfilled! Ceylon's spicy breezes, after all, were not to fan our fevered brows, neither were Cingalese to minister to our need with "tea in the morning, tea in the evening, tea in the afternoon." Early in the morning of January 12 we got word that a special squadron of three ships was to be detached from the main fleet, and with Colonel Ryrie in command, steam straight to Aden. So we stood on deck and swore unrestrainedly.

However, there was still corn in Egypt, and we would be the first to get there. Besides, there was quite a chance that there was something doing—a *dervish* expedition or an Arab raid might be on, and we would have the laugh at the other chaps if we could have first smack at the unspeakable Turk. So by the time the bugle sounded for the usual inspection, we were all in high good humour again. The three liners swung out from the convoy and, cheering a farewell, were soon steaming westward. One after another the transports dipped down under the horizon, and soon a few grey smudges on the rim of the ocean were all that remained to remind us of the fleet.

We had seen no land since leaving Australia. It seemed such a long time. So when, a couple of days later, somebody shouted "Land-ho," we rushed to the nearest post of advantage. Far away to eastward, like a green pimple on the blue face of the waters, was a tiny little island. In an hour we were abreast of it—Minikoi, surely one of the islands of the blessed; how green it looked after the everlasting blue of the Indian Ocean; from end to end it was covered with cocoa-nut palm. A long line of snow-white surf beat upon the sandy shore. Gleaming in the tropical sun was the lighthouse—a silent sentinel. And in the offing were a score of picturesque canoes, and dhows, with brown hempen sails, managed by gaudily-dressed islanders, who seemed rather annoyed that the transports did not stop and purchase their fruit-offerings.

Passing by the rugged Socotra, we soon sighted the mountainous southern coast of Arabia, and by midday on January 20 we were focussing our binoculars on the picturesque gate of the Indian Ocean, Aden. Curious it is how Britain has secured all the great strategical points of the world—Gibraltar, Suez, Aden, Singapore, Thursday Island, the Cape of Good Hope, and the rest. And one has only to see Aden, with its rocky peaks piercing the skyline, to realize how strong it is, and how futile would be any effort to capture it. For all the defences of Aden seem to be hewn out of solid granite.

No sooner had we got anchored in the harbour than the *Suevic* was surrounded by swarms of boats, in which were crowded Asiatics of all descriptions yelling like demons in wild anxiety to sell their wares. Then the colliers came alongside and proceeded to coal. Scores of thin, undersized, but wiry Arabs did the work, and as they loaded the bunkers they kept up a perpetual yelling and singing, and the weird cacophony lasted all through the night.

Aden is a curious mixture of the Orient and the Occident. In the streets silent Arabs stalk along with camels, and Europeans buzz around in automobiles. One section of the port belongs to the Asiatics; the other is all Western. Arab dhows float across the harbour and steam tugs scurry hither and yon. One section of the town has thatched roofs; the other is all galvanized iron. And one of the natives sang us "Songs of Araby." They yelled harshly for *baksheesh* all the while. Clad in their own coloured loin cloths, or in discarded khaki tunics from the Force, they were a motley tatterdemalion crowd. Here East and West met—but did not mingle.

We had had no word of news for weeks. So we eagerly searched for the newspapers, and demanded news of the outer world. The war was still on. The Allies were more than holding their own. Here was news indeed!—news such as *The Transport Trumpeter* (published aboard the *Suevic*) had never heard of. Yet we loved that little paper of ours on the transport—"a little thing, but our own." If it lacked news it did not lack reporters whose imagination made up for the deficiency. We were all reporters for *The Transport Trumpeter*. Even I. And I am wondering to this day about a certain curious coincidence connected with one of my painstaking efforts. I wrote on December 28, 1914, a skit on Lissauer's "Hymn of Hate," and Arthur Adam's reply to it—"My Friend, Remember." A month later I got the Sydney *Bulletin*, and there I saw almost exactly the same article with the same excerpts from each poem. They were probably written on the same day, a thousand miles or so apart. You who delve into the mysterious, will you explain?

******

Egypt! What memories! What life here! What a quest we have set out upon! What Alexanders are we!

I feel the blood coursing through my veins as I have never felt it before. I live in the present, but the past stands up before me. Dead kings and emperors pass in endless succession. Libyans and Ethiopians pass by, Assyrians and Macedonians, Babylonians and Persians, Romans, Arabs, Turks and Mamelukes—and French and British. Great names are sprinkled over the pages of Egypt, from Menes, the first king, and Rameses the Second, down to the present day. Nebuchadnezzar and Alexander the Great, Constantine, Saladin and Napoleon, Mohammed Ali and Kitchener have all left their mark on the Nile Delta. What history! and here are we—soldiers of King George V, from Australia—treading this historic ground, making new history. Nebuchadnezzar knew us not. Constantine never dreamed—and they used to dream dreams in those days—that from a land he knew not of would one day come armed men marching on the wonderful city he built.

Nor did I, nor did any of us, know it—well, not yet.

I know what it means to see the blush clouds beating the night shades back in the van of a golden morning, but there is a quality of richness about the sunrises of Egypt that Australia lacks. Egypt has the glint of gold, the cloud ridges of rosy red, the blaze of amethyst and opal. So also has the Australian sky. But Australia has no pyramids. The first beams of the sun in this land tip the cones of the age-old pyramids, and soon these drab giants shine like molten copper. Then the sky turns all gold, and the scene is duplicated in the placid bosom of the ancient Nile, which skirts our camp. In the murky distance the desert is shrouded in a misty haze which has the same blue that one sees in the distance on the Blue Mountains of New South Wales, but once the sun is fairly above the horizon, the brilliant transformation scene dissolves itself into a glaring white light that lasts till sunset. Then the morning's glory is re-enacted with softer tones and a riot of colour that I can never describe.

Then, as the Pyramids of Gizeh were due west from Ma'adi, we always saw these giant triangles sharply silhouetted against the red horizon. They looked like little toy tents, yet when alongside them their magnitude staggered us.

The day was so hot that helmets were necessary. Some "went down" under the fierce rays of the sun, but there were some with us who said it was not hot at all. They spoke of the sun-baked Western Plains. They spoke of Bourke. They spoke of Northern Queensland. But they wore helmets, nevertheless.

Yet was Ma'adi, for all its heat, a joy to the senses. If we had the everlasting desert wilderness on one side, we also had the oasis of Ma'adi on the other. The irrigationist has caused the desert hereabout to blossom as the rose, and Ma'adi is like an English village, with gracious gardens and green, luscious fields and rippling canals.

I have spoken of the blue of the desert haze that is like that of the Blue Mountains. And here and there one finds other touches of old Australia. I went out one day to Sir Alexander Baird's beautiful mansion near Zeitoun, and there I saw some fine old gums and wattles; and it just felt like home.

And the people, how kind they all were! Even the shopkeepers did all they could to make us feel at home. "Special Australian Shop," "Australian Soldiers' Rendezvous"—signs like these met us at every turn. Especially grateful did we feel for the warning one Cairo shopkeeper gave us: "Don't go elsewhere to be cheated, Australians. Come here!" Nor shall we ever forget the laborious days and nights which that shopkeeper who put out the sign must have spent in mastering our language—"English and French spoken; Australian understood."

Truth to tell, the Australian soldiers were as a shower of gold to the thirsty Cairo traders. They all loved the Australians. We scattered money far and wide—till we had none left. We threw *piastres* to the winds—thinking nothing of them, they were such little coins—till we had none left. From morning till night we distributed largess. It was *baksheesh* everywhere and all the time. Whichever way we turned we found somebody dangling something in front of our eyes—ready to sacrifice it for our sake. Even Trooper Newman, who previously had expressed his best wishes to the ship, comes up to me with a gaudy handkerchief he has just bought for ten *piastres*. It has King George in one corner, Kitchener in another, French in another, Jellicoe in another, and generals and admirals and dukes and earls all round it. "It may be the only chance I'll get," says he, "of poking my nose into high society."

Chapter 3

The First Fight

I am living Egypt, living. . . . Your pyramids and your mosques and your old Nile can talk to me of things long past and gone, and I shall listen with interest to what they have to say, but I would rather be a living dog of an Egyptian than the dead lion of an Egyptian king—I would rather be a moving, talking native dressed in garish clothes than a prince of the House of Rameses, *sans* eyes, *sans* ears, *sans* tongue, in the shrivelled brown form of a mummy.

For there is something about these living ones that brings the dead to life. Sometimes when I look into their eyes I seem to see a strange, mysterious light in them—a light that never was on sea or land. It is then that I think of the things these people have seen in the forty centuries of which Napoleon spoke. I don't believe in magic, but I have seen strange things—things that make me remember that the magicians of Pharaoh were able to turn their rods into serpents!

There came one day a very wise Egyptian—one whom I know as a Freemason—and he gave a valuable scarab, mounted in a gold ring, to Major Lynch. There was no doubt that the wise man valued it, and there is no doubt that he left an impression on Major Lynch. It is a talisman and a protection to the owner, but it has deadly powers. Nothing can harm the owner so long as he has it in his possession, and the owner can shrivel up an enemy by merely pointing at him and muttering incantations—just as the Northern Territory natives in Australia can *will* an enemy to die by pointing a bone at him. Major Lynch lost no time in putting the scarab to the test. There was a very troublesome native who used to bother him several times a day about things that don't matter, and the day after the wise Egyptian had made his presentation the major pointed at the native and muttered a powerful Australian incantation. Since then the native has not been seen.

A *dragoman* wanted to sell me some scarabs.

"You like fine scarab?"

"No scab here," said I, "all good Unionists."

"Not scab. Scarab—good scarab."

"Oh!"

"Beautiful scarab. Very precious."

"Ah!"

"I buy them for English officer; beautiful scarab. Now he go to Suez Canal. I sell cheap."

"Very cheap?"

"Yes, very cheap. Sell now, lose plenty money, sir."

"How much?"

"Five pounds."

"Ah! Is it really worth five *piastres?*"

"*Piastres!* Ach! No, no, no! Five *pounds!*"

"Five pounds a dozen!"

"No, no, no! Five pounds for one beautiful scarab."

"Ha ha!"

"Not ha! ha! It is three thousand years old! Time of Rameses II."

"Too old. Got any nice *new* ones?"

"No, no. Not *new.* Old—very valuable—three thousand years!"

"Too old. Show me a new one."

"You no understand. Very old, very valuable, out of tombs in pyramid."

"Any more there?"

"No more—all gone."

"Oh, well I oughtn't to take them from you."

"Yes, you take. I sell you for five pounds."

"Not me."

"Yes, you. *Four* pounds!"

"Try again."

"Three pounds ten."

"Once more."

"Two pounds ten. Finish."

"No business; *Imshi.*"

Then the old man went away, muttering angrily in his beard because I would not pay three golden sovereigns for a little stone that looked like a petrified beetle. Even if it had been genuine—even if it *was* three thousand years old—I would have thought it a shame for him to take the money. But the reputation these "gyppies" have for faking antiquities and curios made me sceptical. In the Cairo Museum are genuine thousand-year-old relics from the tombs and pyramids, and the natives copy them and sell the replicas as the genuine article.

When I was leaving the museum one afternoon a *dragoman* shuffled up to me in a mysterious kind of way and thrust an antiquated statuette into my hand. "Five shillings," he whispered hoarsely. He wanted me to think it genuine, and, I suppose, stolen. (Even honest people don't mind being "receivers" when they can get a genuine relic of antiquity cheap.) I examined it with the concentrated gaze of a connoisseur in Egyptology, scratched it with my knife, and then exclaimed, "Bah, rubbish! One *piastre*." And the old sinner cried, "Yes, yes," and put his hand out eagerly for the money.

And all this time we were "training for the front." We did not know when we were likely to leave for the front, nor what front it would be, but already some of the Australians and New Zealanders had been in a fight. That was before we came. Egypt had been "invaded"; there had been a fight at El Kantara, some prisoners had been taken, and then the invaders turned their heads north and eastward, folding their tents, like the Arabs they are, and silently stealing away. The Great Invasion of which Kaiser Wilhelm had dreamed for months had simply petered out.

I am no historian—I write only of the little things I care about—but I would be no Australian if I failed to mention this invasion which some of the Australians helped to stamp out. It was almost inconceivable that the "thorough-going, methodical" Germans could have started an army of 75,000 men across the desert, sent only 25,000 of them into action, and then decamped. But that is what happened.

Although the Australians and New Zealanders saw but little of the actual fighting, they played no unimportant part in the scheme of things. The seeds of disloyalty and discord had been assiduously sown by German spies and agents all over Egypt. The so-called Nationalist party was intriguing to oust the British and facilitate the entry of the Turks. It was confidently anticipated by the German wire-pullers that the moment the invaders appeared on the Canal the Egyptians and Arabs would rise *en masse* and drive the British into the sea. Drastic measures were taken months ahead for dealing with the English residents in Cairo and elsewhere. Everything seemed to be going nicely for the plotters. Obvious signs of disaffection were noticed all over Lower Egypt. The British were so few; the German-Arab-Turkish combination was so strong. It only wanted a favourable opportunity to fire the train.

Then the Australians arrived.

There may be a tendency on our part to exaggerate the influence of the Australian and New Zealand troops on the Egyptian situation; but there is not the slightest doubt that the presence of 50,000 Colonial troops had a wonderfully steadying effect on the disaffected natives. They suddenly became loyal again. All talk of sedition ceased. The best-laid schemes of the German plotters went "agley."

One could not help contrasting this large force from Australia and New Zealand—a force that was to be doubled and trebled ere long—with the little force of 500 men which William Bede Dalley, Australian orator and patriot, sent from New South Wales to the Sudan just thirty years before. It spoke not only of the wonderful growth in population of Britain's Dominions of the South, but it was a living proof that the years had only served to cement the bonds of love and loyalty that bind the grand old Motherland to her Oversea Dominions. The rising in India, the intention of the Australians to proclaim their independence the moment when Britain found herself in peril—where were they? Where now was the "disintegration" of the British Empire which the German emperor and his war lords had so confidently predicted?

With Cairo and the Nile safe, General Wilson was able to deal effectively with the invaders. Towards the latter end of January, Northern Sinai was overrun with them. From a couple of captured *Shawishes* of the 75th Turkish Regiment I learned that the staff arrangements by the German officers were excellent. Everything had been foreseen and provided for—or nearly everything. Water was available at each stage of the journey across the desert. Many boats and pontoons were dragged by oxen and camels along the caravan route from Kosseima, El Arish, and Nekl. A few six-inch guns were also transported to the Canal. To supplement the Turkish force on its south-westerly march all the pilgrims and Bedouins met with were pressed into service and rifles were given to them.

It was on the morning of January 28 that the initial conflict took place at Kantara. A reconnoitring party from Bir El Dueidar attacked the British outposts but was repulsed, our losses being only one officer and one soldier killed and five Gurkhas wounded. Further south, near Suez, a nocturnal demonstration by the Turks merely served to prove the alertness of the defenders, though unfortunately two of our air scouts met with disaster. Their aeroplane came down outside our lines, and on returning on foot they were both shot dead by our own

Indian patrols. The pity of it.

The main attack developed on the night of February 2-3, and a determined effort was made to cross the Canal at several points. A number of boats, each carried by forty men, were silently hurried to the front. A small force attacked Kantara, but after losing twenty-one killed, twenty-five wounded and thirty-six prisoners, they decamped. Later on they renewed the attack from the south, with no more success, for they lost eight men killed, whilst a number were wounded. Our losses were four killed and twenty-four wounded.

Meantime a more vigorous assault was made at Toussoum to pierce the line just before daybreak. An infantry attack was followed by artillery fire, and under cover of the maxims a more determined effort was made to cross the Canal by means of boats, rafts, and pontoons. A shrapnel shell smashed the first boat and killed several Turks. Other boats followed and met with a similar fate—most of their occupants were killed or drowned. Not a single boat crossed. About twenty-five men swam across, however. Four penetrated the lines and escaped to Cairo, where they subsequently surrendered. The rest were captured.

Serapeum was attacked about the same time, and at dawn the battle raged along the Canal for about two and a half miles. H.M.S. *Hardinge* moved up and down the Canal, responding to the enemy's artillery. Two Turkish shells landed on our warships, and ten men were wounded. For a couple of hours the battle raged, and although the Turks outnumbered the defenders at Toussoum by ten to one, they were repulsed all along the line.

Further north, at Ismailia Ferry, the enemy entrenched 800 yards away, and a battalion of Turkish infantry (entrenched overnight) opened fire. But they did little damage. They blazed away all day, and our casualties were only six men wounded. Then we drove them off.

So the great Germano-Turkish attack resolved itself into simultaneous onslaughts at Kantara, Ismailia, Toussoum and Serapeum; and when all attacks had failed the guns of the British and French cruisers and the shore artillery harried the enemy in their retreat and added considerably to their losses. Our casualties were only about twenty killed and 100 wounded. The invaders lost more than 420 men killed and over 700 prisoners. Their total casualties—killed, wounded, and prisoners—were computed at 3,000.

Yet it was a small thing, after all—a small thing when I look back and think of all that has happened since. But it was the first fight in the Great War that Australians and New Zealanders had a hand in.

We of the Light Horse were not in it. We saw the Turks away on the rim of the desert horizon; but the enemy attacked where we were not. We never fired a shot.

Chapter 4

In Egypt Still

Yes, we were biding our time in Cairo; and I am telling no secrets when I say that the Australians swore terribly in Cairo. We had left our happy homes in order to take part in the war, and here we were burning our heels on the Egyptian sand—day after day, week after week. No wonder many of us, as we tramped along on a route march to Helwan on the day preceding Good Friday, said we would prefer to be spending the day at the Royal Easter Show in Sydney.

On the right of our line of march lay the Nile with its green strip of verdure on either side, and a dozen pyramids out westward. The day was as hot as a furnace. The mirage seemed to shimmer on the rim of the earth, and horsemen, camels and Bedouins a few miles away seemed to be floating in the air. Like white wings gliding up and down the Nile were the triangular sails of the native *dhows*—wonderfully picturesque, with their tremendous spars that tower into the sky. At old Cairo there was a veritable forest of masts. The rudders of these river boats are huge things, and the noses are painted in gaudy colours, and are always turned up disdainfully, as if they had been bumped against a pier.

You had heard of the Plagues of Egypt; we have seen them, and are able to vouch for the authenticity of the Scriptures. Instead of hot cross buns, Easter brought us a plague of locusts. The entertainment started at about three o'clock in the afternoon and lasted till after sundown. Millions and billions and quadrillions of locusts danced and sang for us. The air was absolutely full of them, darkening the sun—big yellow and brown and black things, mostly about two inches long. They sounded like thousands of whirring wheels, and they dropped on the roofs with a noise like rain. Where they landed they left everything bare as a bone. All along the Nile the "gyppies" turned out and banged tin cans to drive them off. Here was an invasion, if you like! The telegraph wires were black with them—like long beads. Some of the beautiful Ma'adi gardens were quite spoilt. These locusts of Egypt have absolutely no love for the beautiful—in fact, the more beautiful a thing is the more delight do they take in devouring it.

But even a plague of locusts does not last for ever—and Egypt does. Egypt the wonderful! Egypt the kaleidoscopic! No, gentle reader, do not waste your sympathies on us. It was tiresome work, marching, training—training for the front, which for months never seemed to get any nearer, and some of "the boys"—those of them who were "spoiling for a fight," as the saying is—used at times to kick over the traces and paint the town vermilion; but there are compensations in Egypt for all who would seek them. What did it matter that we had no hot cross buns for Easter, no hard-boiled eggs, no ling, no salmon? We had omelettes and quail on toast, and chicken and curry and strawberries (no cream) and oranges and custard and jelly and Turkish coffee and Nile fish and pancakes and fritters and iced butter and beautiful jam and marmalade—and cigars. So we managed to get "a snack," you see. And I know that I, for one, had no desire just then to swap places with any man in Australia.

On Easter Sunday some of us went out to see the Barrage—one of the most wonderful works in Egypt. Mohammed Ali started it to irrigate the Delta, but his engineers made some mistakes and the works were looked upon as a white elephant—until Britain took charge. Wonderful the things that Britain does! A board of eminent engineers examined the whole scheme and decided that it would cost over £2,000,000 to complete it. But a Scotsman came along—Sir Colin Campbell Scott-Moncrieff—and he fixed the whole show up for £1,200,000. Right at the apex of the Delta triangle they have laid out beautiful gardens, with lovely flower-beds, canals and grassy lawns; and it was a treat to rest our tired eyes on the green grass after the everlasting sand, sand, sand of the desert.

It was night when we got back to camp. Oh, those Egyptian nights! The winter cold has gone, and spring is in the air. The nights are fine and fair, clear and cloudless, with the moon pure silver. The reflections in the Nile are just wonderful. The huge date palms stand out sharply from a star-spangled sky that somehow has a tint of green in its blue. One thinks of the Arabian Nights. The very street scenes make one think of them. Motors glide up and down the streets with rich Syrians, Greeks, Egyptians, Italians, Frenchmen and Englishmen, going to the Continental, or to Shepheard's, or to private entertainments. It is a gorgeous splash of colour. They had no motor-cars that I remember in those old Arabian Nights, but the magic of the thing and the colour of it all were surely much the same. And the roads of Egypt—how beautiful they are!—clean and smooth as a billiard table. Are there any finer roads in the whole world than the Mena road and that to Heliopolis? Fifty miles an hour is easy. I sometimes shudder now when I recall the races that we used to have along those roads at night, crying "*Egre! Egre!*"—Faster! Faster!

One night stands out—a gorgeous night—a carnival in honour and aid of brave little Serbia. Kipling says that "*East is east and west is west, and never the twain shall meet*"; but he surely has not seen a Venetian carnival in Cairo, with its intermingling of the progressive Occident and the picturesque Orient. One will always remember that. When the tourists from the West overrun the land of the Pharaohs, as they do once a year, a Venetian *fête* is held at Shepheard's—the social event of the season. Sightseers from England, idle rich from the Continent, plutocrats from America, tourists from the four quarters of the world, all meet and make merry here. This year of grace witnessed a somewhat different spectacle, it is true. It was a polyglot gathering of all nations, to be sure, but the tourist element was wanting.

In the place of the tourists, however, was the "Army of Occupation." Hundreds of officers, British, French, Egyptian, Australian and New Zealand, in smart uniforms, gave striking colour to the scene, which was made additionally picturesque by the vari-coloured silks and satins, scarfs and veils of the ladies. The garden was a blaze of splendour. There were the flags of the nations, there were flowers and palms and purling fountains, mirth and music, lights and laughter, and over all—confetti. All night the air was thick with confetti, like snow falling off a rainbow. Revellers flew hither and thither, flinging it everywhere. Merry maidens threw handfuls of confetti and eyefuls of bold glances at the sun-tanned colonials. There was no respite until the ground was ankle-deep with confetti.

Tired at last of the revelry, we adjourned to the Moorish Hall, and while the orchestra played the ravishing strains of the *barcarolle* we danced the red stars to their death.

Loud explosions in the courtyard sent us rushing forth once more. And then we saw the most wonderful pyrotechnic display in all the world. Without warning, odd corners of the garden burst into a blaze of light. Rockets, Roman candles, Catherine wheels, shooting stars and all the fireworks we loved as youngsters were there in full working order, but ever so many more and ever so much grander than at those "Queen's Birthday" exhibitions which ourselves when young did eagerly frequent. Shall we ever forget that final burst of coloured lights outlining the words "Hurrah for Serbia!" Not *I*. No more than I shall ever forget the deeds of glory of the Serbians.

And I remember another *fête*—the *Grande Fête du 75*, held in the Cairo International Sporting Club's grounds, in honour of the 75 millimetre field gun of the French, and in aid of the sick and wounded soldiers of the "Army of the East," then at the Dardanelles. There was a great crowd present. In the vice-regal stand was a distinguished gathering of generals, consuls, ministers and diplomats. Scores of beautiful French girls, escorted by British officers—by way of emphasising the *Entente Cordiale*, no doubt—meandered amongst the crowd selling commemorative medals. There were military sports by day, and there was a torchlight procession round the arena and through the streets of Cairo by night.

Then we went back to our camp in the desert to wait for the word to "move on." But I will never forget those Egyptian nights . . . and one girl of girls. Tall and stately, like a queen she moved amongst the revellers. The rest of the dancers were just the frame round her picture. . . . We danced. Her blue eyes laughed into mine. . . . And the world has never been the same world since.

CHAPTER 5

Heroes of April 25

Some of the Australians and New Zealanders had already got the call, but we of the Light Horse still waited—growing more and more impatient every day. I have vivid recollections of a captain swearing. I have still more vivid recollections of a certain private's reminiscences. It was generally thought that he had spent some time in hell, or *Booligal*, so familiarly did he speak of the infernal regions. I remember his saying—but no, I will not repeat it.

Chiefly do I remember the riot. It seemed that something must be done to stir the authorities up; and some of the "hot heads" got up a riot in Cairo. They went into Cairo singing "There'll be a hot time in the old town tonight"; and sure enough there was. It was not meant to be quite so hot as it turned out. Things have a way of shaping themselves sometimes. Nobody could tell afterwards exactly how it all happened; but before the night was spent some houses had been burned down, some shots had been fired and some men had been wounded. There were some Australians, some New Zealanders, some Maoris and a few Territorials in it. And it all happened so simply. Some publicans and other sinners presumed to treat the Maoris as "niggers." This was too much for the New Zealanders, and they began to pull some of the furniture out of a public-house, and to make a bonfire of it in the street, the while the Maoris danced a war dance round it.

One or two other bonfires were started. The native police rolled up and kept the crowd back, one of the police inspectors remarking that it would be a good thing for Cairo if a few more of the "dens" were burned down. "I've been wishing for a fire among these rotten tenements for a long time," he said, "and now the fire-engines are coming, and it looks as if they'll be saved again!"

The fire-engine came clattering up the street. The soldiers raided it. In self-defence the firemen repelled the attack with the fire-hose. The soldiers renewed the attack and, reinforcements having arrived, captured the hose and turned it on the firemen, completely routing them. Then they cut the hose up—and the Maoris went on with their "*haka*."

But in the end, of course, law and order had to prevail. Other engines came upon the scene, escorted by a squadron of Territorial dragoons. The soldiers cooled down. The fires were put out. There's a lot more about this Battle of the Wazir, but I cannot tell it.

Not creditable, of course. Not quite the sort of thing they had been sent there for. But human nature is human nature, and a crowd of soldiers is a crowd of soldiers, and bad grog will make the best of soldiers bad, especially in Cairo; and the evil that's in men must come out of them as well as the good. Hence to call the Maoris "niggers"—well, who can blame the New Zealanders for resenting it, and who can blame the Australians for siding with the New Zealanders, or the Territorials for assisting their Oversea brethren, when we have Mr. Asquith's own word for it that "*Who touches them touches us*"? Not creditable!—but human nature—British brotherhood! And high spirits, and the chafing under the monotony of camp life in Egypt! Trooper Bluegum, at all events, long ago forgave them. The same men were among those who were to create for themselves and their country, in the words of General Ian Hamilton, "*An imperishable record of military virtue.*" Many of them are no more. Maoris and all have given their lives cheerfully for their Empire and the sacred cause of Right. Let us remember their virtues and forget their faults.

There came a day when there was sudden movement in the camp. General Birdwood had arrived—one of Kitchener's "hard riding" generals, with a wonderful string of medals and decorations—and there were other "signs of the zodiac" pointing to our early departure. When at last, at the "Stadium," Colonel Ryrie announced to us of the 2nd Light Horse that we were to make ready, you could have heard the cheering miles away. The residents of Ma'adi, when they heard it, thought peace had been declared!

It was the arrival of our Australian wounded back from the Dardanelles that settled it. It was a wrench to leave our horses behind—the dear old horses that we petted and loved, the horses that were a very part of us—but it had to be done. When we saw our fellows coming back with their wounds upon them—when we heard of what they had been through—when we listened to their story of that wonderful landing on Gallipoli on April 25, and of the wild charge they made up the frowning hill—all of us, to a man, begged to be sent to the front as infantry! We were Light Horsemen, and we hadn't been trained as infantry, but it didn't matter—we were soldiers of the king!

I saw the Red Crescent train as it steamed in loaded with the wounded, and I went to the base hospital to see and chat with the men who knew now what war was—the men who had clamoured so impatiently for so many weeks to be sent where "the fighting" was, and then came back again to be nursed in an Egyptian hospital! Yet they were happy. They had "done their bit." They smoked cigarettes and yarned about their experiences. I watched the slightly wounded ones marching from the train to the hospital—an unforgettable sight. Most of them were shot about the arms or scalp. Their uniforms had dried blood all over them, and were torn about where the field doctors had ripped off sleeves or other parts to get at the wounds. As they marched irregularly along, one young fellow with his arm in a sling and a flesh wound in the leg limped behind and shouted out: "Hey, you chaps, don't make it a welter!"

Our men were just splendid in the fight. An Imperial officer who has been all over France and Flanders said that Colonel Maclagan's Australian Brigade was the finest brigade of infantry in the whole of the Allied armies. That was praise indeed. And I remember another fine tribute that was paid to them. "No troops in the whole world could possibly have done better than those magnificent Australian infantry. They performed the impossible. In the face of exploding mines and withering fire from machine guns, shrapnel and rifles, they stormed the hills and, with bloody bayonets, routed the Turks and Germans." That was a tribute the more valuable because it was not an Australian who spoke, neither was it an Englishman, but a Frenchman. It was the remark of a French naval officer who watched the landing of the Australian division on Gallipoli. And when the whole tale was told the world saw how rightly our boys deserved all that was said of them.

What a terribly expensive business it was all to be! How many brave Australians and New Zealanders—yes, and Englishmen, Frenchmen and Indians—were yet to be sacrificed! It is well that the Great Ruler over all, Who holds us in the hollow of His hands, does not permit poor mortals to see into the future. The "forcing of the Dardanelles"— the words were on the lips of all of us and were printed in newspapers all over the world—it seemed only a matter of a little while, and then——

Great is the British Navy, magnificent are its officers and men, but hellish was the work of "forcing the Dardanelles." You remember how the *Goliath* and the *Irresistible* went down. You remember how a great French ship—the *Bouvet*—was sunk. You remember the mines that came down the waters, and the shore torpedoes, and the strength of the Turkish forts, the power of the Turkish guns, erected and manned by German officers. The navy could not force the Dardanelles alone! It was necessary to have the co-operation of land forces. Perhaps the operations should never have been begun until the army was ready to co-operate. I do not know; it is not for me to judge.

General Sir Ian Hamilton first visited the Dardanelles and carried out a reconnaissance on one of the warships and then came to Egypt—a lightning visit—and our forces began to move. Australia, for the first time, was right up against the Hun! South Africa was a picnic to it.

There were spies everywhere. There were spies in the transports, spies amongst the interpreters, spies in the supply depots. The Turks, or rather their German officers, were kept informed of every move the Allies made. They knew exactly the hour of disembarkation and the places of landing. They learned all the Australian bugle calls and used them with telling effect. The French landed and formed up as if on parade, and then, with beautiful precision, marched on and drove the enemy before them. The British, despite the fusillade which greeted them on landing, were steady as veterans and there was no hope of withstanding their landing.

But there was an electric quality about the charge of the Australians that inspired panic in the Turkish trenches. Fiercely angry at the loss of several of their officers, they charged with fixed bayonets, not waiting for supports.

One charge was led by a doctor; another by a priest. Several times they charged so fiercely that they looked like getting out of hand. Scorning cover, they also scorned rifle fire. They scaled the steel-lined heights like demons. It was the bayonet all the time. One huge farmer actually bayoneted a Turk through the chest and pitch-forked him over his shoulder. The man who performed this feat was a huge Queenslander—Sergeant Burne, of the 9th Battalion, who was afterwards wounded and returned to his Australian home—a man whose modesty is as great as his size. We smiled at first when we heard the story, and people in England and Australia read of it with amazement. But Sergeant Burne, standing over six feet high, and massively proportioned, looks quite capable of the feat. He himself tells the story in these words:

> It is not a case for me to take any credit at all, I was in the platoon that landed first on the right. Our lieutenant was the first man to get ashore—and as game a man as ever faced fire. I followed him. I was ordered to take in hand a line of Turkish sharpshooters who were causing a lot of trouble. There was also a machine-gun on the hill. Somebody had to stop it. Myself and two lads went up, and we stopped it. That's all. There were ten Turks there. We got the Turks and we got the machine-gun, but I lost my two lads. They were only boys, but let me tell you the Australians are the best fighters in the world. One of the lads 'fixed' the German officer who was working the machine-gun. The Turks were higher up than we were, and I suppose that is how I was able to throw one of them over my shoulder. It's an old trick that is taught in the Guards.

Sergeant Burne once served in the Irish Guards, and he carries a scar on his forehead, the result of a blow from the butt-end of a rifle at Rhenosterkop, during the South African war. He had been living in Australia for about six years when the Great War broke out, and he was one of the first to answer the Empire's call. His stay on Gallipoli was short, for on the same day as that on which he performed the feat of which I have written he received a bullet in the shoulder.

"It was a very short experience," he said, "but I'll be back there again."

And that was, and is, the spirit of them all.

It is sad to think that so many senior officers lost their lives right at the outset of the fighting in the Dardanelles. Australia could ill afford to lose men like Colonel Onslow Thompson, Colonel MacLaurin, Major F. D. Irvine and Colonel Braund. Colonel MacLaurin was in the act of warning soldiers to be certain to keep behind cover when he was shot in the head. He was hurriedly conveyed to the rear, but only lingered half an hour. Curiously enough, he had a presentiment that he would be killed, and mentioned it to one of our Light Horse officers just before leaving for the Dardanelles.

It was a wicked trick that resulted in the slaughter of so many gallant men of the 1st (N.S.W.) Battalion. They had been holding the line splendidly, despite shrapnel and maxim fire and rifles, and had repulsed several attacks by the enemy. Then a message was passed down the line

1. Col. McCay, Brigadier 2nd Australian Infantry Brigade. Wounded.
2. Lt.-Col. C. F. Cox, C.B., Commanding 6th Light Horse Regt.
3. Lt.-Col. Hubert Harris, 5th Light Horse Regt. Killed.
4. Col. M. Laurin, Brigadier 1st Australian Infantry Brigade. Killed.
5. Lt.-Col. Braund, V.D., O.C., 2nd Batt. 1st Infantry Brigade. Killed.
6. Lt.-Col. Onslow-Thompson. Killed.

for the battalion to attack and capture the guns in front. Not doubting the genuineness of the order, the battalion charged, only to be met with a withering fire, which immediately told them that a trap had been set.

Their leader, Colonel Onslow Thompson, was killed instantaneously by a cannon shot which struck him in the head. He was one of the first to volunteer in Sydney when war broke out. Colonel Arnott knew that Colonel Onslow Thompson was a splendid Light Horse officer, and begged of him to wait for a mounted regiment. "No," he replied, "I'm going, and I'll take the first chance that offers."

The casualties among the officers were tremendous—brave men who led Australia's soldiers in that awful charge! And among the bravest of them were the young officers from the Duntroon Military College that stands amid delightful country surroundings near the capital of Federated Australia that is now in the making in the Mother State of New South Wales. These young fellows fought in a way that showed their native courage and the excellence of their training. Only the year before, when Sir Ian Hamilton, as Inspector-General of the Oversea Forces, visited Australia and inspected these lads who were training for the army at Duntroon, as the representative of the *Sydney Morning Herald* I remember seeing them laugh and cheer when Sir Ian Hamilton, on leaving Duntroon, jokingly wished them "plenty of wars and rapid promotion."

And it seems only a few days since we were dancing and flirting in a Cairo ballroom. Now many of them lie sorely wounded at the base hospital, and several will never again hear the *réveillé*. But the College will not forget its first-fruits offered up so gladly for empire. Officers and men, it was all the same—they went to their death with a cheer for King and Country. I heard an Imperial officer, newly returned from Flanders, say that the 3rd Australian Infantry Brigade was the finest brigade of infantry in the whole of the allied armies. In physique they were far superior to any of the British, French, or Belgian troops. Whether this be true or not, there is no doubt that the sturdy Thirds under Colonel Maclagan fought like Trojans on the Gallipoli Peninsula, and covered themselves with glory. Incidentally, I might mention, some of them never fired a shot during the fierce fighting of April 25. They simply trusted to the cold steel, and flung themselves at the Turkish trenches.

The 1st Brigade (Colonel MacLaurin), the 2nd (Colonel McCay), and the rest of the Australians and New Zealanders fought with equal valour, but the brunt of the attack was borne by the Thirds. So many hundred gallant lives was a heavy price to pay for a footing in Gallipoli, but those impetuous charges, absolutely irresistible in their fury, would, we knew, bear rich fruit, for the Turks could never again withstand a bayonet charge by the Australians.

It was noteworthy that only a few thousand prisoners were taken. I asked one of the 1st Battalion boys (Lieutenant-Colonel Dobbin's command) why that was. He replied: "How could 12,000 of us take prisoners when we were up against 35,000?"

And through it all our Army Medical Corps [1] did yeoman service. Several stretcher-bearers were shot, for they dashed forward too soon to succour the wounded. The doctors were right up in the firing-line all the while. Colonel Ryan and some other doctors were attending to serious cases on the beach, where the landing was effected, and snipers shot two orderlies who were assisting, one on each side of the colonel.

I doubt if there was a single branch of the service that did not suffer and share in the glory of that charge.

General Bridges handled his gallant Australians with consummate skill. He seemed to anticipate the Turkish attacks. His dispositions for defence were brilliant. Then General Godley and his New Zealanders landed and threw themselves into the fray. General Birdwood came and took charge of the Australian, New Zealand Army Corps . . . A.N.Z.A.C.! From that fateful day, April 25, Anzac[2] has been a name to conjure with.

---

1. *The Australian Army Medical Corps in Egypt During the First World War* by James W. Barrett & P. E. Deane is also published by Leonaur.
2. *On the Anzac Trail* by "Anzac," the experiences of a New Zealand soldier in Egypt and Gallipoli during the Great War, is also published by Leonaur.

Chapter 6

Light-Hearted Australians

"Bah!" he exclaimed as he lit his cigarette. "The Turks can't shoot for nuts! But the German machine-guns are the devil, and the shrapnel is no picnic!"

His arm was in a sling, and his leg was bandaged from hip to ankle. But he was cheerful as could be, as proud as Punch, and as chirpy as a gamecock. For he was one of the band of Australian heroes, wounded and back from the front. And we who listened to the deathless story of the wild charge they made could not help wishing we had shared in the glories of that fight.

"It's the Germans we're up against," he went on. "You see they have taught the Turks all sorts of nasty tricks. One of the tricks is to surrender just at the last minute. One Turk in a trench shot my pal on my right and a chap on my left; then when we got right into the trench he suddenly dropped his rifle and put up his hands. I reckoned that wasn't fair, so I jammed my bayonet into him. Time and again the Turks would shoot till we were right on top of them, and then drop guns and surrender. Call that fair fighting?"

Another chap with his tunic all clotted with blood and his head in a bandage here interpolated: "Say, you needn't fear the Turks' shooting. It's safer to be in the firing-line than in the reserves. But look out for those machine-guns; they spit death at you at the rate of ten a second. Also, keep your eyes open for the snipers. We drove them back for miles behind Sari Bair, but there were snipers everywhere. They never minded being killed so long as they could pick off a few officers. One black devil shot our captain at only fifty yards. Five of us got to him, and gave him just what Brutus, Cassius, Casca and the rest gave Julius Caesar."

"We fought them for three days after landing," said a big bushman in the 2nd Brigade, "and they made about a dozen counter-attacks. But when we had a chance of sitting down and letting them charge us it was dead easy—just like money from home. They never got near enough to sample the bayonets again. But on the 27th they tried to get all over us. They let the artillery work overtime, and we suffered a bit from the shrapnel. The noise was deafening. Suddenly it ceased, and a new Turkish division was launched at us. This was just before breakfast. There is no doubt about the bravery of the Turks. But we were comfortably entrenched, and it was their turn to advance in the open. We pumped lead into them till our rifles were too hot to hold. Time and again they came on, and each time we sent them about their business. At three o'clock we got tired of slaughtering them that way, so we left our little home in the trench and went after them again with the bayonet."

"Say, what do you think of *Big Lizzie*?" asked another blood-bespattered Cornstalk. "Ain't she the dizzy limit?"

Is it necessary to explain that this was the affectionate way our fellows alluded to the super-Dreadnought *Queen Elizabeth*? The soldier continued: "All the while our transports were landing, *Big Lizzie* just glided up and down like an old hen watching her chickens. Every now and then the Turkish destroyers from Nagara tried to cut in and smash up the transports. But the moment '*Lizzie*' got a move on they skedaddled. One ship was just a bit slow. Didn't know that *Big Liz* could hit ten miles off. Shell landed fair amidships, and it was goodnight, nurse."

One of the 9th Battalion (Queenslanders, under Colonel Lee) chipped in here: "Ever tried wading through barbed wire and water with maxims zipping all round you?"

This pertinent question explained the severe losses of the 3rd Brigade. The landing was effected simultaneously at several points on the peninsula, but one spot was a hornet's nest and they started to sting when the Australians reached the beach. A couple of boats were upset and several sailors and soldiers killed. Others dashing into the shallow water were caught in the barbed wire.

"My legs are tattooed prettier than a picture," added the Queenslander, "and I've a bit of shrapnel shell here for a keepsake, somewhere under my shoulder."

"Fancy ten thousand miles and eight months' training all for nix," said a disgusted corporal. "Landed at 4 a.m. Shot at three seconds past four. Back on the boat at 5 a.m."

And so on.

To have gone through all they had gone through, and then to treat it all so lightly, seemed an extraordinary thing. All the doctors and nurses commented on the amazing fortitude and cheerfulness of the Australian wounded. I used to think the desire to be in the thick of things, that I had so often heard expressed, was make-believe, but I know better now. I used to say myself that I "wanted to be there" (and *sotto voce* I used to add "I don't think"); and now, in my heart-searchings, I began to wonder if I didn't really mean it, after all. I used to strike an attitude and quote, "*One crowded hour of glorious life is worth an age without a name,*" whilst all the time I felt in my heart that I would prefer a crowded age of glorious life to an hour of fame. Now I began to wonder whether in my heart's core, in my very heart of hearts, I did not agree with the poet. The proper study of mankind is Oneself. And what was I doing there, anyway?

Yes, it was extraordinary—not a doubt of it. Doctors and nurses said they never saw anything like it in the world. Those soldiers back from the Dardanelles, many of them sorely wounded, were laughing and joking all day, chatting cheerfully about their terrible experiences, and itching to get back again and "do for the dirty Turks"!

"Nurse," said one of them, with a shattered leg, as he raised himself with difficulty, "will you write a little note for me?"

She came over and sat at the side of the bed, paper and pencil in hand.

"'My dear mother and father, I hope this letter finds you as well as it leaves me at present.'. . . How's that for a beginning, nurse?" he said with a smile.

I heard of another man who sent a letter from the Dardanelles. It ran:

> Dear Aunt, this war is a fair cow. Your affectionate nephew.

Just that, and nothing more. The censor, I have no doubt, would think it a pity to cut anything out of it.

I heard of another, and at the risk of an intrusion into the private affairs of any of our soldiers, I make bold to give it. It was just this:

> My darling Helen, I would rather be spending the evening with you than with two dead Turks in this trench. Still it might be worse, I suppose.

Those cheerful Australians!

Can you wonder that the Light Horse wanted to get a move on and make a start for the front? Can you wonder that when we heard of the terrible list of casualties which were the price of victory, and when we saw our men coming back, many of them old friends, with their battle-scars upon them, we fretted and fumed impatiently? We had a church parade, and the chaplain, Captain Keith Miller, preached from the text, "*Let us run with patience the race that is set before us*," and it only made us angry. There was only one text that appealed to us, and that was "*How long, Oh Lord, how long?*"

We could stand it no longer. Our boys needed reinforcements, and that was all we cared about. They must have reinforcements. It would be some days before men could arrive from England and France. Sir Ian Hamilton wanted men to push home the attack and ensure the victory. We knew that no cavalry could go for a couple of weeks, and our fellows were just "spoiling for a fight." They were sick and tired of the endless waiting, with wild rumours of moving every second day. Men from all the troops and squadrons went to their officers and volunteered to go as infantry, if only they could go at once. B Squadron, 6th Regiment, volunteered *en masse*.

Colonel Ryrie, accurately gauging the temper of the men, summoned the regimental commanders, Lieutenant-Colonel Cox, Lieutenant-Colonel Harris and Lieutenant-Colonel Arnott. What happened at this little Council of War we don't know. But we guess. Word was sent on to the general that the whole brigade would leave for the front within an hour, on foot if necessary.

A similar offer had just been made by the 1st Light Horse Brigade (Colonel Chauvel) and the 1st Brigade of New Zealand Mounted Rifles.

What it cost these gallant horsemen to volunteer and leave their horses behind only horsemen can guess. Colonel Ryrie's brigade was said to be the best-horsed brigade in Egypt. Scores of men had brought their own horses. After eight months of soldiering we were deeply attached to our chargers. Fighting on foot was not our *forte*. We were far more at home in the saddle. But Colonel Ryrie expressed the dominant thought of the men when he said:

> My brigade are mostly bushmen, and they never expected to go gravel-crushing, but if necessary the whole brigade will start tomorrow on foot, even if we have to tramp the whole way from Constantinople to Berlin.

There was cheering all along the line when the news filtered through. Men who had of late been swearing at the heat and dust and the flies and the desert suddenly became jovial again. At dinner they passed the joke along, sang songs, and cheered everybody, from Kitchener to Andy Fisher, and the brigadier down to the cooks and the trumpeters.

So we are off at last, after weary months of waiting—on foot. Blistered heels and trenches ahead; but it's better than sticking here in the desert doing nothing.

Chapter 7

At the Dardanelles

As I sit and gaze over the limpid waters of Aboukir Bay I think of the old-time rivalry of France and Britain, and the struggle for the possession of Egypt.

*In 'ninety-eight we chased the foe
Right into Bouky Bay!*

These are the opening lines of the old sea ditty which describes how Nelson won the Battle of the Nile. Right here it was that the *Orient*—flagship of the French admiral—was blown up.

And now, a hundred years after, we see French and British warships again off Alexandria. But this time the Union Jack and the Tricolour are intertwined, and in the streets of Alexandria French and British soldiers and sailors walk arm in arm, while the ancient city is gay with flags and bunting. For big things are brewing in the Levant. Before the eyes of the citizens during the past week was a unique international naval and military pageant—*Zouaves*, with their blue jackets and red trousers, French infantry in their blue-grey uniform, cavalry with gay tunics, British Jack Tars in blue and white, Australians in sombre khaki, swarthy-skinned Maoris from the Wonderland of the Southern Seas, and dusky warriors from the Punjab. British troops—and especially those young giants from Australia—had the better of the Frenchman in the matter of physique; but there was clear evidence of "grit" in the intelligent, humorous faces of the French, which helped one to understand why, for instance, they are said to be the finest marchers in Europe, and why the Germans never got to Paris!

At last the Australian Division is on the move. After weary weeks of waiting the order has come. There were wild cheers at Mena when the news buzzed round; lusty cheering at Zeitoun when the New

Zealanders heard it; more wild cheering at Heliopolis and Abassia as the message flashed further afield. Out at Mena camp there was great excitement as battalion after battalion marched away, encouraged by the cheers of their comrades behind. Trams brimming over with jubilant human freight moved off from Mena House, and glided along the well-known road to Cairo, where trains were waiting to convey the men to Alexandria. At Alexandria the transports were waiting to take us to the Dardanelles. Turkey, forgetting the traditional friendship of Great Britain, had allowed Germany to bluff her into invading Egypt. Now, in return, Britain was knocking at the front door—the impregnable front door of Constantinople.

We had a final concert in the cinema tent, and it was a huge success. The good folk of Ma'adi rolled up in full force. Charles Knowles, the famous baritone, came out and sang "The Trumpeter" and "My old Shako" and "The Old Brigade" and "Land of Hope and Glory," and we all joined in the choruses. The brigadier made a farewell speech, and thanked the residents for all their kindness to the men of the 2nd Brigade. He said we were sorry to part with such good friends, but were glad at last to have a chance of striking a blow for freedom and justice and the grand old flag of the Empire. Of course, we cheered all the time, and we laughed when genial Mr. Hopkins, President of the Citizen's Committee, farewelled us with the words, "God bless you" and "God help the Turks if you get at them with the bayonet."

We marched away at last. British folk at Ma'adi and Cairo were enthusiastic, and gave us a great farewell. Some of the "gyppies" and Arabs along the roadway were sullenly passive and apathetic. At the main station, Cairo, crowds of soldiers assembled to cheer the horseless horsemen. "We went to South Africa as infantry, and they mounted us," said a philosophic Riverina grazier. "Now, we come to North Africa as Light Horsemen, and they bundle us off as infantry."

We profited by the experience of the infantry. Our officers dressed exactly like the men. They carried rifles and wore bandoliers. All their pretty uniforms that they "swanked" in at the continental dances and dinners went by the board, and they roughed it in service jackets and hobnailed boots.

Seen from aloft, the 2nd Light Horse embarking resembled nothing so much as a swarm of khaki ants covering the quays at Alexandria. They scurried hither and thither, and to the onlooker it seemed all confusion worse confounded by the arrival of additional trains from Cairo.

But the confusion was more apparent than real. One noticed soon that all the soldiers going to the transports were loaded with arms and ammunition and stores. Those coming from the ships were empty-handed. And soon the trains rattled off, the wharves were cleared and all the troops were aboard. But there were no fond farewells this time. All the folk who were near and dear to us were far, far away. A coffee stall on the quay[1] "manned" by the Y.W.C.A. worked overtime from four o'clock in the morning, and our fellows were very grateful to the ladies of Alexandria who did us this kindness. They wished us "Good luck," and we glided out. There were no cheers or sirens to hearten us. That was all past. We were starting off in grim earnest this time. A few embarkation officers and transport officials on the wharf called out "Good luck, boys"; and that was all.

Half an hour later we were out on the Mediterranean—the blue Mediterranean—and we thought of all the fleets that in the centuries gone by had sailed these waters—Greeks, Romans, Carthaginians, Spaniards, Turks, French and British. Our ship was numbered A25—the *Lutzow*, one of the many German liners that had fallen to the mighty British Navy. And on board were crowded 2,000 men. No horses! Our gallant steeds had all been left behind at Ma'adi, ready to follow the moment we drove the Turks from the hills and reached "cavalry country." Our boys had had the chance of coming without horses or stopping behind; they never hesitated for a moment.

"Submarine," whispered someone the first day out. And all eyes searched the waters round us. But no submarine had been seen. We had simply been warned that there was a Turkish submarine somewhere outside the Dardanelles. So the brigadier, Colonel Ryrie, took steps to give it a warm reception in case it poked its nose—its periscope—above the surface of the sea.

The whole brigade was remarkably happy. Despite the fact that within a couple of days these men would be fighting for their lives, despite the fact that their comrades of the Australian Infantry had just suffered 4,000 casualties in four days, they went as cheerily forward as their relations in Sydney went to the Easter Show. And that reminds me that right here near the Dardanelles I came across a copy of the Easter number of the *Sydney Mail*. What a joy it was to escape the war pictures for a brief while and see, instead, the photographs of prize

---

1 *Nothing Like A Nice Cuppa* (containing *The Canteeners* by Agnes M. Dixon, *Red Triangle Girl in France* by Cairns Collection of American Women Writers & *Betty Stevenson, Y. M. C. A* Edited by C. G. R. S. and A. G. S.) is also published by Leonaur.

pumpkins, of milking shorthorns, and the great stock parade, and the high jump, and all the other attractions of one of the greatest shows on earth! It was just like a message of good cheer from sunny New South Wales.

We had left Alexandria under sealed orders. We had to meet a certain warship in a certain place and get certain instructions. We travelled at night with all lights out, and threaded our way with care through the Archipelago. Passing Rhodes and Crete and Tenedos, we reached the scene of what has been described as the most picturesque phase of the Great World War—the attack on the Dardanelles.

There had been many changes in the brigade, since the men first went into camp at Rosebery Park, Sydney, nine months before. Nearly a thousand men passed through Colonel Cox's regiment before it finally started out to smash the Turk and thrash the Hun. There had been changes also amongst the officers, and as the exact list has never been published and many of these officers were soon to lay down their lives in the service of their country, let me give their names here—a permanent record which will be cherished by those officers and men who remain and by the families of all the brave dead.

Headquarters Staff: Brigadier, Colonel Granville Ryrie; Brigade Major, Major T. J. Lynch; Staff Captain, Captain R. V. Pollok; Orderly Officer, Lieutenant Oliver Hogue; Field Cashier, Lieutenant B. E. Alderson.

5th Light Horse Regiment (Queensland): Lieutenant-Colonel Hubert Harris, V.D., Major L. C. Wilson, Major H. H. Johnson, Major S. Midgley, D.S.O., Captain P. D. Robinson, Captain Donald Cameron, Captain J. C. Ridley, Captain G. P. Donovan, Captain J. E. Dods (Medical Officer), Chaplain Captain Michael Bergin, Lieutenants Pike, Nimmo, Chatham, Wright, Hanley, Fargher, Rutherford, McNeill, Irving, Bolingbroke, McLaughlin, Lyons and Brundrit.

6th Light Horse Regiment (New South Wales): Lieutenant-Colonel C. F. Cox, C.B., V.D., Major C. D. Fuller, Major W. T. Charley, Major F. D. Oatley, Major J. F. White, Captain G. C. Somerville, Captain (Medical) A. Verge, Chaplain Captain Robertson, Captain H. A. D. White, Captain M. F. Bruxner, Lieutenants Richardson, Ferguson, Anderson, Huxtable, Cross, Roy Hordern, H. Ryrie, Robson, Cork and Garnock.

7th Light Horse Regiment (New South Wales): Lieutenant-

Officers of the 6th Australian Light Horse Regiment, 2nd Light Horse Brigade.

Left to right.—Standing at back: Lieut. R. N. Richardson, Lieut. J. M. Chisholm, Lieut. D. Drummond, Capt. L. McLaglan, Lieut. G. Ferguson, Lieut. R. Hordern, Lieut. H. S. Ryrie.. Sitting: Capt. H. O'Brien, Capt. M. F. Bruxner, Major F. J. White, Major C. D. Fuller, Lt.-Col. C. F. Cox, C.B., V.D., Lieut. M. D. Russell, Capt. A. Verge, R.M.O., Capt. H. A. D. White.. In front: Lieut. N. M. Pearce and Lieut. W. M. Anderson.

Colonel J. M. Arnott, Major G. M. Onslow, Major E. Windeyer, Major T. L. Rutledge, Major H. B. Suttor, Captain (Medical) T. C. C. Evans, Chaplain Captain J. Keith Miller, Captain J. D. Richardson, Lieutenants Board, Elliott, Fulton, Bice, Higgins, Hession, Gilchrist, Stevenson, Maddrell, Bird, Barton and Lake.

Brigade Train: Lieutenant R. G. Bosanquet and Lieutenant G. D. Smith.

Field Ambulance: Lieutenant Colonel Bean, Major D. G. Croll, Captains Fraser, McDonnel, Pitcher and Buchanan.

Signal Troop: Captain R. A. Stanley.

The exact strength of the brigade as it entered Turkish waters was 76 officers and 1,455 other ranks. Back at Ma'adi we had left about twenty-five *per cent* of our men and all our horses. Major Righetti, of the 5th Light Horse Regiment, had been appointed Camp Commandant, and we were hoping that in a couple of weeks at the latest he and his merry men would join us and then, once more mounted, we would canter gaily along the Gallipoli road to Constantinople. We were mostly young and optimistic! We were soon to find what a long, long road it was.

It seemed as if they had made special arrangements for a fine big bombardment just to let the Light Horse see how it was done. As the 2nd Light Horse Brigade arrived off Gallipoli we were eyewitnesses of a spectacular bombardment that thrilled us. It was about seven o'clock on the evening of May 18 that our transport glided in between Tenedos and Imbros and anchored off Helles. Long before we anchored we could hear the rumbling of heavy artillery, and we knew that the fleet was busy. Soon we saw the intermittent flashes of the guns, and then there loomed up out of the dusk the spectre-like shapes of the allied warships. A long, impregnable-looking line they made, stretching from Kum Kale north and west, and north again, till they were lost to sight in the murky pall which was fast settling down on the Ægean Sea.

All night long the firing continued, but we slept just as soundly as we had done out on the desert at Ma'adi. By sunrise the troopers were astir, crowding the rigging and watching with intense interest the panorama spread before them. As the sun peeped over the hills we could see the tents of the field hospital whitening in the growing light. All around us were warships and transports and colliers and supply ships of all descriptions. Here and there were the low grey hulls of destroyers streaking across the waters. From our warships came a desultory fire on the Turkish trenches.

So intent were we as we watched the camp of the Allies that we never noticed that our own vessel had dragged its anchor and was fast bearing down on a French transport a few cable-lengths off. The ships came together with a crunch that startled us. We thought for the moment that we had either been torpedoed or rammed. Then the nose of the Frenchman crunched along our port side, smashing stanchions and gangways, twisting sheet iron into fantastic shapes and breaking horse-boxes into matchwood. The active troopers all sprang free of the danger—all but one, who was so intent on adjusting his puttees that he never noticed what was happening. First thing he knew was when an anchor fluke caught him bending and drove him with the force of a battering ram headlong amongst the pans and dixies. His angry "*Imshi yaller*" was drowned in the roar of laughter from his comrades.

Just before breakfast an airman went up—up with the lark. He flew up the Dardanelles towards the Narrows, cut across Maidos to the Australian Division, doubled back, then swung round over our heads and turned in and landed. A valuable reconnaissance was made, the report was sent to headquarters, and then the airman strolled into breakfast. This man and his aeroplane were a target for Turkish shells and German gunners all the time. Shell after shell burst around him, but he took not the slightest notice—he said afterwards, with a laugh, that they were quite "beneath his notice." At one time we counted eight shell-bursts round about the aeroplane. It seemed to us who watched him that the aviator must have borne a charmed life.

Every time I see an air pilot I feel like saluting him. Colonel Ryrie said that morning, when he saw the spot on which our infantry had landed: "After that, I'll take off my hat to the Australian soldier every time." And that's how I feel about those gallant airmen.

The enemy's gunners were good; there was no doubt of that, even though they failed to "wing" the aeroplane. They next turned their attention and their fire on the British trenches. For a while the shells flew wide. Some fell into the sea; others burst high. Then they got the range, and kept it. To what extent our comrades suffered, or how well they were dug in, we could not see. But the warships soon got to work and silenced the enemy's guns. Then we went in to breakfast.

Just before we disembarked Colonel Ryrie addressed the assembled soldiers. He said his only fear was that they would be too impetuous. Their comrades who had gone before had made history. Their courage and dash and their invincible charge on a well-nigh impregnable position would be a theme for historians throughout the ages. Their only fault was—they were too brave. They were ordered to take one strongly-fortified line of trenches and they actually took three. Concluding, the brigadier said:

> If I get back to Australia and some of you fellows don't, I know I shall be able to tell your people that you fought and died like heroes. If you get back and I don't, I hope you will be able to tell my countrymen that Colonel Ryrie played the game.

Chapter 8
Anzac

We've had our first week in the trenches. The Turks have killed some of us, and we have killed some of them. They certainly fared the worst; and we agree with the chaplains that it is more blessed to give than to receive.

In some places our trenches are only seven yards from the Turks; in others they are 700. All day and night the sniping continues. Hand grenades and bombs are thrown to and fro. Aeroplanes circle aloft and drop bombs on the opposing trenches. When our aeroplane goes up the boys yell out: "Lay an egg on the Turkeys!" When the Taube drops bombs we "duck" to shelter. Most of our spare time we spend in dodging shrapnel. It's fine fun, but no one can guess where the splinters will fly to. We've all had the sorrow of seeing old comrades struck down at our sides, and yet we carry on cheerfully.

On Empire Day—five days after we landed—the Turks asked for an armistice to bury their dead. It took eight hours. In front of our trenches were 3,500 dead. We reckon that in the attack on our position on May 18-19 the enemy had at least 10,000 casualties. The Australians lost about 500. Time and again the Turks charged in solid phalanx, but withered away before the deadly fire of our riflemen. Whenever they did effect a breach they were speedily ejected by dashing bayonet attacks by the Australians and New Zealanders.

Today—May 28—we are all in the highest spirits, for we have received a special "Force Order" from General Sir Ian Hamilton, and it shows that we have not been idle. Here is the order:—

Force Order No. 17.

General Headquarters,
May 25, 1915.

1. Now that a clear month has passed since the Mediterranean Expeditionary Force began its night and day fighting with the enemy, the General Commanding desires to explain to officers, non-commissioned officers and men the real significance of the calls made upon them to risk their lives, apparently for nothing better than to gain a few yards of uncultivated land.

2. A comparatively small body of the finest troops in the world, French and British, have effected a lodgement close to the heart of a great continental empire, still formidable even in its decadence. Here they stand firm, or slowly advance, and in the efforts made by successive Turkish armies to dislodge them the rotten Government at Constantinople is gradually wearing itself out. The facts and figures upon which this conclusion is based have been checked and verified from a variety of sources. Agents of neutral powers possessing good sources of information have placed both the numbers and the losses of the enemy much higher than they are set forth here, but the General Commanding prefers to be on the safe side and to give his troops a strictly conservative estimate.

Before operations began the strength of the defenders of the Dardanelles was:—

Gallipoli Peninsula, 34,000 and about 100 guns.

Asiatic side of Straits, 41,000.

All the troops on the Gallipoli Peninsula and fifty *per cent* of the troops on the Asiatic side were Nizam, that is to say, regular first line troops. They were transferable, and were actually transferred to the side upon which the invaders disembarked. Our Expeditionary Force effected its landing, it will be seen, in the face of an enemy superior not only to the covering parties which got ashore the first day, but superior actually to the total strength at our disposal. By May 12 the Turkish Army of Occupation had been defeated in several engagements, and would have been at the end of their resources had they not meanwhile received reinforcements of 20,000 infantry and twenty-one batteries of Field Artillery.

Still the Expeditionary Force held its own, and more than held its own, inflicting fresh bloody defeats upon the newcomers; and again the Turks must certainly have given way had not a second reinforcement reached the Peninsula from Constantinople and Smyrna, amounting at the lowest estimate to 24,000 men.

3. From what has been said it will be understood that the Mediterranean Expeditionary Force, supported by its gallant comrades of the Fleet, but with constantly diminishing effectives, has held in check or wrested ground from some 120,000 Turkish troops elaborately entrenched and supported by a powerful artillery.

The enemy has now few more Nizam troops at his disposal and not many Redif or second-class troops. Up to date his casualties are 55,000, and again, in giving this figure, the General Commanding has preferred to err on the side of low estimates.

Daily we make progress, and whenever the reinforcements close at hand begin to put in an appearance, the Mediterranean Expeditionary Force will press forward with a fresh impulse to accomplish the greatest Imperial task ever entrusted to an army.

W. P. Braithwaite, Major-General,
Chief of General Staff,
Mediterranean Expeditionary Force."

And I have by me a copy of the little one-page *Peninsula Press* published at Sir Ian Hamilton's headquarters some distance from Anzac. It is No. 13, and is dated May 25, 1915; and it gives this "Official Account" of the enemy's losses:—

> The burial of the dead on the Australian and New Zealand front was completed yesterday under the armistice asked for by the Turks. The number of the enemy's dead lying between the trenches was estimated at 3,500, counting only those who have fallen since May 18. Rifle fire broke out soon after the close of the armistice.

That *Peninsula Press*, little thing though it was, used to be read and re-read till we could almost repeat all its contents word for word. It gave us the war news on all fronts in a nutshell. In this particular number we read of the great Russian victory in East Galicia, when the Austrians were pushed back from the Dniester to the Pruth, and on a 100-mile battle-front the Russians took 20,000 prisoners in five days. We read of von Bethmann-Hollweg's threat to Italy—his threat to punish Germany's "faithless ally" who had seen fit to throw over the Powers of Darkness for those of Light and Freedom and Civilization. We read of the German losses between Steenstraete and Ypres, despite their use of asphyxiating gas which their enlightened scientists had been able to place at their disposal. We read this:

The British Navy has rescued 1,282 German seamen and marines from German warships sunk. Not one British seaman or marine has been saved by Germans in like circumstances.

We read an extract from the Greek newspaper *Athinai* relating to the elections in that country:

> If the people give the victory to the party of M. Venizelos, then the Entente Powers will have no further anxiety concerning us; Greece will be ready for war in accordance with the programme of M. Venizelos and with the engagements he has assumed.

(And the people did give the victory to M. Venizelos—but Greece, oh, where was she?) And this also we read in our paper. A Turkish correspondent says:

> The people of Gallipoli Town "have seen only four British (Australian) prisoners of war. The men excited great admiration among the people, because it was seen that they were indeed soldiers. They wandered about freely and drank coffee, creating great excitement by their queer remarks and causing no ill-feeling.

And the *Lusitania!* We read the lines from *Punch* of May 12—Britain to America, on the sinking of the *Lusitania*:

> *In silence you have looked on felon blows,*
> *On butcher's work of which the waste lands reek;*
> *Now, in God's name, from Whom your greatness flows,*
> *Sister, will you not speak?*

We ourselves had seen a ship go down. We saw the *Triumph* torpedoed. We saw her shiver from stem to stern—and then go down in the sea. She was a triumph of man's handiwork, and man's handiwork had destroyed her. The sea was very calm, but submarines and mines lurk in still waters as well as rough—and out of the calm sea came the thing of death. From the moment she was struck till she turned turtle but fourteen minutes elapsed. A dozen launches and torpedo boats rushed to rescue the crew, and all were saved except about forty. And we who saw it all from the trenches looked on at it stupefied. With a mighty lurch—as it were a giant in the agonies of death—the *Triumph* heeled over and was gone.

Such things are done, and will be done, as long as there are Hymns of Hate in the world. War is a gruesome business.

Just as I walked out of my dugout this morning two men were shot by a machine-gun not ten yards off—one in the shoulder and the other in the eye. Two seconds ago a big shrapnel shell burst right in front of our dug-out. The bullets flew everywhere, and we bolted to shelter. No one was injured. It is marvellous. Up to the present it has been the most wonderful week in my life—full of excitement and hair-breadth escapes.

Sunday came—May 30. The day dawned peacefully, minus the artillery duel which ordinarily heralds the coming day. The blue Mediterranean lay like a sea of glass at our feet. Imbros Island, opposite Anzac Cove, lay wreathed in the morning mists. Torpedo boats glided to and fro across the waters, lest some adventurous submarine should attack. All was peaceful. Ashore, the wild flowers blossomed on the hillsides. Birds chirruped contentedly in the scrub. Soldiers released from a night's vigil in the trenches sauntered along the winding road to the beach, dived in and sported freely in the sea. The transport mules munched contentedly, and the Indians lay back smoking hubble-bubbles. Light Horsemen (minus their horses) and infantrymen emerged from their dugouts and stretched themselves lazily in the sun.

It was too good to last—too good altogether. Some activity behind the Turkish trenches attracted the attention of our artillery observation officers, and our guns boomed out a warning. It was evidently disregarded by the enemy, for more of our guns opened fire. Then the Turks replied. The hills around spat fire, and the valleys echoed and re-echoed with peals of thunder. Shrapnel shells and "Jack Johnsons" went screaming overhead, to burst with a deafening report over our trenches and bivouacs. Our guns were so cunningly concealed that the German artillery officers could not locate them, and for the most part their shells ploughed up the unoffending earth, or made harmless rents in the atmosphere. Our artillery had better success. Our guns tore down the Turkish trenches, and the Turks flying to shelter were met with a devastating fire from our machine-guns. Still, we did not have it all our own way. Now and then a shell landed in our trenches, and the story of it was told in the casualty lists.

About one o'clock the artillery duel began, and it continued without cessation for over an hour. The roar was awful. Bullets spattered everywhere. The marvel was that our losses were so few. Gradually the big guns grew silent. Our warships aimed a few salvos on to the enemy's position, then drew off. Soon there was comparative calm.

There remained but the interminable fusillade of musketry which never wholly ceased on the trenches round Anzac.

At eventide the Ægean Sea took on new colourings. The sun set in a blaze of splendour; the whole western horizon was alight with its reflected brilliance. The islands seemed to rest against a superb canvas on which Nature had splashed lavishly a wealth of gold and rose-red and saffron and purple and amethyst. The sea in turn mirrored and accentuated the beauties of the scene. The angry armies gazed in quiet contemplation of Nature's craftsmanship, forgetting their mutual hate.

Up on Braund's Hill—where Colonel Braund, who used to sit for Armidale in the New South Wales Parliament, had met with a tragic fate soon after the historic landing was made—right at the entrance to the trenches in the firing-line, Divine Service was being held. In the days of my wanderings I have attended many church services, in shearing-sheds and on mining fields, on board troopships, and in the bush; but never had I attended such a service as this. Captain McKenzie, of the 1st Infantry Brigade, and Captain Robertson, of the 2nd Light Horse, were the officiating chaplains. Soldiers, unkempt, unshaven, unwashed, lolled around on the path or the hillside. Men coming from the trenches joined in the singing. Men going to the trenches for the night lingered awhile. And they sang the old well-known hymns. None asked for "Onward, Christian Soldiers," or any of the warlike hymns at all. They wanted the old gospel hymns. So we sang, "Jesus, Lover of My Soul," "Sweet Hour of Prayer," and "Abide with Me." . . .

Firing had recommenced before we finished the service, and the chaplain's voice was now and then drowned in the rattle of musketry or the bursting of shrapnel. And because of the shells and bombs which continually burst overhead, we meant it when we sang "Cover my defenceless head with the shadow of Thy wing."

A few words of prayer, a few words of exhortation and commendation, and then the service was over. Some filed off to the trenches for the vigil of the night. Others formed up for the reserves. The rest of us returned to our dugouts, to snuggle in while the roar of battle raged overhead. And one soon gets used to the battle noises. I fell asleep thinking of dear old New South Wales, my dear old home, and—my dear old mother.

CHAPTER 9

Stories That Will Never Die

Life in the trenches became quite bearable—after a time. But it took time. At first when a bullet skimmed the parapet and went whistling overhead we ducked instinctively. But the experienced infantry laughed, and said, "They're only 'canaries'." Again, when the shrapnel came hurtling aloft and burst with an ugly roar, we crouched and waited for death; but the old hands explained that if we could hear it burst we were pretty safe. It was the shells we couldn't hear that we ought to dodge. We understood that epigrammatic utterance better later on.

But one thing is absolutely essential for a philosophic enjoyment of trench life—and that is a sense of humour. Failing that, most of the soldiers would in the end go stark, staring mad. It is this saving grace which makes our Australians such a wonderful fighting force. They go laughing into the firing-line. They come laughing out again. They laugh as they load and fire. Nearly every wounded man I've seen laughs. A staff officer said the other day: "It's only when they're killed that these Australians cease laughing."

Our three Australian Light Horse brigades have now been in the trenches for some time. "We came to Egypt as horsemen," said a Hunter River man; "then we did foot-slogging at Cairo and Alexandria, and now we're living in caves and tunnels, like rabbits or troglodytes."

Since the days of Darwin quite a lot has been written about evolution. But we never thought of evolution in connexion with our Light Horse Brigade. We soon found that we couldn't escape the process any more than the rest of the universe.

One would have thought that as new and awful weapons of destruction were evolved, battles would become short, sharp, and decisive. Instead of that, they are toilsome, long-drawn-out, and indecisive. I cannot say why. The elucidation of the problem I leave to the "experts." All I am concerned with is the story of how the 2nd Light Horse Brigade became the Lost Horse Brigade. Australia sent four Light Horse brigades to uphold the honour of the Commonwealth; first, Colonel Chauvel; second, Colonel Ryrie; third, Colonel Hughes; fourth, Colonel Brown. At first we thought we were going to be armed with swords as well as rifles. When first mounted, despite our sombre khaki, we felt as proud as Life Guardsmen. And we saw visions and dreamed dreams, and pictured the Australian Light Horse on the left wing of the Empire army driving the Huns in confusion over the Rhine and back to Berlin.

Hope on, hope ever. All we have done so far is, by process of devolution, to change from prospective cavalry to mounted infantry, to foot-sloggers, to pick and shovel artists, and finally to troglodytes. The pen is mightier than the sword—but so is the spade.

We did not like the packs at first. Our horses used to carry our kits, and it was rather irksome to be transformed suddenly into beasts of burden. Also, we imbibed a new respect for the infantry, who seemed to carry their heavy packs with consummate ease. Ours at first felt like the Burden to Christian. But gradually we, too, developed the necessary back and shoulder muscles for the infantryman's job. We trudged up and down the hills of Anzac; we filed into the trenches and took our stations at the loopholes; on the day of the armistice we helped to bury the dead Turks whom Enver Pasha had ordered to drive the Australians into the sea. Then it was that the infantry, seeing "2 L.H.B." on our shoulder straps, called us the 2nd *Lost* Horse Brigade.

But we didn't mind losing our horses so long as we had a finger in the Gallipoli Pie. Trench warfare suited us well enough. The firing-line was always interesting. Everybody was light-hearted. Jokes and laughter passed the time pleasantly when we were not sniping or observing. It meant a little more work when the Turkish (or German) guns smashed in our parapets and half-choked, half-blinded and half-buried us. Now and then some of our chaps stopped a bullet or a bit of shrapnel. But we dealt out more than we got. Every day the officer commanding and the brigadier made a tour of the firing-line, while we often had three generals to see us on special days. The day after the big attack General Birdwood asked one of the 1st Light Horse Regiment if he had killed many Turks, and he answered, "Yes, miles of the cows."

As a matter of fact the Australians were almost quarrelling for positions in the firing-line that night. When the fight was at its hottest, men in the supports were offering bribes of tobacco and cigarettes to the men in the firing-line to swap places with them just for ten minutes. Our night patrols had great fun harassing the enemy; but for the bulk of us it got monotonous. It was nothing but dig new saps, new tunnels, new trenches, day after day and night after night.

The 6th Light Horse Regiment changed its badge and its motto. When we left Sydney we had beautiful badges with a fighting cock and the motto "Fight on, fight ever." We've got a new badge now—pick and shovel, argent, crossed on an azure shield, and our new motto is "*Dig on, dig ever.*"

The 7th Light Horse Regiment also changed its motto, which used to be "*Patria te Salutamus.*" Now the troopers sport a shield with a picture of a rabbit, and Colonel Arnott's new motto is "*Infra dig. Tunnelabit.*"

The A.L.H. did their share of the trench fighting quite as well as their infantry comrades. Day after day they took their posts as observers or snipers. Night after night they manned the loopholes or did patrol work or sapping. When off duty they bolted to Anzac Cove, and all the shrapnel shells in the world didn't keep them out of the water.

The truth is, a lot of our soldiers grew to be rank fatalists. "If I'm to be killed, I'll be killed," they said. On the night of the big attack the men in the supports were begging the men in the first line to give them a chance: "Come on down, and let's at 'em; I'm a better shot than you." With men clamouring for positions in the firing-line, no wonder the Turks had 10,000 casualties. When it came to the armistice to bury their dead, a soldier exclaimed, "I don't mind killing, but I bar burying the cows!"

The Turks made the same mistake about the Australians that the Yorkshiremen made about the Australian cricketers. They thought we were all black. (The Germans knew better, but encouraged the false idea.) In a Gallipoli paper we were referred to as Australian blacks, with the comment that this was "the first time cannibals had landed on Gallipoli." But after the wild bayonet charges our men made at Anzac they called the Australians "the White Gurkhas." Later on when our first few prisoners were taken to Gallipoli, the Turks admired their physique, and exclaimed: "These are indeed soldiers."

"*Our army swore terribly in Flanders,*" it is written. I'm afraid that our historian will say the same of the army in Gallipoli. But this is about their only vice, and they have all the soldierly virtues that a general could desire. When the Turks made their big attack, and advanced yelling "*Allah, Allah!*" "*Mohammed!*" "*Allah!*" one of our devil-may-care infantrymen yelled as he fired: "Yes; you can bring them along too!"

Then there was the Turk who bowed. It was when the burial parties met between the trenches to bury the dead. The Turkish officers were polite and the Germans surly. A Turk picked up a bomb and started to run back to his trenches. A Turkish officer ran after him, kicked him, and returned the bomb with a bow to one of our officers, thus observing chivalrously the letter and spirit of the armistice. A Turkish soldier came up to one of our men and volunteered the information: "English good—German no good." It wasn't much, but it told a lot.

A number of prisoners were taken, and several more surrendered. But the Turks were between the devil and the deep sea. If they came with their rifles towards our trenches we shot them. If they came without them, their own soldiers shot them. So they had to sneak in as best they could, and risk being shot front and rear.

One of the finest things done in those first fatal days at Anzac must be put to the credit of Murphy's mules. Murphy's ambulance was looked for as anxiously as Gunga Din. It was "Murphy! Murphy! Murphy! an' we'll thank you for your mules!" As a matter of fact "Murphy" was a Scotsman, though he hailed from South Shields, County Durham. His real name was, I believe, John Simpson Kirkpatrick; some say it was Latimer, and others that it was Simpson; and he was a stretcher-bearer. He used to hurry up with water to the firing-line, and carry back the wounded. It was a terribly heavy pull up and down Shrapnel Gully, from the cove to the top of Braund's Hill, so Murphy "pinched" a couple of mules, and did yeoman service. He used to leave the mules just under the brow of the hill and dash forward himself to the firing-line to save the wounded. "Murphy's" voice near them sounded like a voice from heaven. Time after time he climbed the hill and did his noble work. Day after day he smiled and carried on. The mules were missed, and they found out who stole them. But they also found out what splendid work "Murphy" was doing; so the officers connived at the theft. They became accessories after the fact.

There came a day when "Murphy's mules" came not. Stretcher-bearers were working overtime, and the wounded cried "For God's sake, send 'Murphy's mules'!" Later on they found the mules grazing contentedly in Shrapnel Valley. Then they found poor "Murphy"....

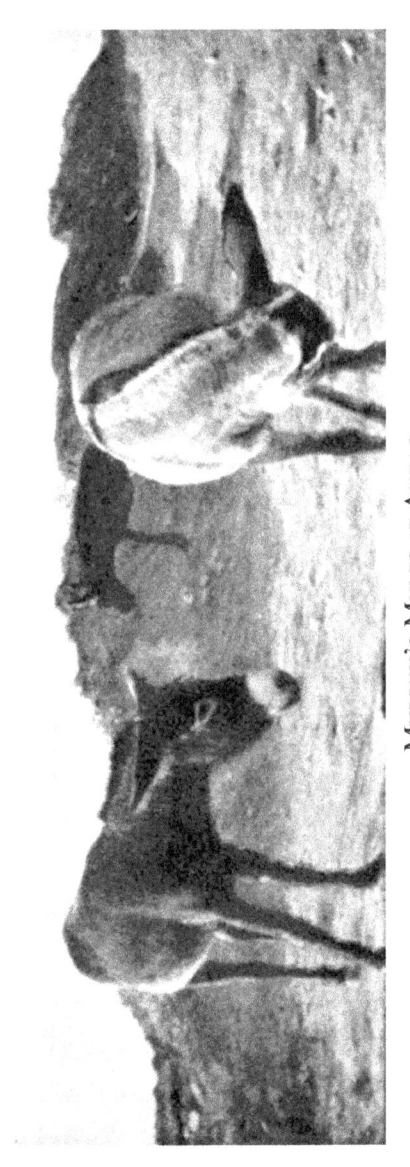

Murphy's Mules at Anzac.

"Murphy" on the left, his mate on the right, and little "Shrapnel" in the background.

He had done his last journey to the top of the hill.

"Where's Murphy?" demanded one of the 1st Battalion.

"Murphy's at heaven's gate," answered the sergeant, "helping the soldiers through."

CHAPTER 9

To Drive Back the Turk

We had scores of little affairs of outposts, and our patrols enjoyed some fine skirmishes and night encounters. None of them, however, quite deserved mention in the official chronicle. But the affair of *July 12*—of "*glorious and immortal memory*"—was more important.

It began and coincided with an advance down south at Helles. The plan of operations there was to seize the right and right-centre sections of the foremost system of Turkish trenches, from the spot where the Kereves Dere meets the sea to the main Seddel-Bahr—Krithia Road, a front of about 2,500 yards. The object was to complete the driving back of the Turks to their second system.

It was a double-barrelled attack, and was opened after the shore batteries and the ships' guns had completed the preliminary bombardment. The first phase was an assault by the French and our 155th Brigade, who captured the enemy's trenches after a splendid charge. But they had to fight like grim death to withstand the fierce counter-attacks which were made from the maze of Turkish trenches in the vicinity. This done, the second phase was entered upon by the 157th Brigade. They, too, after fierce fighting, gained their objective, with the help of the Royal Naval Division. Meanwhile the French pushed their extreme right on to the mouth of the Kereves Dere, where it runs into the sea. The whole position was maintained, despite the persistent counter-attacks of the Turk.

So much for the southern—and main—operation. Our rôle up north at Anzac was so to harass the enemy that he would expect a big attack, and so be unable to reinforce his comrades down south. The Australian and New Zealand Army Corps early in the morning engaged the enemy, and after our artillery had opened the ball, the 2nd Light Horse Brigade advanced from the new position it had taken up at Ryrie's Post towards the Turkish trenches. The 6th Light Horse (Colonel Cox) and the 7th Light Horse (Colonel Arnott) sent a squadron over their trenches. The troopers jumped on to the parapet with a cheer, and swarmed down the hill to the comparative safety of the valley below. By a stroke of luck not one man was hit in this charge, though they encountered a hail of bullets. The Turks were too surprised to shoot straight. Later on the enemy's shrapnel did much execution, but the only casualty in this initial manoeuvre was when a trooper of the Sixth tripped over some of our own barbed wire and rolled, kicking and swearing, down the hill, to the huge delight of his comrades.

Pushing out over Holly Spur, towards Pine Ridge, the Light Horse advance, under Lieutenant Ferguson, drove the enemy's patrols back and opened a hot fire on their trenches. Meanwhile, to stimulate a general attack, the parties were sent forward in full view of the enemy, and withdrawn under cover to their original position. Long lines of bayonets were seen passing along our trenches and disappearing at the communication tunnels, thus lending additional colour to the idea of a general attack. Further demonstrations by the 5th Light Horse (Lieutenant-Colonel Harris) on the right wing provoked a wild fusillade from the enemy, who promptly reinforced his position all along the line, and the fusillade became general.

Most noticeable was the rapidity with which the Turkish—or German—artillery came into action. Within three minutes of the commencement of operations the Turkish shells were falling thick and fast on Holly Ridge. They had the range to a nicety, and it was a miracle how any of our advance parties escaped annihilation. As it was, we had five killed and fourteen wounded. It is estimated that the Turks fired two hundred rounds of shrapnel on the Light Horse position in one hundred minutes. Our artillery was by no means idle. Colonel Rosenthal concentrated a devastating fire on to the enemy's trenches and gun emplacements. Our howitzers landed high explosives amongst the enemy's reserves, while the enemy's guns battered our trenches. The roar of the cannonade was terrific.

We did not know exactly how fared the infantry on our left, or the New Zealanders further north. But we did know, by the rapid reinforcement of the enemy's position, that our demonstration had achieved its purpose.

One would like to mention all the acts of gallantry which were done on this occasion. But no one saw them all. I was so busy dodging shrapnel shells that I saw only a few. Anyhow, our chaps did not come with a view to getting medals. Other gallant soldiers of the Seventh and Sixth and Fifth will never get mentioned in dispatches.

After eight weeks on the inhospitable shores of Gallipoli, the Turks at last took pity on the Australians. They promised us excellent treatment and ample provisions. All we had to do was to "Come and surrender."

This cheery invitation was scattered broadcast over the Gallipoli Peninsula by a German aeroplane. But the pilot was such a poor shot that not one of the messages fell in the league-long trenches of the Australians and New Zealanders. The wind wafted them all across into the Turkish lines. But our friends next door (they are only ten feet away in one place) wrote nasty messages on the papers and threw them back into our lines.

It was a most interesting document, the one we received. It informed us that the British navy had abandoned us to our fate. Unfortunately for the Turks, half a dozen warships and a flotilla of submarines were at that moment thundering away at the Turkish batteries. Another bit of news to the Australians was that "Greedy England made us fight under a contract." Anyway, as we had not completed the contract we did not like the idea of quitting the job.

However, here is the grandiloquent German-made proclamation:—

> Proclamation to the Anglo-French Expeditionary Forces.
> Protected by a heavy fire of a powerful fleet, you have been able to land on the Gallipoli Peninsula on and since April 25.
> Backed up by those same men-of-war, you could establish yourself at two points of the peninsula. All your endeavours to advance into the inner parts of the peninsula have come to failure under your heavy losses, although your ships have done their utmost to assist you by a tremendous cannonade, implying enormous waste of ammunition. Two fine British battleships, *Triumph* and *Majestic*, have been sunk before your own eyes by submarine boats, all protective means against them being found utterly insufficient. Since those severe losses to the British navy, men-of-war had to take refuge, and have abandoned you to your own fate.
> Your ships cannot possibly be of any help to you in future, since a great number of submarines are prepared to suppress them.

Your forces have to rely on sea transport for reinforcements and supply of food, water, and every kind of war material. Already the submarines have sunk several steamers carrying supplies for your destination. Soon all supplies will be entirely cut off from your landed forces.

You are exposed to certain perdition by starvation and thirst. You could only escape useless sacrifice of life by surrendering. We are assured you have not taken up arms against us by hatred. Greedy England has made you fight under a contract. You may confide in us for excellent treatment. Our country disposes of ample provisions. There is enough to feed you well and make you feel quite at your comfort. Don't further hesitate. Come and surrender.

On all other fronts of this war, your own people and your allies, the situation is as hopeless as on this peninsula. All news spread amongst you concerning the German and Austrian armies are mere lies. There stands neither one Englishman, nor one Frenchman, nor one Italian on German soil. On the contrary the German troops are keeping a strong hold on the whole of Belgium and on conspicuous parts of France since many a month. A considerable part of Russian Poland is also in the hands of the Germans, who advance there every day. Early in May, strong German and Austrian forces have broken through the Russian centre in Galicia. Przemysl has fallen back into their hands lately. They are not in the least way handicapped by Italy's joining your coalition, but are successfully engaged in driving the Russians out of Galicia. These Russian troops, whose co-operation one moment you look forward to, are surrendering by hundreds and thousands. Do as they do. Your honour is safe. Further fighting is mere stupid bloodshed.

Lovers of peace will regret to learn that the hard-headed and ferocious Australians rejected this kind invitation, and persisted in "stupid bloodshed." Incidentally, it might be mentioned, most of the blood shed was Turkish.

One other literary effort from our friend the enemy reached us about the same time. It was issued by the Director of the Military Museum at Constantinople, and was to the following effect:—

The public are hereby informed that the 700 British *mitrailleuses* and 300 French cannon captured during the Battle of

Ari-Bournu at Gallipoli by our heroic troops, in the course of bayonet charges in which they drove into the sea and drowned more than twenty thousand of the enemy, will be on exhibit in the foreign gallery of the Museum immediately after the cessation of hostilities.

This startling item of information was so unexpected that it made us all long to get to Constantinople to see the trophies of Turkish prowess. It was solely with this object in view that we began making fresh preparations for a special trip to that city beautiful.

Chapter 11

War Vignettes

Vignettes of battle!

These are the kaleidoscopic pictures that remain mirrored in the memory. I have forgotten what the transports looked like when we reached Gallipoli. I only half remember the panorama of battle when we first tackled the Turk. Yet there is no forgetting these little snapshots of soldiering, the vivid vignettes which stand out in clear-cut silhouette against the background of our experiences. Somehow they seem more like *tableaux vivants* than a moving picture show. Certainly the impression is not blurred by action, so the mind, like a camera plate, retains the scene down to the minutest details. Perhaps, when we think of the big things that our lads have done, these little visions may seem hardly worth chronicling. But the Censor will not let me take photographs, and after all it might interest the old folks at home to scan these hurried lines and construct their own mental pictures of the rugged and inhospitable Gallipoli Peninsula where so many young Australians have fought and died for empire.

First, the Cove! It was in Anzac Cove we first landed. In spite of the shrapnel shells which burst on the beach or plunged into the sea, we could take stock of the whole scene before us—afloat and ashore. Straight ahead the hills rose almost from the water's edge to a height of 400 feet. To right and left were the army stores: little mountains of bully beef and biscuits. Scores of soldiers moved hither and thither on fatigue duty, giving Anzac the appearance of a thriving port. At least five hundred men were swimming in the Cove entirely indifferent to the enemy's shells. Under the sheltering shadow of the hill was the field ambulance—doctors working overtime, orderlies running here and there, stretcher-bearers coming and going with their burdens of wounded and dead; seaward, transports lolled lazily on the placid bosom of the Mediterranean; torpedo boats streaked about looking for submarines; warships wreathed in battle-smoke belched broadsides; aloft, a circling aeroplane.

. . . . There are weird names on Anzac. Hell Spit, Shell Green, Casualty Corner, Valley of Despair, The Bloody Angle, Dead Man's Hill, Sniper's Nest, and Cooee Gully. Every name conjures up memories. At the Bloody Angle Turks and Australians were at death-grips, day after day, and week after week, with the trenches only a few yards apart. It was back through the death-strewn Valley of Despair that the Australian infantry withdrew after their first glorious charge inland. On Dead Man's Hill the Turks lay slaughtered in hundreds after their fierce attack on May 19.

And we all know Shrapnel Valley. Here the Light Horse lay all through the night of the 20th, learning what shell-fire really meant. Since the first landing on April 25 the Turks must have landed tons and tons of lead and iron in Shrapnel Valley, but we soon knew the safety spots and the danger zones. The tortuous, waterless creek bed wound its aimless way to the sea; steep hills, scrub-faced, rose on either side; wild flowers, pink and white and lilac and yellow and blue, graced the uplands where we first landed; but they were all gone now. On the crest of the hill, sharply silhouetted against the skyline, were our trenches, so manned that the devils of hell could not break through, let alone the turbaned and malignant Turk. On the ledges behind—rather ragged and unkempt now—lounged the reserves, ready in case of attack, but knowing well that their comrades in front could easily hold the line. MacLaurin's Hill is at the top. A little further down projects Braund's Hill. Little graves dot the hillside; little wooden crosses mark the graves.

. . . . And then the Mules! Just mules and donkeys; but they play no unimportant part in the war game at Anzac. They too, with their Indian attendants, landed at Anzac with only the Turkish guns to voice a welcome. They too sheltered in dugouts when the artillery duel waxed warm. But day after day, and night after night, they toiled for the transport. Water and ammunition and stores of all kinds had to be carried from the depots to the firing-line, and the bulk of the burden fell on the mules. Along the meandering paths they filed, scrambling up the stiff pinches, resting awhile on the crests. Now and then a shell would slaughter a few. *Anon*, snipers' bullets would take toll. But the imperturbable Indian would just carry on. We had two little donkeys in Shell Green.

They divided their time between the 2nd Light Horse Brigade and the 3rd Infantry Brigade, and the boys gave them biscuits. Morning and evening the Turks shelled our lines, and Shell Green was plastered with pellets and splinters. Yet by some miraculous chance the donkeys escaped harm. Men were struck down on either side, but for a couple of months the lucky animals escaped scatheless. The soldiers swore by the donkeys' luck, and when the shells burst stood by the animals rather than fly for shelter. At last the luck turned. A high explosive burst over thirty men, scattered everywhere, wounded both donkeys, and never touched a single man. We buried one of the donkeys next day. The other, wounded and lonely, wandered about disconsolate.

. . . . Night at Anzac! The sun, a sphere of flaming red, sank into the sea. The western horizon glowed rich and splendid, while the waters of the Archipelago shimmered like molten gold. Imbros and Samothrace stood out in bold relief on the crimson skyline, while the coast of distant Bulgaria softened till lost in a purple haze. Down south spurts of fire and booming thunder told of the British warships still hammering away at the forts of the Dardanelles. Slowly, there was unfolded for the millionth time the miracle of nature's transformation scene. Like a white-hot furnace cooling, the blazing west turned to rose-red and amethyst, lilac and purple. Faithful as an echo, the mirroring sea reflected the softened shades of the sky, and the chastened waters grew mystic and wonderful in the afterglow. As the deepening twilight mantled the Ægean Sea, twinkling lights appeared on land and water, while one by one the little stars joined the crescent moon for company. All blurred and indistinct were the hills and hollows, and during a brief respite from the never-ending fusillade we forgot the war. But just behind was the long line of Australian bayonets pointing towards Constantinople.

. . . . The Guns! Thick-lipped and cold, cruel and menacing, were the Guns of Anzac. Death-dealing monsters were they, heartless and vindictive, but, oh, how we soldiers loved them! For they were our very best friends; field guns, mountain guns and howitzers. We knew when the German and Turkish artillerymen started their snarling hymn of hate that our gunners would soon be barking defiance. Enemy shells might roar and thunder, and shrapnel claim its victims; high explosives might wreck parapets and trenches, but we knew our guns and our gunners, and that was enough. We lay low while the artillery duel raged overhead and the echoing hills reverberated with the thunderous roar of battle. So cunningly concealed were our guns, with such acumen were our emplacements selected and built that Tommy Turk had continually to be guessing. His shells searched the hills and the valleys in vain. His gunners too were skilful and brave. They took position in gullies, behind hills and in villages, and blazed away at our lines. But our aeroplanes circled overhead to spot them. Then our guns got busy and fired like fury till the Hun cried "Hold!"

Then when our spell in the trenches was over, and we sought the seclusion of our dugouts, there came visions that are not vignettes of war. I saw the old homestead in the Hunter Valley. Hard by Erringhi it stands, where the Williams River meanders through the encircling hills and flows on towards Coalopolis. There are roses 'neath the old-fashioned windows, and in the fields the scent of lucerne ripe for the scythe. Magpies yodel in the big trees, and the wattle-gold is showing down the river. I wonder will I ever see dear old Erringhi again?

CHAPTER 12

"George"

George was the cook.

He blew into the Light Horse Camp at Holdsworthy when we were training. The staff captain gave him the job because he was a sea cook. Any man who can cook at sea ought to be able to cook on dry land. And all through the weary weeks of waiting and working, George kept on cooking.

George was small, not to say puny. His height was five feet, and his chest measurement nothing to cable home about. Had he gone to Victoria Barracks in the ordinary way to enlist he wouldn't have passed even the sentry at the gate, let alone the doctor. But George knew the ropes. He had "soldiered" before. That's why he took the short cut direct to camp.

We never saw much of him on the *Suevic*; when off duty he used to climb to some cosy corner on the uppermost deck and read dry textbooks on strategy and tactics. At odd times he would seek relaxation in *Life of Napoleon*, *Marlborough*, or *Oliver Cromwell*, but this was distinctly "not a study, but a recreation." Passing through the Suez Canal we saw the Turks miles away on the rim of the desert. George got out his rifle, set the sight at 2,500 yards, and waited. But the invader kept well out of range, and George went back to his cooking.

It was mid-winter in Egypt and the nights were bitterly cold. Greatcoats were vitally necessary. How welcome were the mufflers and Balaclava caps and warm socks knitted by the girls we left behind us! Welcome also was the hot coffee George provided to fill in the shivering gap between *réveillé* and stables. And after the horses had all been fed and watered, we returned with zest to breakfast—porridge and meat and "eggs a-cook" and bread and marmalade. I've heard some grumblers complain of the "tucker" in Egypt, but I've seen a bit of war by this and I'm convinced that the Australians are the best-fed army in the world. And George by the same token was not a bad cook.

Summer swooped down on Egypt. In its wake came heat and dust and flies and locusts. Over the scorching sands of the desert we cantered till the sweat poured from us and our horses, and the choking dust enveloped all. "Gyppie" fruit-sellers scurried hither and yon yelling "Oringes—gooud beeg one." And as we regaled ourselves with the luscious thirst-quenchers we thought of camp and the dinner that George was preparing. We trekked along the Nile, and almost before we halted George was boiling the billy. We bivouacked at Aaron's Gorge, or the Petrified Forest, or in a desert waste, and always George was on the spot with his dixies and pans. The cook's cart was a pleasing silhouette against the pyramid-pierced skyline, when we turned our eyes westward in the long summer evenings.

When at last we started for the Dardanelles, we of the Light Horse Brigade had (as you know) to leave our horses behind, and the cook's cart stopped too. But George came along all right. Despite the activities of the submarines we reached Gallipoli in safety, and witnessed the allied warships pounding away at the Turkish defences. Historic Troy was on our right; before us the entrance to the Dardanelles; and on the left, firmly established on Helles, was the great Mediterranean Expeditionary Force, making its first halt on the road to Constantinople. But we had to go further north, a mile beyond Gaba Tepe, where the Australians—particularly the 3rd Infantry Brigade—had performed such deeds of valour that Dargai, Colenso, and Magersfontein were declared by old soldiers to have been a mere picnic in contrast.

We landed amid a hail of shrapnel. Transhipping from the transports, we crowded into launches and sweepers and barges. These little boats, heavily laden with khaki freight, made straight for Anzac Cove. Fair targets for Tommy Turk, of course; so the guns of the Olive Grove Battery sent us anything but peaceful messages. *Plug-plong* went the shells into the water. *Zip-zip* hissed the bullets all round us. But, marvellous to relate, not a man was hit. Next day some infantry reinforcements, landing in the same place and manner, sustained forty casualties. That's the luck of the game—the fortune of war. We landed everything satisfactorily.

George brought up the rear, with his pots and dixies. It is because of George that I recapitulate.

In a long, straggling khaki line ("Column o' lumps," said the brigade major) we meandered past Casualty Point and Hell Spit, and up to our bivouac in Shrapnel Valley. Snipers on the hill up beyond Quinn's Post sent long-range shots at random down the track. Shells burst over our heads, and the leaden pellets spattered over the landscape. It would take too long to recount half the miraculous escapes some of our chaps had. Our artillery worked overtime, and the row was deafening. But our gunners could not silence the elusive cannon in the Olive Grove. After a time, wherein the minutes seemed like hours, we reached the camp site, and started to dig in feverishly. We burrowed like rabbits. Picks, shovels and bayonets made the earth fly till we had scratched a precarious shelter from the blast. Like troglodytes we snuggled into the dugouts, waiting for the bombardment to cease.

But George went on with his cooking.

Next day we changed our quarters. The German artillerymen were too attentive. We had sustained a few casualties, so we sought a more retired spot under the lee of the hill. For the first time since we had landed we were able to look about us. There was a lull in the cannonade, though the musketry fusillade proceeded merrily. We saw the long line of Australian and New Zealand trenches whence the Turks had been driven in rout the night before, leaving 3,000 dead to mar the landscape. We heard too, definitely, for the first time of the good Australians who on this inhospitable shore had given their lives for King and Empire—General Bridges, Colonel MacLaurin, Lieutenant-Colonel Braund, Lieutenant-Colonel Onslow Thompson, Sergeant Larkin (who used to sit on the opposite side to Colonel Braund in the New South Wales Parliament, but found in war the leveller that makes us all one party), and hundreds of others. Looking up to the precipitous cliffs above, we marvelled anew at the reckless daring of our infantry comrades who had scaled those heights in the face of rifle, machine-gun and shrapnel.

But we had not long to saunter and wonder. Our brigade was sent straightway into the firing-line. We were initiated into the mysteries of trench warfare, sapping and mining, bombs and grenades, observing and sniping, posies and dugouts, patrolling and listening, periscopes and peepholes, demonstrations and reconnaissance, supports and reserves, bully-beef and biscuits, mud and blood and slaughter, and all the humours and rumours, the hardships and horrors of war.

And all the time we were doing our little bit George went on with his cooking. He may have been thinking of Napoleon, or Marlbor-

Major-General W. T. Bridges.

ough, or Cromwell, but he did not seem to be thinking much about this war of ours—except that he had to do some cooking for it. The Turks were shooting many of our officers down, and many of our dear old pals, but George remained—and we hoped that they would spare him. Good cooks—real, good cooks like George—are scarce.

Chapter 13

"Robbo"

George and Bill, Tom and Dick and Harry—all a happy family, having a wonderful time. You never knew what was going to happen next. At any moment your turn might come. You could not tell. But you saw old pals in the morning, and you didn't see them in the evening. Sometimes the mate who had shared your tent and fought alongside you in the trench—the mate who was with you at Holdsworthy, who was with you in Egypt, and laughed and joked with you at Anzac—was suddenly snatched away from you, and then you realized what a thin line it is that separates life from death. Have you ever dreamed that you were standing on the edge of a precipice and that an enemy was racing along behind you to push you over? That was how we felt during these days on Gallipoli. A moment, and then you too might be falling headlong down the precipice. But we found it best not to let our minds dwell upon it.

So we went on burrowing into the side of the hill. We banked up the sides of our dugouts with sandbags and tins and earth. Most of the fighting was being done in the trenches. In some places they were now 1,500 yards apart, in some only twenty-one feet apart; and in the latter case life was all excitement. It was sap and mine and bomb and fusillade all the time. My brigade had now been here for some time, and despite the "accidents" which were always occurring we all had, somehow or other, a feeling of absolute security. We laughed at the Turks, and we smiled at what Liman von Sanders said—that he would drive us into the sea. We were just waiting, content and confident, for the big move that was going to lead to Constantinople!

And as I have said, we were a fairly well-fed army. We had none of the luxuries that the British Expeditionary Force had in France and Flanders. But on the whole we did not do too badly. The brigadier ate the same "tucker" as his batman.

We were given meat and vegetables and biscuits and cheese and jam. If only we could have had a lump of bread for a change! For the biscuits were so hard that they could be used to defend the trenches, if necessary—either as missiles or as overhead cover. Colonel —— broke one of his teeth on one. So we tried to soak them in our tea. Then we made them into porridge.

There was fighting on land and sea, in the air and under the water. Aeroplane reconnaissance was a daily spectacle. Our airmen would go aloft and have a good look at the enemy's position. The enemy's guns would boom out all the time, and shrapnel shells would burst all round the 'plane without ever seeming to hit it. We thought it was great sport watching the white puffs of smoke where the shells burst. Then the aeroplanes would drop bombs on the Turks for spite—"throw-downs" we called them. Sometimes the position was reversed, and the Germans dropped bombs on us. Two can play at the same game in war. Take the hand grenades. You should have seen Corporal Renwick take them! Before he became a soldier Renwick was well known on the cricket field—as indeed were hundreds of others—and on Gallipoli he used to catch the bombs and throw them back before they exploded. Nor was he the only one who did this. It was like tossing live coals back and forth—playing with fire. Some of our boys used to say it was the best "slip practice" they ever had! Sometimes a bomb would explode prematurely and a man's fingers would be blown off, and worse than that. But the others went on with the game.

And we went swimming down at the beach, just as if it had been Manly or Coogee. Only it was more exciting: Shells took the place of sharks. Instead of the sudden cry one would sometimes hear at Manly or Coogee of "'Ware shark," it was "'Ware shell!" The Turks are not the surfers that the Australians are. They had little sympathy with such healthy exercise, and they showed their disapproval of it by opening fire on the beach; and then there was a warning whistle, and we all rushed in to shelter. Afterwards we had the pleasure of initiating some Turkish prisoners into the joys of surf-bathing, but the majority of them did not take kindly to it.

And all the time the fighting went on. One night we had a great set-to. The Turks mined one of our trenches and rushed in and captured it. This was the affair at "Quinn's Post." We counter-attacked and re-took the trench, killed and captured some of the Turks, and then took one of their trenches. Then the hand grenades began to come, and the cricket commenced. It was an exciting match. The Turks made a determined attempt to recapture the position. They charged in strong force, but our chaps all along the line "hit them to leg." We enfiladed them with rifle and machine-gun fire, and they were eventually repulsed with a loss of about 2,000.

Wiggins, of the Field Ambulance, was sitting in his dug-out, and two of his mates went out and called to him. He leaned out and said: "Not yet; the shrapnel hasn't stopped." Then a shrapnel shell passed between the other two and struck him on the head and killed him.

Life and death! A very thin line. . . . One never knows. "In the morning the grass growth up, in the evening it is cut down and withered."

One day the word went round that "Robbo" had been killed. We would not believe it at first. It seemed a silly lie, one of those baseless camp rumours that some fool starts for a joke. Some of the officers went round to see for themselves. Colonel Cox stood by the dug-out, looking old and stricken. "Robbo's killed," he said. Then we knew it was true. Alas, alas, here was a loss! For "Robbo" was great.

The Turks had been subjecting us to a heavy bombardment for some days, and our artillery had been responding vigorously. Mostly their shells buried themselves in the sides of the hills, or exploded somewhat harmlessly in the air. Then one unlucky shrapnel shell burst right over the headquarters of the 6th Light Horse Regiment—and "Robbo" was there.

Lieutenant Henry Robson lay on the floor of the dugout, a shrapnel bullet in his breast. And we who had lived with him in camp and on the march for eight strenuous months, sorrowed as keenly as will his North Coast friends. To Colonel Cox it was not only the loss of an officer; it was also the loss of an old friend who years before had shared the dangers of battles and the stress of war.

All of us liked Lieutenant Robson. His bark was far worse than his bite. He'd give a shirking soldier the full force of his tongue, but his heart—"right there" as "Tipperary" has it—was in the right place. Kind of heart, genial of temper, and always willing to help others along, we mourn a man that can ill be spared. He was reckoned the best transport officer in Egypt. He knew horses as few men did. Australians are reputed to be good horsemen, but poor horse-masters. But Lieutenant Robson was good all round with horses. He would get more work out of a team than any one I know. He could get a full measure of work from his men also. But he never overdrove man or beast. That's why we liked him.

Harry Robson was forty-eight years of age when he died a soldier's death on Gallipoli Heights. He was one of the original Northern River Lancers, and went to England with the New South Wales Lancers in 1893. Later on he went home with the lancers under Colonel Cox in 1899. Standing six feet two in his socks, he was as straight as the lance he carried. He was an expert swordsman, and won several prizes at the tournaments in Scotland and at Islington. At tent-pegging he was an acknowledged champion. On the transport and in Egypt we had many bouts with the sword and singlesticks, but none of the younger officers could worst Robson, although he was old enough to be their father.

When the South African war broke out, he was sergeant-major in the New South Wales Lancers under Colonel Cox, they being the first Colonial troops to land at the Cape. He went right through the war, and participated in the battles of Modder River, Magersfontein, Grasspan, Paardeberg, Driefontein, and the Relief of Kimberley. He was with French's column during the main advance. When the 3rd Imperial Mounted Rifles were formed, Lieutenant Robson became transport officer under Colonel Cox, and saw a lot of service in Natal, the Orange Free State, and Eastern Transvaal. He participated in Kitchener's big drives, wherein his resourcefulness was of great help to the column. On one occasion Remington's column was held up by an impassable, boggy morass. The Inniskillens and Canadians were bogged. The Australians halted. Lieutenant Robson improvised a crossing with bales of hay and reeds, and got his transport over while the others were wondering how far round they would have to go. On another occasion in the Transvaal, by a simple device, he crossed the Wilge River with all his mules and wagons at a place reckoned absolutely hopeless for wheeled transport.

After the South African war he settled down on the Northern Rivers, and prospered. But when this great cataclysm convulsed the world, he heard the call of Empire, and responded like a patriot. He wired to Colonel Cox, offering his services, and left the comforts of home for the discomforts of war. On board the transport he was most painstaking and zealous in the performance of his duties. At Ma'adi he had his transport running as smoothly as a machine. When we found we were going without our horses, we thought that Lieutenant Robson would be left behind. But at the last moment the regimental quartermaster fell ill, and Robson filled the breach. And so for nine weary weeks of fighting he looked after the needs of the regiment, and not one trooper ever went to bed hungry. (I say "bed," but none of us has seen a bed for many months.)

As quartermaster, there was no need for him to be poking about the trenches and up in the firing-line as he did. But it was not in the firing-line he was killed. That is the fortune of war. He was standing just near headquarters watching the warships gliding over the Ægean Sea. Then came the fatal shell, and "Robbo" passed out to the Beyond.

Chapter 14

"Come and Die"

We were told at the outset that the trenches were the safest place to be in, and this is quite true. Shrapnel now and then knocks down the parapets and does a little damage, but in Shrapnel Valley and Suicide Walk it bursts at all times. And even in the dugouts one is not wholly safe. Many a brave spark has gone out in the dugouts. The Turks have their snipers, and we have ours, as the sea hath its pearls. A good sniper is indeed a pearl—unless he is fighting on the "other side," and in that case he is "a cow." Most of us try our hand at sniping, with more or less success—climbing up and down these hills in search of what we call "big game"—but although I am a tolerable shot myself, I have come to the conclusion that your true sniper, like your true poet, is born, not made. I have heard it said that a good tennis-player makes a good sniper (providing he can shoot) because he has the knack of anticipating his opponent's movements.

It is not enough to see your man and have a "pot" at him, for the chances are that just as you let go, he stoops down to pick a pretty flower, or he stumbles over a scrub-root. Now, the successful sniper is he who anticipates that stumble, or with an uncanny sort of second sight sees that pretty flower which the enemy gentleman is going wantonly to pluck, and aims low accordingly. Only by some such sort of intelligent anticipation could some of our men have put up the astonishing records that stand to their credit. But of that more *anon*.

Just at the moment I am out of the firing-line, and it is time enough to write of snipers and shot and shell when I get back to it—lots of time. For the present I am otherwise engaged. I have seen a girl—several of them—real girls—beautiful girls. To one who has not seen a girl for nearly six weeks girls seem wonderful. It is a red-letter day. For the first time for five weeks I feel absolutely safe from snipers and shells. I'm on the hospital ship *Gascon*, a couple of miles off Anzac. No, I'm not sick, neither am I wounded; it is just a little matter of duty that has brought me over, and I'm having a glorious holiday—two hours of real holiday. Presently I shall go back to my little grey home in the trench; and so I am enjoying every minute of my time on the ship. After weeks of bully-beef and bacon and biscuits I have had a *dinner*. Can you who live at home at ease realize what that means? I had soup, fish, grilled chop, sausage, potatoes, rhubarb tart, cheese, bread and butter, coffee—fit for a king! Before dinner I hungrily watched the stewards as they walked in and out of the saloon. And after dinner I bought two cigars for two shillings and smoked the smoke of absolute peace and contentment.

I quite forgot the war. I could scarcely hear the sound of the fusillade and bombardment of Anzac, and I kept on the other side of the ship so that I should not see the place. The only thing to remind me of the war was the occasional booming of the guns of our warships. After the trenches it was just like heaven. The view was delightful. Imbros, Samothrace and Tenedos were near by. The sea was smooth; the weather perfect, the blue of the sky rivalling the blue of the Mediterranean.

And the girls! There were *nurses* on board. I shook hands with them all and talked to half a dozen of them. One was a very sweet little thing—an angel! I longed for a broken arm or leg, so that I might stay there.... Come, shade of brave old Sir Walter, and help me here.

> *O, woman! In our hours of ease,*
> *Uncertain, coy, and hard to please,*
> *And variable as the shade*
> *By the light quivering aspen made;*
> *When pain and anguish wring the brow,*
> *A ministering angel thou!*

But they are all angels, ministering angels, tending the sick and wounded, whispering sweet words into the ears of brave men who lie there, suffering tortures of mind and body, but never uttering a complaint.

There were several doctors on board, and quite a lot of officers and men, some wounded, others sick and broken down with the stress of the last few weeks. Several of our brigade were among them. Heroes all.

Yes, I felt that if anything happened to me I should like to be taken aboard that hospital ship. But nothing had happened to me worth recording—only a few narrow escapes such as we all have in war time. I never felt better in my life. My appetite was of the best. My tongue had no coat of fur upon it. I had no excuse for remaining. I commandeered a few sheets of paper and some envelopes (precious things!). I went in and had a *bath*—none of your ordinary swims, with one eye on the shrapnel and the other on the shore, but a real bath with soap and fresh water—and then I said goodbye to the nurses, goodbye to the doctors and the men, and went back from this heaven on the water to that hell upon the earth.

It *was* hell! All war is hell, as General Sherman said. And there never was one that better deserved the name than this one. Oh, God! I have stood on Braund's Hill admiring the sunset views, when the islands of the Ægean Sea seem to be floating on the edge of a gorgeous canvas of shimmering gold, and I have stood on other hills and watched the dawn-blush and the rising sun, and I have said to myself, What a blot upon God's beauties is war!... And then I have taken up my rifle and gone forth to kill men! Every prospect pleases and only the enemy is vile. Oh, these shifting scenes and changing moods!

On the other side were forty thousand Turks (we are told) watching for the opportunity to kill us. Our mission was to get to Constantinople; theirs to drive us into the sea. We were "dug in"; they were "dug in." If we found it a long, long way to Constantinople, they were finding it's a long way to the sea, which is much nearer as the crow flies. They shivered at the sound of our land guns; they heard the broadsides of our ships; they watched the *Queen Elizabeth* fire her 15-inch gun; the shells landing on the sides of the hills, tossing hundreds of tons of earth and rock high into the air, so that when the smoke cleared away they would not know those hills; and they trembled, as all men who have seen have trembled at the fury of the monstrous gun!

But they fought on. Every yard of ground won cost us dear. I have seen our boys fall like ninepins before a hail of bullets. I have heard the cry "Lie low" in an advance, and every man has fallen flat upon the ground to escape certain destruction; and I have heard that other pitiful cry, time and time again, of "Stretcher-bearers wanted!" Once the men lay prone for four hours in the midst of the scrub, with the air full of bursting shells and rifle and machine-gun fire passing just over them. I do not wonder that some men lost their nerve during those terrible hours.

But never yet did Australian officer call upon his men to take a position, no matter how impossible the feat, and find them wanting. "Impossible!" There was no such word in their vocabulary. Nothing was impossible to them—until they died. Colonel McCay, Brigadier in Command of the Second Infantry Brigade, spoke the truth when he said:

"The way, the cheerful, splendid way, they face death and pain is simply glorious, and if no Australian ever fought again, April 25, April 26 and May 8 specially mark them as warriors. On the eighth of May I said in effect to them (my own brigade), 'Come and die,' and they came with a cheer and a laugh. They are simply magnificent."

The men were led by brave officers—officers who would not ask their men to go where they themselves were afraid to go. It was thus, leading their men to the fight, that General Sir William Throsby Bridges, commanding the Australian Imperial Force when it made its historic landing, Colonel MacLaurin, Colonel Onslow Thompson, Lieutenant-Colonel Braund, and other gallant officers fell. And it was thus that, later, Colonel McCay received the wounds that put him out of action. Australian officers, like any other officers, are human and have erred at times, but they have never asked their men to take risks they would not share themselves. There is a letter written by Colonel McCay in which he says:

> When my men have to go into a veritable hell, as they did on April 25, April 26 and May 8, I must lead them, not send them. I won their confidence because I shared the risks with them.

And that is the spirit of all the Australian officers—gallant leaders of gallant men.

Such was the spirit of Lieutenant-Colonel Hubert Harris, V.D., commanding the 5th Light Horse Regiment, who was killed in action on Gallipoli on the night of July 31. Curious it was that the only man hit in the regiment that night was its commander. They were firing from the trenches and occupying the attention of the Turks while the infantry on our left blew up the enemy's trench, dashed out, bayoneted the defenders, and captured the position. There was a wild fusillade by the enemy's riflemen, and a heavy bombardment of our lines. One unlucky bullet came through a loophole, struck Colonel Harris in the neck, and he died in a few minutes.

There was heavy fighting along the whole league-long line that night. But the main work was left to MacLagan's famous 3rd Infantry Brigade. The Turks had sapped in and dug trenches opposite Tasmania

Post. They looked dangerous, and it was thought they would try to undermine our trenches and blow us up. So we mined in under them, and blew up their advanced trench. On our left the New Zealanders made a lively demonstration to keep the enemy opposite engaged, and the big guns blazed away at the main Turkish position. From the sea a warship fired high explosives in the same direction. Then Captain Lean with a storming party of the 11th Infantry Battalion, dashed out with great gallantry and seized the objective. They used boards to surmount the barbed wire entanglements, swept down on the Turks, bayoneted and shot about fifty of them, and entered into possession. Engineers immediately bolted out under a heavy fire, and hurriedly built up sandbag defences. And having got it, the Eleventh held on.

Meanwhile the 2nd Light Horse Brigade on the right poured a heavy fire into the Turkish trenches on the immediate left of the captured position. All attempts at reinforcing the Turkish advanced line were thus frustrated, and no counter-attack had any chance of getting home. Thinking a further attack was intended from Ryrie's Post, the Turkish artillery concentrated their field guns on the Light Horse, and the bombardment was terrific; yet—and here is the luck of the game—not one man in the firing-line of the 6th Light Horse was wounded. I was up with B Squadron, and the hail of shrapnel was something to remember. That was about half-past ten at night; and the moon having just risen, we concentrated our rifle fire on the enemy's trenches, leaving our artillery to deal with their reserves. Then it was that the fatal bullet killed Colonel Harris.

In a special order issued by General Birdwood next day reference was made to the excellent qualities of Colonel Harris, and to the conspicuous ability he had shown during the few months he had led his regiment on Gallipoli. We of the Sixth knew his value, and liked him; the Queenslanders loved him, and would have followed him anywhere.

Colonel Harris was a comparatively young man, not yet forty-five years of age. He started his soldiering in the Brisbane Grammar School cadets, and then became a bugler in the Queensland Rifles. Later on he joined the Mounted Infantry, volunteered for the South African War, going with the second Queensland contingent as a lieutenant, and returned a captain. He maintained his interest in the military forces after his return, became adjutant, and later on succeeded to the command of the 13th Australian Light Horse Regiment. Curiously enough, Colonel Spencer Brown, whom he succeeded in that command, and Lieutenant-Colonel Stoddart, who succeeded him, have also come to the war. For five years, Lieutenant-Colonel Harris commanded the 13th Regiment, and then was placed on the unattached list. When the war broke out he offered his services, and in November, 1914, took command of the 5th Light Horse Regiment in Colonel (later Brigadier-General) Ryrie's 2nd Brigade. He wore the Victoria Decoration and the Queen's South African ribbon with five clasps.

So here in the hills of Gallipoli there passes to the Great Beyond another good Australian, a brave and gallant officer, a kindly and courteous gentleman. The Americans used to sing "John Brown's body lies a-mouldering in the grave; his soul goes marching on." So the 5th Regiment may well feel that the spirit of Hubert Harris will go with them on to victory.

We buried him next night. The Dean of Sydney, Chaplain-Colonel Talbot, officiated, assisted by Chaplain-Captain Gordon Robertson. Officers and men of the regiment—all who could be spared from the trenches—attended with Major Wilson, who assumed command of the Fifth. Brigadier-General Ryrie and staff, and Lieutenant-Colonel Arnott, of the Seventh, were also present. As the earth was heaped upon him, the brigadier remarked sadly: "The brigade has lost a gallant officer, and Australia a patriot."

Chapter 15

The Bombs

Some talk of Alexander,
And some of Hercules,
Of Hector and Lysander,
And such great men as these:
But of all the world's great heroes
There's none that can compare
With the tow-row-row-row-ri-ro,
The British Grenadiers!

A year or more ago, (as at 1916), when we sang this old song, we thought that the days of the grenadiers were numbered, that future warfare would know them no more.

Yet here we were on Gallipoli, reverting to the grenades of the Peninsular War, and the old Roman catapult, and even the bows and arrows. The enemy was so close to us that we could not use some of our guns to demolish his trenches. We even had to take some of our howitzers back a mile in order to hit the enemy in front of us. What a conglomeration of anomalies this war presents! In an age when our big guns can hurl huge projectiles many miles, we are compelled to fight with bows and bayonets and bombs and brickbats.

Bricks were not often used. But when the Turkish snipers "sneaked" close up to our lines through the scrub, we threw stones at the likely places. Thinking these missiles were bombs, the Turk would often run, or else disclose his position. Then we gave him a few rounds rapid.

One day a German aeroplane flew along the coast, and in plain view of the army dropped a huge bomb at our hospital ship, only missing the target by about fifty yards. There were no other ships near, so there was no excuse. This cowardly act so incensed our medical officer that he went straight out to our firing-line and threw a brick at the Turks, forty yards off. "I wear the Red Cross," he apologised, "so I cannot fire at them, and they are not supposed to fire on me. But I must show my indignation somehow."

As to the bows and arrows: this was Major Midgley's idea. At night the Turkish patrols crawled up close to our lines, and sniped away without being seen. Our flares could not be thrown far enough to show them up. So we made bows out of pine saplings and wire and sent fiery arrows into the scrub. This made the unwelcome visitors keep a respectful distance.

But if bows and bricks were only incidentals, the bombs were the real thing. In the wild bayonet charges our footballers were simply irresistible. But with the bombs our cricketers excelled. One of them exclaimed: "We've got the cows bluffed." Another boasted: "We've got 'em beaten to a frazzle"—shade of Roosevelt! Anyhow, our chaps could beat the Turks at the bomb business. Have I not already told how some of our cricketers caught the enemy's bombs and hurled them back again?

There was a picture—in *Punch* I think—of the incident of the Irishman who yelled out to the Germans, "How many of yez are there?" and on getting the answer "T'ousands," he heaved a bomb, saying, "Well, share that amongst ye!" The Australians have quite the same humorous appreciation of the situation. With the trenches anything between 10 and 1,000 yards apart, there was ample scope for the passing of compliments as well as bombs between the contending forces. It was quite common for a trooper to cry out: "Are you there, Abdul? Well, here's *baksheesh*." Or may be, "Here you are, Mohammed, here's a Christmas box"; and a hand grenade would accompany the sally. When a Turkish bomb arrived the Australian merely observed: "*Maleesch*," or "Ver' good, ver' nice," in imitation of the "gyppie" *dragoman*. If a bomb exploded right in the trench or on the parapet the real Australian "Slanguage" was sure to be heard. One Light Horseman was heard to observe as a bomb exploded over his head: "These Turks are clumsy cows; they'll be killing some of us if they ain't more careful!" Once the voice of a Hun sounded from a Turkish trench: "Come on you—kangaroo-shooters!" But prisoners told us that the German officers were rarely seen in the firing-line. They felt safer further back.

A curious incident happened in the infantry lines. A kangaroo-shooter from the Kimberley country threw a bomb at a Turkish trench only fifteen yards away, and the cries of "*Allah*," "*Allah*," told him that his aim was true. He turned to his mates and remarked casually, "That's the first man I've killed without getting into a heap of trouble." A much more unsophisticated youth—one of the recent reinforcements—had been a week in the trenches without actually seeing one of the enemy. Then a Turk jumped on the parapet, threw a bomb, and jumped down again. And the guileless one exclaimed, "That's the first Turk I've seen in his wild state!"

Lieutenant Massie, the giant Varsity cricketer, son of the General Manager of the Commercial Banking Company of Sydney—known in the 1st Brigade as "Massive"—was throwing bombs one night (he can throw bombs farther than any man on Gallipoli), and after landing a few in the Turkish trenches, he accidentally struck his hand on the back of the trench. The bomb he was about to throw rolled along the bottom of the trench and then exploded. Everybody in the vicinity bolted to the nearest traverse, so no one was hurt badly. But Massie was kept busy for a week picking bomb splinters out of himself.

Massie had several miraculous escapes since landing on Gallipoli. The closest shave occurred when he was out in front of the firing-line fixing some barbed wire. He was clambering back over the parapet when one of his own men mistook him for a Turk and lunged at him with his bayonet. Massie ducked just as if he were dodging a "straight left," but the point of the bayonet caught him in the neck, inflicting, fortunately, only a slight wound. Later he was seriously wounded, and was taken off to hospital.

There was one senior officer in the Light Horse who occasionally enjoyed fresh fish for breakfast. This was very rare on Gallipoli. The cook would never tell whence the fish came, but it was noted that the regimental supply of bombs was always one or two short. Nobody ever connected the absence of bombs with the presence of fish. But one morning very early the officer noticed the cook making stealthily in the direction of the cove. He followed. Then he saw the bombs explode in the water, and he saw the cook swim out and gather in half a dozen fine big mullet. An hour later he had delicious fresh fish for breakfast, while most of the officers had bully-beef and bacon. The officer was in a quandary. He did not know whether to court-martial the cook or promote him!

One other bomb incident I hesitate to give, as I did not see it, and cannot vouch for it. But up at Quinn's Post they swore it was true. I give it in the words of the callous-hearted soldier who told me the story.

We were giving Abdul a 'bit of hurry-up up' at Quinn's. Jim always was slow, and it settled him. He had a 5-seconds bomb, made out of a 'baccy' tin, and he was told to count one, two, three, and on the 'three' chuck the blame thing into the Turkish trenches. Well, he lit it, and it never burned too good, so he starts blowing at the fuse. He looked awful comical, and we yelled at him to 'shot.' But he kept on blowing till the dash thing exploded, and blew half his head off. He was a humorous bloke.

Chapter 16

Aeroplanes

A gunner of the 6th Battery, Victorian Division of Artillery, Anzac, at a time when victuals were not too plentiful, wrote:

> My turn at cooking comes round every third day. I give them bully-beef and biscuits one day, and biscuits and bully-beef the next for a change. How I think with envy of the wonderful messes of pottage the mater used to make for the hens at Sandringham! . . . It is a most peculiar sensation at first to have 'Weary Willies' bursting over you and to see the pellets dropping on the dusty road like rain after a dry spell.

And another wrote:

> The trenches are certainly the safest place to be in. One 8-inch shell took the roof (blankets) off our officers' heads, just missing Major Hunt, O.C., Lieutenant Smith and Lieutenant Perry, of our company, by inches—not the whole shell, but a piece of it. The shell killed a couple of our men when it burst. . . . We were continuously at it for five solid weeks, and then we were taken to Rest Gully for a rest, which consisted of fatigues, sapping, trenching under fire and working parties on the famous beach, where 'Beachy Bill' and 'Lonely Liz' used to scatter men by the score, with also an 11-inch shell dropping now and then from the Straits. Splendid rest, this!

Change! What change could one have there? Rest! What rest? John Bright in one of his most memorable orations said:

> The Angel of Death is abroad throughout the land. You can almost hear the beating of his wings!

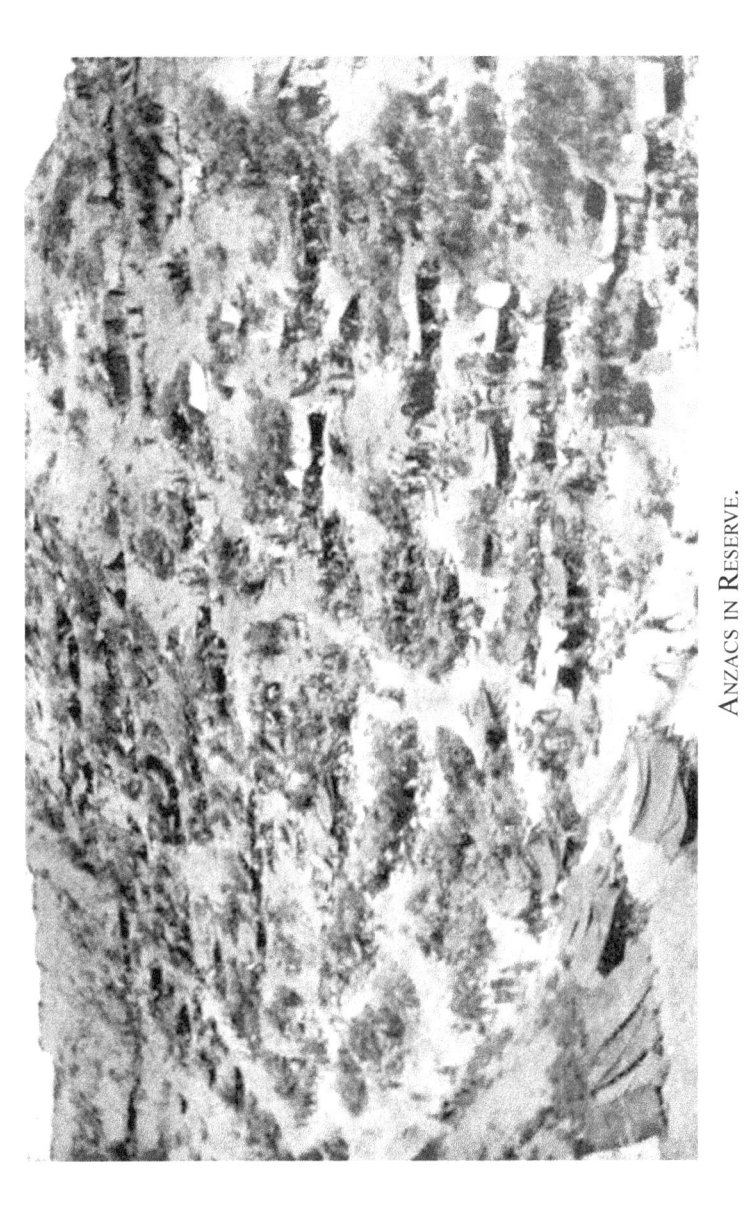

Anzacs in Reserve.
An Australian Brigade in dugouts in Rest Gully

But on Gallipoli you could hear the beating of his wings day and night, knowing not what the next moment might bring forth.

There were three mates in Junee, a western town of New South Wales, who used to play cricket and football together. When their country asked for soldiers they answered the call. The three enlisted together, shared the same tent in camp, and fought side by side in each successive engagement, from the landing to the fight for Lonesome Pine. One of them—Reg. Humphreys—fell with a bullet in his brain, and died in the arms of his comrade, Joe Charlton. Later in the day, Charlton fell, and the third man, Paul White, carried him back to the ship, where he died of his wounds. Out of 120 men of A Company only White and one other man remained. The rest were all killed or wounded or sick.

Such is war. And yet our boys went cheerfully on with their work. Hard work—hot work, so hot that we followed the example of the Indian Army and cut our trousers short. Very comfortable were these "shorts" when climbing about the hills. We looked like Boy Scouts. You should have seen the gunners on a hot day, stripped to the waist, and stripped from the knee to the feet—wearing their "shorts" and nothing but their "shorts"! Infantry and Light Horsemen, you could scarce tell one from the other. "Shorts" put us all on the same level. And we were all as jolly as sandboys, having our fun and cracking our jokes, reading the official *Peninsula Press* and enjoying the unofficial humour of our own trench organs, such as the *Dinkum Oil News* and *The Dardanelles Driveller*. We knew that Death was near, but we laughed in his face.

One day a bread ration was issued, instead of the inevitable biscuit ration. "Well, they might have given us butter with it!" exclaimed one trooper, with a smile. "Butter!" cried his mate—"you'll be wanting flowers on your grave next!"

They had many names for the Australians on Gallipoli, and one of them was "The Linguists." Some of the British Tommies used to stand in awe when they heard an Australian bullock driver giving vent to his feelings. I have even heard it said that a reputable Australian curate who went to the front in the ranks used the most disreputable language in charging a Turkish trench. One morning a German aeroplane dropped two huge bombs behind our lines. They exploded with a terrific blast, but did no damage. As the glistening bombs shot earthward, one of the men exclaimed, "'Ere comes 'er 'ymn of 'ate from 'ell!"

Another day we thought we would see an aerial duel. Already we had seen about everything else that twentieth-century war could show us. But the duel never came off. One of our 'planes took wing and flew north from Helles, over Anzac, towards Enos. Shortly afterwards, a German aeroplane took the air, and hovered over our lines. Evidently our airman could not see the Taube, for he circled aimlessly about over the Ægean Sea. Meanwhile, the German got quite venturesome. He sailed low—barely 2,000 feet above us—and though we blazed away with rifles and guns, he managed to have a good look at our position. Also, he dropped a couple of bombs at the right of our line before he bolted. But they fell harmlessly into the sea.

We got several good laughs every day. It made life worth living to note the wonderful good humour of our soldiers. Sometimes we laughed at the Turks, sometimes at each other. We had one great laugh at a German airman. He went up with a big bomb, evidently intent on some frightfulness. A British aeroplane immediately sighted him, and started in pursuit. Then a couple of French airmen took the air, and joined in the chase. With three of them hot on his trail, the German fled over the Turkish lines. The Allies gained on him, so to lighten his load he dropped his bomb overboard. But it landed on the Turkish trenches. They thought he must have been an enemy, for they at once opened fire with rifles, machine-guns, and anti-aircraft artillery, and the poor Taube had a very sultry time.

The Germans erected a new aerodrome, "somewhere on Gallipoli." The French airmen sighted it, dropped a few bombs, set fire to the petrol store, and did considerable damage. We had an aerial night attack on the Turkish camps at the Soghan Dere. Our aeroplanes first fired with their machine-guns at the flashes of the enemy's rifles. Then they dropped a couple of 20-lb. bombs, which burst in the centre of the Turkish camp. Finally they dropped 300 arrows amongst the bewildered enemy.

After watching the airmen operating over the Suez Canal and the Mediterranean, and in Gallipoli, we came to the conclusion that flying is easily the safest job in war time. We used to think otherwise. To the onlooker it appeared so hazardous, that the marvel was that those dare-devils were not all blown to smithereens. But for about three months, we watched them at work, and not a hair of one of their heads was harmed. Time and again the airman sailed across the enemy's lines, while their anti-aircraft guns worked overtime. The blue of the sky was flecked with white puffs of smoke where the shells burst, yet the aeroplane flew on serenely. I counted forty-one shells one day, which burst all round one of our airmen on reconnaissance. Many seemed to go very close indeed; others flew wide of the mark. The Turkish trenches would spring to life as our 'planes passed over, and thousands of rounds would be poured into the atmosphere. Their machine-guns would sound the *rataplan* as the belts were emptied. But the wild fusillade never disconcerted the airmen. All of which proves what an exceedingly difficult target the aeroplane must be.

We did not have any Zeppelins buzzing round the Dardanelles. Perhaps they were too busily engaged on their baby-killing enterprises on the east coast of old England. The nearest thing we had was an observation balloon, looking for all the world like a huge German sausage suspended in mid-air. But it was very helpful to our warships for observation purposes.

Chapter 17

"Padre"

In the training camps in Australia the chaplains conducted services, helped at the concerts, and generally made themselves useful and agreeable. On the transports they did pretty much the same thing; but somehow we never seemed to know them, and they, in turn, knew very few of us by name. It was when we settled down in Egypt that we first began to know them, and to appreciate their work. And since Cairo has the reputation of being the wickedest city in the world, there was ample scope for the operations of the chaplains.

But one of the chaplains had adamantine ideas on theological subjects. He was a great scholar, and had other virtues, but his conscience would not let him participate in the combined services with the other ministers. So when we came away to thrash the Turk we left him behind in Egypt.

In his stead we took an Irishman—Father Bergin. He was a good sport, a good priest, brave as a lion, and with wounded soldiers gentle as a nurse. His only fault was that he always wanted to be right up in the firing line, for he dearly loved a "scrap"—being Irish. When the 5th Light Horse Regiment had their fight near Gaba Tepe, Father "Mike" was everywhere tending the wounded, and as a water-carrier he rivalled Gunga Din. Those of us who were not of the "faithful" learned to like him more and more, and if the campaign had lasted much longer I fear we would have all been "Romans."

Then there was Captain Robertson, young and quiet, and kind of heart. I don't think any of us ever saw him in a pulpit. Mostly he had to preach in tents or in the open air. I have heard him hold forth in an Anzac gully, with the shells bursting overhead. Again, I have sat at his feet right in the support trenches, just behind the firing-line, while his sentences were punctuated by the report of snipers' rifles. He used to dwell on "historic associations." He told us that our feet had trod the same streets and fields as Moses and Aaron and Pharaoh, Joseph and Mary, the Apostle Paul, Antony and Cleopatra, Helen of Troy, Mahomet Ali, Napoleon and Byron, and a host of others. His *forte*, however, was not preaching, but practising. He practised most of the Christian virtues. He was the soldiers' friend, and when we'd sit and smoke and yarn round the camp fire at night, and some one swore inadvertently, he was not righteous overmuch.

Our third *padre*, the senior chaplain of the brigade, was Captain Keith Miller. As the Americans say, he was "some preacher." At Ma'adi we used to have the big tent packed with 2,000 soldiers. Visitors from Cairo and beyond used to go from our services as much impressed with the preacher as with the physique and bearing of the Light Horsemen. Sermon-tasters from St. Andrew's, Cairo, nodded their heads in grave approval. Elders, with an air of finality, said, "Yon's a fine deliverance"; and other elders answered "Aye." The *padre's* final oration and peroration before we left for the front won the special commendation of General Birdwood, who was present. I forget now what the sermon was about—but I know I wanted to cheer at the end of it.

On one of the Turkish prisoners captured, we found a copy of a divisional order, in which the O.C. stated:—

> I have many times been round the fire trenches, but have never met any Imam. I lately gave an order that Imams were to be constantly in the trenches, in order to keep up the morale of the men by preaching and exhorting; and whenever possible men should be assembled for prayer, and the call for prayer should be cried by a fine-voiced Imam.

Now, it is pleasing to record that no such order was necessary in the ranks of the Australian division. Our chaplains since the memorable day of the landing played their part manfully in the great game. McKenzie of the Salvation Army was real grit; one of the finest of our militant Churchmen. They were in the trenches day and night, talking with the men, writing letters home to their people, visiting the sick; and every man in our brigade was supplied with a neat little pocket Testament by a friend of the New South Wales Auxiliary of the British and Foreign Bible Society. And on Sundays there were services in all the brigades—in the gullies, or under the crests of the hills behind the firing line. And sometimes we couldn't hear the singing because of the cannons' roar; there was not one solitary spot in Anzac absolutely safe from the enemy's fire. And yet I have never heard of any soldier being wounded at any of these services! Once Padre Miller was conducting a service in Shrapnel Valley, and had finished his firstly, secondly, and thirdly, and was just coming to the peroration, when shrapnel shells burst overhead. So the service had to be abandoned. That was a "sair" trial to the "Meenister."

Yet, in spite of his many estimable qualities, I regret to state that Padre Miller had one besetting sin. It was a secret sin. Only a few of us knew of his weakness. He played chess. Yes, played chess over and over and over again. When in Cairo others of us would play tennis, he would slink away with some old crony and play chess. I have known him play till two o'clock in the morning at a game. (There is no doubt about the hour, because he called for me on the way back to camp.) He was often late at mess, playing chess. He scarce had time to dress, playing chess. Admittedly he played well, and after defeating the Ma'adi champions he sought fresh victims in Cairo. The Scotch engineer on the transport was a fine player, but he couldn't checkmate the *padre*.

When we landed in Gallipoli the first thing the *padre* did was to dig a dugout. The second was to seek a chess-mate. There was no chessboard, so he got the lid of a box. There were no chessmen, so he carved queens and bishops and knights and pawns out of the flotsam and jetsam on Anzac Beach. Then, safely ensconced in a snug little dugout, the *padre* and his mate stalemated and checkmated to their hearts' content, oblivious of the shells which burst around. Immediately after his tour of the trenches, and his visit to the sick, the *padre* would make for his chess-mate.

Later on we found him making periodical visits to the hospital ship. I admit he religiously did the rounds of the wards, and looked after the wounded, and I frankly admit that I went on board to see the nurses, but I'm positive the driving force behind the *padre's* visits was the prospect of a game of chess with the skipper.

After a few months on Gallipoli the *padre* was transferred to the hospital at Lemnos. We all sympathized with him, stuck at the base, and missing all the fun of the fighting. Then we heard that the M.O. at the hospital was a great chess-player, and we knew that the *padre* never deserved our sympathy. [1]

---

1. *Fighting the Good Fight*, Two Accounts of Chaplains During the First World War, *The Church in the Fighting Line* by Douglas P. Winnifrith and *In the Northern Mists* by Montague Thomas Hainsselin is also published by Leonaur

Chapter 18

"Stunts"

They are not battles or fights; they are hardly skirmishes even. They are just "stunts."

I don't like the word "stunt"; it sounds like an American vaudeville turn. But somehow it attained a general vogue on Gallipoli, and it meant any of the little incidents, episodes, and brushes with the enemy which served to relieve the monotony of trench warfare.

Having been ousted from their "impregnable" positions on the coast, the Turks dug in deep to block the advance of the Australians on the west and the Allies on the south. Slowly they were being shifted; more by the pick and shovel than the rifle. The trenches were only a few yards apart in some places; several hundred yards apart in others. And it was in the neutral zone between the hostile armies that these "stunts" took place.

Mostly they were planned and executed under cover of darkness, for a head couldn't be shown above the trenches in daylight without getting a score of bullets. Our chaps were far more enterprising and venturesome than the Turks, but the latter were better patrols. The reason was that the Turks know the country, wear a kind of moccasin on their feet, and move about quite noiselessly. With our heavy service-boots silence is impossible. So we got out early—just after dark—waited in ambush, and caught Tommy Turk when he came poking his nose into our business.

One fine "stunt" was spoilt by a cough. Lieutenant Chatham, of the 5th Light Horse, had a troop out in ambush near the Balkan gun pits, where the Turks were working each night. Just when the enemy's patrol approached, one of our troopers felt a tickling in the throat. He tried to swallow the tickle and couldn't. He gulped, but the tickling continued aggravating. At last he stuffed his handkerchief in his mouth and coughed. It was only an insignificant little cough; but it sufficed. The Turkish patrol halted and the leader investigated. Stealthily he crept up till he could almost touch the crouching Australian. *Bang!* Finish Turk. Patrol "*imshi.*" That was one to us. But for the unfortunate cough we might have got half a dozen.

The enemy scored next time. One of their snipers, over-bold, crept up in the scrub to within twenty yards of the trenches of the 7th Light Horse, and started blazing away. Our fellows could not get him from the trenches, so Sergeant Ducker and three others volunteered to rush the Turk's "posey" and bring him in, dead or alive. Cautiously they fixed bayonets, climbed on to the parapet, and then dashed out. They found the sniper's nest, but the bird had flown. A number of empty cartridge cases bore testimony to his activity. But the scrub was full of snipers, and as our dashing quartet dashed for home a hot fusillade was opened on them from the Turkish trenches and the scrub. Ducker dashed into shelter so fast that he landed on General Ryrie's back. No. 2 sent a miniature avalanche of dust and *débris* on top of Colonel Cox; No. 3 landed on my pet corn; and No. 4, Trooper Edgeworth, got a Turkish bullet in the arm. "*Maleesch.*"

One of our best exploits was "White's one-night stunt," as it was called. The general wanted a certain position taken and occupied. Our brigade had to do it. Under cover of night a patrol went out, reconnoitred the position, and formed a covering party for the work to come. Major Fred. White then took 150 men of the 6th Light Horse, armed with picks and shovels as well as their rifles, and dug a long sap six feet deep, right out to Harris Ridge. Then the trenches were dug, and the position occupied. The Sixth dug like miners, and burrowed like rabbits. Next morning when Abdul awoke he beheld the smoke of the Light Horse camp fires and the hill in possession of the enemy. And the Turks wondered what had happened.

One morning early, Major Windeyer, of the 7th, poked his head over the parapet to enjoy the panorama, and a Turkish sniper let fly, the bullet just whizzing past his ear. Several snipers had been heard in front of our lines, but not located. So it was decided to drive them off. Fifty volunteered for the job; six were chosen, but it was found that a dozen joined in the rush. The Turkish patrol was easily driven back by Sergeant Walker and his comrades, and the Turks in the foremost trench were so surprised that about fifty rounds were poured into them before they got busy. At least one was killed before their reinforcements came tumbling up. Then the Australians bolted for home, and reached safety without any casualties, though the Turks blazed away like fury. That's the luck of the game.

Sergeant Brennan, who used to be in the Dublin Fusiliers, and whose camp kitchens at Liverpool have often been admired by Sydney visitors, was in charge of the cooks and dixies of the 7th Light Horse. Every morning, breakfast over, he took down his rifle, strolled across to the trenches, and had innumerable duels with Turkish snipers. He had the range of all their trenches, and when he saw a sniper's "posey" he blazed away till he silenced the enemy. Now and then an unwary Turk showed half a head, and this Irish sharpshooter was on to him like a shot. Some days he would come back to camp angry and disappointed. "Thirty shots and not a single scalp," he exclaimed, kicking aside some innocent mess tin. But at other times he stalked back as if he had won the Battle of Anzac "on his own." "Killed three Turkeys," he cried. And then he was as happy as Larry all day.

But there was one man in the 5th Light Horse Regiment whom we called "The Murderer." He played the Turks at their own game, and beat them badly. He himself admitted it was "a shame to take the money." He used to sit with his rifle set at a certain track which the enemy thought was well concealed behind the hills. His mate had a telescope, and spotted for him. They waited till they saw a head appear, and they knew that three seconds later a Turk would be in full view for two seconds. That was quite enough. "The Murderer" was ready. The spotter said "Right"; the rifle fired, and another victim of German "*kultur*" fell.

The man's name was Billy Sing, a Queenslander, belonging to "Midgley's Myrmidons." The 5th Light Horse Regiment was nominally composed of Queenslanders; but the North Coast rivers of New South Wales were included in the 1st Commonwealth Military District. A great many men from the Tweed, Richmond, and Clarence Rivers enlisted in Brisbane. This was particularly true of the 5th Light Horse, for the majority of Major Midgley's squadron hailed from Northern New South Wales. They revelled in the exploits of the gallant little Major, swearing to follow him anywhere, so we called them Midgley's Myrmidons. If he were casually to remark, "Come on, boys, I think we'll take Achi Baba tonight," not one of them would have hesitated an instant. Major Midgley reckoned that since the glorious game of war degenerated into a battle of troglodytes, we might as well make it interesting and diverting. So, in this particular section of our line of battle, things were always happening. We never wanted for diversion. But this same diversion was always at the expense of our friend the enemy, and poor Abdul was correspondingly angry.

Sing held the Australian snipers' record. He was a crack shot, and had often won prizes at Brisbane and Randwick. Day after day, night after night, he used to settle down comfortably in his "posey" and wait for his prey. His patience was inexhaustible. He would sit for hours on end with a telescope glued to his eye, watching the tracks or trenches, where sooner or later a Turk was sure to show himself. If a Turk looked up, and then bobbed down quickly, Sing only grinned and waited. He would get his Turk later on. Emboldened by fancied immunity, the unsuspecting one would show his head again, then his shoulders, then half his body. Then Sing's rifle would crack, and another notch be made in the stick. There was not the slightest doubt of his performances, for every day an officer or non-commissioned officer checked the shot and recorded the kill. Before he left Anzac Billy Sing bagged over 150 Turks.

One night he went with the rest of Midgley's Myrmidons on a rather hazardous enterprise. It turned out to be one of the most successful affairs undertaken. General Ryrie wanted to know how strongly held were the Turkish trenches on an imposing ridge opposite our lines. The 5th Light Horse Regiment (Major Wilson) had to find out. Major Midgley's squadron had to make the attack. Major Johnson's squadron skirted the coast to keep Gaba Tepe quiet and guard against a flank attack. Captain Pike's squadron manned our outpost, and brought covering fire to bear on the enemy's right. One of our destroyers fired a few salvos at the Turks' position; just something to go on with. Then the Myrmidons sneaked out. It was about four o'clock in the morning. The moon had just set. Through the scrub they crept silently and stealthily. Not a sound escaped them till they were within thirty yards of the enemy's trenches. Then something warned a sentry, and he fired half a dozen shots into the scrub. But our lads lay low and made no sound, and the sentry evidently thought he was mistaken.

At a word from the major the line started slowly forward again, and, unnoticed, reached a little knoll, not ten yards from the Turkish trenches. Then the music began, with a pyrotechnic display thrown in. Our "grenadiers" threw bombs and grenades thick and fast on the bewildered garrison, while on either wing our riflemen blazed away, driving back the supports which hurried up from the enemy's rear. On the shore line, B Squadron opened on the Gaba Tepe defences, while we in the trenches blazed away at Pine Ridge till our rifles burned our hands. The silence of the night was broken by a fierce fusillade, as pin-points of fire burst from the whole length of the Turkish trenches. But the regiments on our left lay low in their trenches, and laughed at the Turks' impotent rage. We on the post had one man very slightly wounded—just a scratch. The shore line squadron had also one man wounded—rather badly.

Midgley's gallant Myrmidons effected a splendid withdrawal, for after they had cleaned out the Turks' advance trench they came back to our lines with only one man wounded in the leg. When he came in Major Midgley reported to the general: "We've got 'em stone cold. My birds simply bombed them out, cleaned out the trench, bagged about thirty, and are now back for breakfast."

CHAPTER 19

Lonesome Pine

August on Gallipoli will be long remembered by the Australian troops on account of the terrific fighting in which they participated. July was fairly quiet. But August witnessed the great flanking movement of the British troops, which we were confident at the time would result in the final defeat of the Turks on the Peninsula.

The new movement took the form of an attack and demonstration in front, while under cover of darkness a new British force landed at Suvla Bay and enveloped the enemy's flank. In the better understood parlance of the ring, we feinted with our right, and landed a terrific blow with our left. So successful was this feint that all the local reserves of the Turks were hurried up to counter it, thus leaving an opening for the main attack from Suvla.

All the honour and glory of the magnificent charge of our Australians and the capture of Lone Pine Ridge belongs to our infantry comrades of the 1st Brigade. We of the Light Horse can claim none of the kudos for that gallant feat of arms, though the 2nd Light Horse Brigade and 2nd Infantry Brigade fought like tigers day after day and night after night to hold the line during the consequent counter-attacks.

There was some fierce and bloody fighting during those early days of August all along the line, but the capture of Lone Pine Ridge stands out, not only because of the complete success of the operation but on account of the irresistible dash and daring of the lads from New South Wales.

Just before the battle we got a message from Sir Ian Hamilton. It was in a Special Order issued from the general headquarters of the Mediterranean Expeditionary Force, and was as follows:—

August 5, 1915.

Soldiers of the old army and the new:—

Some of you have already won imperishable renown at our first landing, or have since built up our foothold upon the peninsula, yard by yard, with deeds of heroism and endurance. Others have arrived just in time to take part in our next great fight against Germany and Turkey, the would-be oppressors of the rest of the human race.

You, veterans, are about to add fresh lustre to your arms. Happen what may, so much at least is certain.

As to you, soldiers of the new formations, you are privileged indeed to have the chance vouchsafed you of playing a decisive part in events which may herald the birth of a new and happier world. You stand for the great cause of freedom. In the hour of trial remember this, and the faith that is in you will bring you victoriously through.

Ian Hamilton, General.

For five days and nights the battle raged on Gallipoli. The cannon roared incessantly; big guns, little guns, field guns, mortars, ships' guns, and howitzers belching forth their iron hail till the earth trembled again.

Hardly heard amid the thunderous roar of artillery were the interminable rattle of musketry, and the spiteful snapping of Maxims. From the firing fine to the base, hardly a square foot of ground seemed safe from shrapnel shells and high explosives. Probably 200,000 men were engaged, hacking at each other day and night; for this seemed the decisive battle of the Gallipoli campaign.

It made one's blood flow faster and tingle with pride to see the magnificent way our young Australians played the great game of war. Hemmed in and cooped up in the trenches for weary weeks, they had at last been let loose upon the enemy at Lone Pine. Like hounds from the leash, they charged across the bullet-swept area between the contending armies. The Turkish lines spat fire from every loophole, and machine-guns seemed to revel in murderous music. On swept the line, thinned but dauntless. Heroes fell on every side. Enfilading volleys swept across from the side. To us on the right the men seemed to falter for a space; but it was only to hack their way through the maze of barbed wire. Then they scrambled over the sandbags, their last obstacle, and bayoneted the Turks by scores. One wild *mêlée* on the parapet—thrust, lunge, and parry—then the trenches were ours.

This charge was only one little episode in the long, long struggle of those early days of August. Each time the Turks massed for a charge Colonel Rosenthal's guns tore great rents in their ranks, and wrought havoc in their trenches. But again and again their bomb-throwers—hidden behind the communication trenches—massed and endeavoured to retake the position.

On the left the Australian and New Zealand Division, with whom were our 3rd Light Horse Brigade, made a splendid advance over shrapnel-swept ravines, defended by trenches and machine-guns cunningly hidden in the scrub. They charged the heights like the Highlanders at Darghai, but against a far more formidable foe. They suffered terribly, especially the Light Horsemen, but there was no stopping them.

Hundreds of prisoners were captured, much ammunition, many rifles, and a few machine-guns. The prisoners stated that the Australians' attack was a complete surprise. But a far greater surprise awaited them. At night in the offing there was only seen one hospital ship, though now and then a destroyer sent its searchlight on to the hills. But when the first streaks of dawn-light fell on the Ægean Sea the amazed Turks beheld a vast flotilla, and in futile anger the German staff officers witnessed another landing on Gallipoli. Almost unmolested, a new British force landed at Suvla Bay, for the Turks had hurried all their reinforcements back to stem the onrush of the Australasians. Several warships and a score of destroyers glided into the bay or round the projecting horns, and sent a veritable tornado of shells on to the enemy's position.

A dozen big transports came up and emptied their khaki freight into a hundred barges, pinnaces, launches, and sweepers. The new force landed, formed up, and marched inland against the Turkish right. At first the resistance was feeble, and the enemy was driven back beyond the salt lake towards the hills. More troops were hurried up from Gallipoli, and the fight waxed more strenuous. Nothing in the war has provoked so much keen disappointment and vitriolic criticism as the Suvla Bay business. We who saw the landing, mingled with the British troops and knew how much depended on the success of the venture, are perhaps not the best critics. We do not know all the facts of the case. We think Sir Ian Hamilton's strategy was brilliant. We know the work of the Navy was magnificent. We fear that after the landing, the attack was not pushed home with that vigour and determination which were essential for the success of the operation. Precious time was lost, and while the British hesitated the Turks hurried up reinforcements and once more barred the way to Constantinople. And we had hoped that August would herald the beginning of the end.

★★★★★★

The First Infantry Brigade of the Australian Division did big things since landing on Gallipoli—glorious deeds that will be the pride and boast of successive generations of Australians. It was Colonel Maclagan's 3rd Brigade that achieved undying fame by the electric daring of its picturesque landing, but it was the 1st Brigade which, following hot on the heels of the gallant Thirds on that memorable day, swarmed up the heights and drove back at the point of the bayonet the successive swarms of fanatical Turks who tried in vain to drive them into the sea. But how dearly was that victory won! How the ranks of these gallant Sydneysiders were decimated! It was small comfort to us to know that Constantinople reported 120,000 Turkish casualties for the three months after our landing.

The list of senior officers killed was appalling; not one of the original battalion commanders retained his command. Not less tragic was the loss of junior officers. In the Lone Pine attack the 3rd Battalion lost eight officers killed and nine wounded; while the 2nd Battalion lost nine killed and eight wounded. We captured many prisoners, several machine-guns, and many thousands of rounds of ammunition. But the cost to young Australia was so heavy!

★★★★★★

Lone Pine Ridge was situated right in front of the centre of the Australians' position, and was strongly held and fortified like a little Gibraltar. The overhead cover was so strong that our shells made little impression on the Turkish trenches. Machine-guns punctuated the line at regular intervals. The open space in front was swept by enfilading fire from the Bloody Angle on the left and the Pine Ridge on the right, while the German gunners behind Gun Ridge had the range to a nicety. A network of barbed wire entanglements provided a nasty obstacle right in front of their trenches, while "posies" for expert snipers and bomb-throwers completed their defence works. To the trained soldier the position looked absolutely impregnable.

But our lads were well trained. They reckoned they were veterans. I who had visited them in camp and on the march round about Liverpool knew the stuff of which they were made. Yet there were those who, ere they left Sydney, said the Australians would only do

Entrance to Lone Pine, which was so hardly won.

garrison duty, as it would be murder to put them in the firing line. Competent critics held that General Birdwood was the luckiest man in the army in getting the command of the Australians, for no troops in the world could do what they have done. Is this boasting? Ask the British staff officers. Ask the French. Ask the Gurkhas and the other Indian soldiers.

The First Infantry Brigade fired not a single shot during the great charge. It was all bayonet work. In the ranks were many of the heroes who landed on the memorable 25th of April, were wounded, and were now back in the firing line. Others had been in the thick of it all the time; no periodical spells such as the soldiers in Flanders get. Others again were the latest reinforcements who left Sydney in June, and landed the evening before the battle. Yet these raw youngsters, having their first experience under fire, charged with the best, and wielded a bloody bayonet within the hour. And many of them—Dr. Digges la Touche amongst the number—perished in their first fight.

Prior to the charge our artillery opened a heavy bombardment of the Lone Pine trenches. Shrapnel and high explosives rained down on the Turkish lines. The Turkish gunners in turn opened on our lines a devastating fire, and the resultant roar of heavy guns and screeching of shells created a veritable inferno.

I don't know how long it lasted, but suddenly our guns ceased, and on the instant our gallant infantry sprang from their trenches and charged straight ahead. They were over our parapets and well on their way before the Turks could realise it. Then rifles and machine-guns started a murderous fusillade, while the guns in the background sent a hail of shrapnel. Thick and fast fell the attackers. One marvels how any escaped that hell of fire. But, fortunately, only a small percentage of the Turks are marksmen. The German machine-gunners, however, were very deadly, and the enfilading fire from Pine Ridge increased in volume and effectiveness and the trail to Lonesome Pine was strewn with khaki figures. Our Light Horse on the right had all their crack shots picking off the Turks on Pine Ridge, while our field guns in Hughes's battery at point-blank range helped to keep the enfilading fire from this quarter down to a minimum.

Meanwhile the Firsts had almost reached their goal. They were checked for a space by the barbed wire; but hacking their way through they scaled the enemy's parapets, tore aside the overhead cover, leaped into the trenches, and then, free from the murderous cross-fire of machine-guns, they resolutely set to work with the bayonet to finish the job. Since the days of Plevna [1] the Turk has been reckoned second to no soldiers in the world behind the trenches and parapets. I am not in a position to dispute this, but I do claim that in the open or with the bayonet the Turk is not a match for the Australians. Right along the trenches and saps the Firsts fought their way, bayoneting every Turk or German who did not immediately throw down his rifle. Here and there the defenders made some resistance, and little knots of them would rally for a minute or two. But the Firsts flew at them like eagle-hawks, and a neat bit of bayonet work settled the Turks for good and all.

As to the part played by the Light Horse Brigades in the general scheme of attack, it fell to General Ryrie's Second Brigade to hold the right of the line opposite Gaba Tepe. We made minor demonstrations against the enemy, cleaned out a few of his trenches, kept his snipers very much in subjection, mined and counter-mined, and blew up Abdul's tunnel just when he thought he was going to do the same to us. Also, we kept each day a fresh squadron in Lonesome Pine to assist in defending against the Turkish counter-attacks. Our losses had not been great, considering the slaughter all along the line. Since landing we had had just over 600 casualties, of whom 105 were killed; also we had had several hundred sent sick to hospital.

General Chauvel's First Brigade had suffered much more heavily. They had well performed their share of the trench fighting since May. In the big battle the First Regiment had to advance under a murderous fire from Pope's Hill, and take the Turkish trenches opposite the Bloody Angle. Captain Laurie, with A Squadron, scaled the parapets and charged across the bullet-swept interval, while Captain Cox, with B Squadron, crawled up a gully; and then both squadrons rushed to the attack.

Without firing a shot, they captured three successive trenches, bayoneting the defenders, and then swept on. Twelve officers and 200 troopers made that dashing charge, and without reinforcements they withstood all the Turkish counter-attacks from four o'clock in the afternoon till half-past six. But the slaughter was cruel. Fewer and fewer were left to defend the hard-won trenches. From all sides the enemy threw bombs and grenades. Our bombs were all gone. At last the remnant had to retire. Major Reid was killed; Captain Cox so badly wounded that he died a few days later; only fifty unwounded

---

1. *Conflict at Plevna* (containing *Under the Red Crescent* by Charles Ryan & *The Third Battle of Plevna* by William V. Herbert) is also published by Leonaur.

men regained our trenches. Of all the officers, Major Glasgow alone was unwounded.

A worse fate befell the 3rd Brigade, under General Hughes. In their attack on Walker's Ridge they lost thirty-two officers and 400 men in ten minutes. They swarmed out of our trenches and sprang forward; and then so terrific was the hail of bullets that they fell in heaps. It almost looked as if they had thrown themselves prone to get cover. Machine-guns swept the area from end to end. The 8th (Victorian) and 10th (Western Australian) Light Horse Regiments just thinned out and wilted away. About a hundred unwounded men came back from that hell.

Later on the 3rd Brigade had their revenge. When the New Zealand and Australian Division swept forward, driving the enemy before them, and capturing trench after trench, there remained one spot on the line of ridges that baffled the attack. Both sides dug in, and had a few days' respite. Then the 10th Light Horse hurled themselves on the stubborn Turks, cleaned out their trenches, and with bloody bayonets stood masters of the hill. It was only a remnant of the regiment that remained, but they baffled every effort of the Turks to dislodge them.

One spot further along the line had at length given way to the pressure of the enemy's attacks. The New Zealanders, after some magnificent fighting for several days, had been driven back from one point on the line. It was essential that the position should be retaken and our advanced line linked up. So the 9th Light Horse Regiment was sent forward to do the job, and they did it brilliantly....

The pen seems so futile a thing to depict the scene. It was the same thing day after day. A stealthy advance through the scrub, a rattle of snipers' rifles, then wild cheers, as the Australians scrambled up the hill; a terrific fusillade as they neared their objective; a glint of gleaming bayonets as they charged the trenches; then the wild *mêlée* of hand-to-hand fighting, when one Australian always reckons himself a match for three Turks; and finally the shout of victory.

And through it all the stretcher-bearers were real true-blue. Under the heaviest fire they went right up to the firing-line, tended the wounded, and carried them back to the field hospitals. Oh, you, who think the Army Medical Corps is always comfortably and safely situated at the base, pray be undeceived! Their part is just as hazardous as that of the soldier of the line.

Soon the cheers of the victors and the cries of the Turks died down. Above the groans of the wounded could be heard the staccato tones of the officers ordering platoons and sections this way and that to defend the position against counter-attacks.

Scores of prisoners were led away. Hundreds of captured rifles were stacked. German machine-guns were faced about and manned. Bomb-throwers were placed in position. Hot tea was served out to the men. Night fell. Lone Pine was ours. The successive ridges on our left towards Hill 971 had all been captured by the New Zealanders, and our 4th Infantry Brigade under General Monash and the 3rd Light Horse Brigade under General Hughes. The big Battle of Suvla Bay was over. But it was only a partial victory. Despite our gains and our losses the Turks still blocked the way to Constantinople.

CHAPTER 20

Lucky Escapes

When I was a good little boy going to Sunday school, teacher gave me a book entitled *Wonderful Escapes*. I read it with absorbing interest, for it told of the marvellous escapes of princes and princesses from fortified castles in the hands of their enemies.

Yet these delightful tales which so thrilled my youthful imagination pale into insignificance and seem quite commonplace when compared with the hair-breadth escapes which I have witnessed, and which I have myself experienced since the 2nd Light Horse Brigade landed on battle-scarred Gallipoli.

With the Taubes dropping bombs and darts from the sky, with the Turks undermining and blowing up our advanced trenches, with snipers cunningly concealed on the ridges, and the enemy's big guns sending high explosives right across the Peninsula, there is really not a single safe spot in all Gallipoli. So, when these Australian soldiers get home again and fight their battles o'er again, don't disbelieve them. The truth here is much more startling than any fiction.

I vouch for the absolute accuracy of the following incidents, for they all came within my own ken. Some will say 'tis "luck"; some, "fate." Others speak of the law of averages. It may be that the prayers of thousands of Australian mothers and sisters beseeching Heaven for the safety of their loved ones are not all in vain. For in very truth there have been occasions when escape from instant death has savoured of the supernatural. Men have left their dugouts for a few seconds, and almost on the instant a shell has wrecked those same dug-outs. Others have seen shells fall on the identical spot they occupied a few seconds before. Men have come back scatheless from the open field which has been ploughed with shrapnel. Some have charged across the hills in the teeth of murderous machine-guns, which were spitting death-pellets unceasingly.

General Birdwood was having a look at the enemy's position when a sniper's bullet parted his hair and split his scalp. Half an inch lower would have been certain death. It would take pages and pages to tell of the lucky escapes I could relate.

Take the case of Colonel Ryrie, now a brigadier-general. There is a very comforting idea that regimental headquarters are always a long way behind the firing-line, while brigade headquarters are further back still. Therefore, it is argued, a brigadier has a nice, safe job. This may be all right in theory, but it does not work out so in practice. I call to mind that hearty send-off given to the then Colonel Ryrie by his constituents at North Sydney, and what the recipient of that favour said on the occasion. "Don't you worry about me," he said, "I'll come back all right. They may knock some corners off me, but they won't get me." Some "corners" have been knocked off him.

I do not believe there has been a day when the brigadier-general has not visited the firing-line of his brigade—up to the time when a bullet got him in the neck and he was lost to us for some time in hospital. Time and again he has taken the sniper's "posey" and mingled in a bit of sharpshooting himself. Also, he has at different times gone in advance of our firing-line to select new positions. Once, with his brigade-major and orderly officer, he suddenly stopped to watch a squadron at bayonet exercise, and a shrapnel shell burst, and the case landed right in front of him. Had he not stopped, it is certain the party would have been wiped out.

On another occasion the Brigadier-General and Major Onslow, Major Suttor, Major Windeyer, Major Rutledge, Captain Miller and Captain Higgins were outside Colonel Arnott's dugout, when three shells burst overhead. No one was hurt, though a fragment of shell landed in the midst of them. There is always so much more landscape to hit than man.

Such incidents can be multiplied by the score. Sergeant Christie Hayden—who was badly wounded in South Africa—emerged from his dugout the other day, and a shell missed him by inches, and wrecked his little grey home. Sergeant Paddy Ryan, Sergeant Ken Alford, and Lieutenant Pearce were standing together on Holly Ridge a few days ago and a sniper's bullet perforated the hats of both the sergeants, and missed the officer by a fraction of an inch. I wonder did that sniper wait till he got the three in line, instead of making sure of one? Trooper Sandy Jacques showed his head over a parapet for a couple of seconds, and a sniper fired, but by a merciful dispensation of Providence, the bullet split just before reaching him. The nickel casing went to the right, and the leaden missile to the left. So Jacques got a slight wound on each side of the head, and was able to walk to the ambulance.

Some wag has suggested that the bullet knew very well what to expect if it struck Sandy's head, so it took the line of least resistance; another said that Jacques was wounded by two different bullets from a machine-gun. Lieutenant Lang sent a man for water. As he walked away a high explosive shell passed right between his legs and then exploded. The soldier merely exclaimed "Strewth!"

Here's an example of good and bad luck following one upon the other's heels. The Turks bombarded our lines, and hurled half a dozen shells into our trench, smashing down parapets, wrecking rifles and gear, splattering bullets and splinters everywhere, and yet miraculously missing everybody. Later on a single stray bullet found its way through a loophole, ran off at an eccentric angle, and killed young Trooper Bellinger, one of the best lads in the Sixth.

I went down to Anzac Cove for a swim. About 500 soldiers were having a glorious time—better than Bondi. Half a dozen shells landed in the water, while the pellets splashed all round like hail. Most of the swimmers sought shelter; some took not the slightest notice. Not one man was hit! But they are not always as lucky as that. Sometimes they pay for their temerity. Trumpeter Newman and I stood outside the field hospital a week ago, and a big howitzer shell burst fairly in front of us, killing or wounding a dozen men. Neither of us suffered a scratch, but there was a ringing in my ears for hours afterwards.

Lieutenant Ferguson was out on Ryrie's Post, beyond the firing-line, for over an hour, while the Turkish artillery just dotted the whole area with shrapnel. Hardly a square yard missed getting something, yet he never stopped one. When Sergeant Shelley walked along Shell Green a shell burst, and we could hardly see him for the dust kicked up by the flying shrapnel bullets, yet he never got a scratch. Another shell just shaved an infantryman, who turned round, shook his fist at it, and swore loud and long. A second shell came after the first, so close that it almost took the soldier's breath away. He did not wait to swear again, but ran like a scared rabbit to his dug-out!

An infantry officer vouched for the accuracy of the following story:—Two "Jack Johnson" shells (probably fired from the *Goeben*) landed in quick succession in a trench occupied by half-a-dozen Australians. The first tore down the parapet and buried one of the soldiers. Before his mates could dig him out the second shell burst in and disentombed him.

CHAPTER 21

The Church Militant

La Touche is dead. . . .

Digges La Touche, the brilliant scholar, the fervid evangelist, the militant divine, the fiery orator, the pugnacious debater, the uncompromising Unionist, the electric Irishman—Digges La Touche, the patriot, is dead: killed in his first battle, yea, in the first minute of his first battle.

It came as a shock to those of us who knew him in camp. It will come as a bigger shock to those who knew him in the Church, for it seems scarcely more than a month since they bade him God-speed in Sydney. He landed in Gallipoli on August 5, the eve of the big battle. That night he went into the trenches. Next day he participated in the gallant charge of the First Brigade which found its culmination in the capture of Lone Pine Ridge. But La Touche never reached the Turkish trenches. Charging at the head of his platoon, he had barely got beyond our own trenches when a bullet struck him in the body. He fell. Later he managed to crawl back to our trenches—and died.

For ten months he had pleaded with Church and State to let him serve as a soldier of the king. For ten weeks he wore the uniform of an officer of the Australian Imperial Force. For ten hours he did duty in the trenches. For ten brief seconds he knew the wild exultation of the charge. Then there passed away a great-hearted Britisher, strong of soul and clear of vision, who counted it a great privilege to fight and die for his king and country. The Crescent had glorified the Cross.

The pity of it all was that none of his friends knew he had arrived. The Dean of Sydney—Chaplain-Colonel Talbot—was about to read the burial service over eighteen soldiers who had perished in the charge. He heard the name, and looked and saw his friend. That was the first he knew of Lieutenant La Touche's arrival on Gallipoli—his arrival and departure.

When we of the Sixth Light Horse first went into camp at Rosebery Park, La Touche was there with the Thirteenth Battalion, under Colonel Burnage, one of the most popular, as he afterwards proved one of the most gallant, officers who ever donned a uniform. Dr. Digges La Touche desired first to go as a chaplain, but was not selected. Far be it from me to reflect on the judgment of the Archbishop of Perth who selected the Anglican chaplains, but I have seen chaplains with not one tithe of the qualifications that La Touche had for the job. Failing selection as a chaplain, he enlisted as a private in the First Contingent. But he was not over-robust and was transferred to the Second Contingent, and rose to be a colour-sergeant in the Thirteenth. The Primate objected to ministers serving as soldiers, and the friends of Digges La Touche time and again urged him to remain behind. But his determination was fixed, and though health considerations compelled his withdrawal from the Thirteenth Battalion he attended an officers' training school and gained a commission as second lieutenant; and he left Sydney in June with the Sixth Reinforcements of the Second Battalion. Then, after a brief spell in Egypt, he came to Gallipoli.

Before he got his commission La Touche was a great recruiting sergeant. He never left in the minds of his hearers any doubts as to his opinion of Prussian militarism and savagery. His addresses on the war were fiery orations, inspiring men to patriotic self-sacrifice and zeal for Empire. He summoned all the riches of his intellect to confound, refute and castigate the nation that had done such scathe to Belgium. And though no Turk or Hun died by his hand, Dr. La Touche inspired many young Australians to take their place in the firing-line. Some of these were with him in the fatal charge. He saw them dash on through the bursting shrapnel, and he heard the cheers of victory as they gained the parapets, bayoneted the defenders and captured the position. As one thinks of him cut off in the prime of life, when the unbalanced enthusiasm of his youth had hardly been tempered by experience, there comes a feeling of revolt against the decrees of the God of Battles.

But Everard Digges La Touche was only one of the many brilliant young men who have laid down their lives in this cruel war. Remembering the inspiration of his example, one feels that he did not die in vain.

Others will speak of his scholarship—he was a student in law, arts and theology, and a lecturer of Trinity College, Dublin, before he went to Australia. I have seen him in the pulpit, in Synod and on the public platform, but I leave it to others to appraise his churchmanship. I merely record, with heartfelt sorrow, how Lieutenant La Touche died a soldier's death on Gallipoli.

The Church Militant! Was it ever so militant as now, when all the powers of darkness, all the forces of the Devil, are arrayed against Christianity and all the manifold blessings of Civilization? Look at stricken Belgium and the battlefields of France, where hundreds of priests combine their holy offices as chaplains with the duties of the soldier, a Bible in one hand, a sword in the other! See, at the head of Russian armies, priests leading the soldiers into battle! And here, on Gallipoli . . .

We have our chaplains, and we have ministers of the Gospel fighting as "happy warriors" in the ranks. Digges La Touche had the character of the happy warrior, who:—

While the mortal mist is gathering, draws
His breath in confidence of Heaven's applause.

But it matters little whether they go forth as armed men in the Great Crusade, or to fight the good fight by ministering to the dying, or to read the burial service over the dead, they all must needs be brave men, ready to risk their lives. Death is very close to all of us in this war—chaplains, doctors, stretcher-bearers and all.

Brave men, yes. Fighting parsons, soldier saints, whether they be chaplains, or whether they have forsaken the study for the stricken field, the pulpit for the platoon, or whether they be in the Army Medical Corps, heroes of the Red Cross of Geneva. Some have been killed, some wounded.

Andrew Gillison is one of those who has gone to his rest—one of Gallipoli's heroes. Chaplain-Captain Andrew Gillison, of the Fourteenth Battalion, Fourth Infantry Brigade, was the first of the Australian army chaplains to be killed. Prior to the war—and that seems a long, long time ago—he was a minister of St. George's Presbyterian Church, East St. Kilda, and before that he was at St. Paul's, Brisbane. He was well known and greatly loved throughout the whole Presbyterian Church of Australia. He was no sour-visaged, long-faced Christian. His religion was cheerful, optimistic and joyous. I met him at St. Andrew's, Cairo, and then I knew why the Fourth Brigade almost worshipped him. On the transport he was a prime favourite. He sang a good comic song. He entered into the boxing tournament. He won his first bout in fine style. Then he got a hiding, and took his beating like a man.

It was meet that such a man should die giving his life for another. Greater love hath no man than this; and Andrew Gillison would not have willed it otherwise. It was while performing a work of necessity and mercy on Sunday morning, August 22, that he was shot, and he died a few hours afterwards.

The New Zealand and Australian Division had made a most gallant attack on the hills occupied by the Turks. Pressing home the attack with the bayonet, they drove the enemy from trench to trench and from ridge to ridge. Deeds of valour were performed day after day and night after night. Heroes died on every side, with no historian to tell how gallantly they died. One of these young Australians was wounded in the charge, and lay some distance behind the advanced position. It was then that two fighting parsons came along a communication trench, which was comparatively safe from rifle fire, but offered little protection from shrapnel. From a slight hollow they saw the wounded man, in evident agony, raise his hand, and try to move. Captain Gillison and Corporal Pittenrigh—who is a Methodist minister when not a soldier—decided to try to effect a rescue, though they knew a machine-gun was trained on the trench, and had been warned to beware of snipers. Mounting the parapet, they crawled along some distance towards the wounded man. A couple of bullets zipped by, but they pushed on. More bullets flew, and both the rescuers were wounded.

Then they tried to regain the shelter of the trench, and Gillison was wounded again, but his companion managed to scramble in. Mortally wounded in the chest and the side, the poor chaplain lay in the open, but was soon carried in and conveyed to the field hospital. He was conscious for a while and cheerful, though he knew his hours were numbered. He was able to greet Chaplains F. Colwell and G.T. Walden, who had just arrived with Colonel Holmes's Australian Brigade, and Chaplain J. M. Dale of Brisbane. Before two o'clock he was dead, dying as he had lived, a gallant Christian soldier.

That night, wrapped in a Union Jack, he was buried. It was bright moonlight. Out in the Ægean the warships and hospital ships lay passive. Back in the hills sounded the ceaseless rattle of musketry. Chaplain-Colonel E. N. Merrington conducted a brief service, at which were chaplains of all denominations and several officers and men of his brigade and battalion. The little shallow grave lies a couple of miles north of Anzac, on the edge of the five-mile beach that stretches on to Suvla Bay. As with the hero of Corunna, "*we carved not a line, and we raised not a stone—but we left him alone with his glory.*" His comrades went back to the firing-line with the memory of his self-sacrifice to cheer them on. And we thought then of Longfellow's beautiful lines—

Dust thou art, to dust returneth,
Was not spoken of the soul.

Soon the battalion will erect a little wooden cross over his grave—one more of those little wooden crosses that are so numerous on Gallipoli. We who knew and loved him will never forget Andrew Gillison.

CHAPTER 22

Sergeants Three

Non-commissioned officers are the backbone of the British Army!

This is high praise, of course, yet it is well merited; and I think the same tribute can be paid to the non-coms. of the Australian Imperial Force.

For our non-coms. hold their office by virtue of their merit. It is simply a case of the survival of the fittest. We all started off scratch. There was keen competition for stripes when our regiment was first formed. The best men were selected. There was no favouritism. Some old soldiers had an initial advantage, but all the appointments were provisional at first, and they were all tried in the crucible. Only the pure gold was retained; the baser metal was rejected.

The result was that when the 6th Light Horse Regiment left Sydney it had a body of non-commissioned officers who would compare favourably with any in the world. It was a great pity that the people of Sydney never saw the "Fighting Sixth" ride through the metropolis. In Egypt they were reckoned the best mounted regiment that ever left Australia. The limelight has been turned right on to subsequent volunteers. Other contingents—months and months and months after we left—bathed in the smiles of the multitude. Special trains were run in order that the country folk should see them. But our brigade, the 2nd Light Horse Brigade, comprising the 5th, 6th and 7th L.H. Regiments, were hunted off like thieves in the night. In deadly secrecy we struck camp. In the dawn hush we stealthily slunk through the city streets.

We were all on board the transports before Sydney was well awake. The papers were not allowed to publish a line about our departure. So the country folk came to see their sons and brothers off—too late. The whole city knew it—too late. Every German spy in Australia knew it—early. When we arrived at Aden a nigger on the gangway of the transport told us to a man the constitution of the force, the number of ships, and our destination. So cleverly had our censors concealed our movements!

★★★★★★

So it is a pity the brigade never rode with clinking snaffles and clanking stirrups through the city—more for the sake of the city than the soldiers themselves. Also because many of our soldiers will never again see George Street, or Pitt Street, or Martin Place, or Macquarie Street. The wastage of war has had its effect. We have been under fire day and night. Snipers have taken their toll. Machine-guns have added to the casualties. Shrapnel shells and high explosives have torn gaps in our ranks. In killed and wounded we have lost over half our original strength.

There were three sergeants of the 6th Light Horse Regiment, who now are resting in little shallow graves in Gallipoli. Never again will they watch the sun go down in splendour into the Ægean Sea. When we go marching into Berlin they will be with us—but only in spirit; and when the war is over and the boys from the bush ride home again, there will be three sergeants missing. But their names will be emblazoned on Australia's roll of honour. And we of the Sixth won't forget Sergeant Sid Parkes, Sergeant F. R. Tresilian, and Sergeant Fred Ellis.

Sid Parkes was small and slight, so small that he was almost rejected by the medical examiner. He had to show his South African record, and remind the doctor that giants were not wanted in the Light Horse, but light, active, wiry horsemen. So he just scraped through and went into camp. I remember him at Rosebery Park. Not much over five feet three, only about nine stone, but active and strong. He knew his mounted drill like a book, and he knew how to handle men; so he soon got his three stripes—and stuck to them. The men liked him. The officers appreciated him. We saw several other sergeants made and unmade, but Parkes of B Squadron was a fixture.

Already he had seen four years' peace service, and eighteen months' active service in South Africa with the New South Wales Mounted Rifles. So he brought the lessons of his previous experience to bear on his new job. On parade he did his duty well. Off duty he was a humorist, and as care-free as a schoolboy. On the transport he entered into all the fun going. In Egypt he played the game. Somehow, I always thought Parkes would come safely through the war. We joked together the night we first went into the trenches, never anticipating ill. Yet he was the first man of the regiment killed in the trenches. A sniper's bullet came through a loophole and killed him on the spot.

✶✶✶✶✶✶

Frederick George Ellis, sergeant in C Squadron, was an Englishman from Hants. He had spent five years in the Royal Navy, some of the time on the China station. He was one of the few survivors of H.M.S. *Tiger*, which was rammed and sunk during the naval manoeuvres off Spithead. Three years ago he came to Australia to get colonial experience, prior to settling on the land. A few years in the nor'-west, at Bogamildi and Terala stations, transformed the sailor into a bushman. So he came to Sydney when war broke out, and joined the 6th Light Horse. He rose to be lance-sergeant. On July 12 he was killed by a shrapnel shell on Holly Ridge. Several of our fellows were killed and wounded that day, for the Turks dropped 200 shells on the Light Horse lines, and for an hour or two it was terrific.

✶✶✶✶✶✶

A strong, dominant personality was Tresilian, one of the very best troop sergeants that ever joined the Light Horse. He seemed to love the firing-line like home. He was quite fearless. Somehow he seemed to revel in the roar of battle. On one occasion the Turks sent a dozen shells at our little section of the trenches, smashing down the parapets, making the place a wreck, wounding two men, and half blinding, half deafening, half choking, half burying six of us. When I could see and hear and breathe again I saw Tresilian laughing merrily. "Hello, Bluegum," he said, "not killed yet?"

He came from Humula, near Wagga, where his people were well-known farmers. Till a young man he remained on the farm, and was known throughout the district as a good "sport"—a good cricketer and footballer, and a fine rider and shot, just the typical Australian Light Horseman, though more sturdily built than the average. He tired, however, of the farm, and yearned for the freer life of the Western plains. So he tackled station life, became a station manager, rode over the whole of the north-west, went to the Northern Territory in search of pastoral lands, and when the war broke out was managing a station in the Boggabri district. He had seen service in South Africa, and he once more volunteered to serve the king.

On Gallipoli his scouting and patrol work were excellent. He seemed to have a charmed life, for he had many narrow escapes in the open and in the trenches. On the day he was killed a bullet whizzed past his head, just wounding his cheek slightly. Later on he and Sergeant Paddy Ryan were putting barbed wire entanglements in front of our trenches. A sniper's rifle cracked. Ryan escaped. Tresilian fell dead.

CHAPTER 23

Mail Day

"Serves 'em right, for sinking our mails and spilling our rum!"

This remark broke from the angry lips of one of our Light Horsemen as our artillery inflicted a terrific bombardment on the enemy. The Turks replied vigorously, and the result was an inferno; shells bursting everywhere, gaping holes torn in the inoffensive earth, trench parapets levelled, soldiers slaughtered. Then, as our warships steamed up and added their quota to the conflict, the trooper reiterated, "Serve 'em right!"

For a moment we wondered what he was driving at. Then we remembered that a few days ago some unlucky Turkish shells had landed on a barge coming from one of the supply ships to Anzac, and had sunk it. This caused us but slight concern till we found out that several casks of rum were spilled, and 250 bags of mails from Australia were sent to the bottom of the sea. Then, as our ships' guns sent another salvo, we too exclaimed, "Serve 'em right."

We did not mind the rum so much, for the Army Service Corps had quite enough on hand for our ration when the issue was due. But every Australian on Gallipoli bitterly resented the loss of the mails. It made us really angry. Some of our chaps reckoned that the loss of the mails and rum was the prime cause of the big battle which ensued during the early days of August. So they have called it the Battle of Mail Rum. Historians, however, will probably call this sanguinary struggle the Battle of Suvla Bay.

Good folk at home, and even of the out-back country, receive mails pretty regularly. We get ours once a fortnight, or once a month, or at even longer intervals. I do not join in the general chorus of condemnation of our postal service, for since the time I enlisted nearly twelve months ago all my letters and parcels have come duly to hand, while, so far as I know, none of my letters to Australia have gone astray. When we came to Gallipoli we naturally expected some break in the continuity of the service—and we got it. One reason is that, while the New Zealanders provided an up-to-date, well-equipped postal service, the Australians had only a skeleton postal corps—shockingly undermanned. Hence the congestion at Alexandria and Lemnos and the belated arrival of letters at Anzac.

There is nothing that cheers the soldiers up so much as letters from home. You see their eyes light up with pleasure as the postal orderlies toil up the hill with the mail bags. The postal corporal is the most popular man in the army. But he always seems so slow with his sorting. Those of us not in the trenches crowd round him and pounce eagerly on our precious missives. I have seen a great, hulking, swearing, unshaven trooper grab his letter, sneak into his dugout, and kiss reverently some love-letter from a sweetheart back in sunny New South Wales; or perhaps it was from his mother or sister away in the great West land. And I've seen anxious troopers, with yearning eyes, hang round till the last letter and postcard were sorted—then wander away silently, and gaze dry-eyed over the blue Mediterranean.

Some of our fellows are married men, and some of these married men used jokingly to say that they had enlisted to get away from ... never mind; but I know that there was not one of them but spent half his time thinking of the old and the middle-aged and the young folks at home—not one of them but would have given the world to be able to take a peep at the wife who scanned the casualty lists so eagerly as they appeared in the papers, and the kiddies who strutted round proudly, saying, "Daddy's gone to the war."

It's cruel to be forgotten by the home folk when fighting the battles of one's country; but most of our chaps are loyal, and they always blamed the post office. One time our 6th L.H. Regiment mail had not arrived, and I stood by miserably watching other lucky devils getting their letters. Suddenly my eye caught the address on a newspaper, "To any lonely soldier in the Australian Army." I immediately grabbed it. There was a protest from the postal official, who said the paper was not addressed to me, and that unclaimed papers are considered as "*baksheesh*" for the postal corporal. I pointed out that it was not unclaimed, since I had claimed it; and that as I at that moment was a lonely soldier it was clearly addressed to me. There was a fine row, but I won my case—and the paper.

Always at the end of the sorting there are many, many letters unclaimed. And the regimental sergeant-major goes through the list, and with heavy red pencil writes "killed," "wounded," or "missing" on the envelope. What a tragedy lies hidden in these little heaps of letters to dead soldiers who can never read them!

It was no small loss, that barge with 250 mail bags from Australia. When I saw the barge sink I repeated the prayer of the popular English preacher, who exclaimed, "God damn the Sultan!" Why should that love-laden barge be the mark for the Turkish gunners? And why, after the hundreds of boats they have missed, should they get a bull's-eye there? It is sad to think of the thousands of soldiers who will never know the loving thoughts penned in those precious missives. Many will wonder why friends and relations have never written. And folks at home will be wondering why they got no answer.

For a time we simply could not write home. There was an envelope famine on Gallipoli. Not a single envelope could be had for love or money. We readdressed our old envelopes, or turned them inside out. We made postcards out of cardboard and cigarette boxes. Some of us even wrote home on the biscuits, which were warranted not to break. We waylaid sailors on the beach and offered fabulous prices for paper and envelopes. We wrote to our friends in Ma'adi and to the stores in Alexandria. But it's a long, long way to Egypt, and it seemed a long, long time before the envelope famine was relieved. That's one reason why some of our chaps never wrote home. Another reason was that we were all so tired after our turn in the trenches and the eternal "dig on, dig ever." As for stamps, everybody in Australia knows the legend on the soldier's envelope: "No stamps available."

Some of the letters home were delightfully ingenuous. Nearly all were brimful of cheerfulness. Now and then there was a growl; but we knew it wouldn't help the home folk if we complained, so I might paraphrase the Psalmist and say that all our men were liars—cheerful liars. I told you of the trooper who wrote home, "Dear aunt, this war is a fair cow." But that was exceptional. Most of the soldiers told cheerful lies about the good time they were having, the romance of war, the excitement of battle, and the exhilaration of victory. They told of the tricks they played on the Turks, the dummies they held above the parapets for Abdul to snipe at, the "stunts" for drawing the fire from the enemy's trenches, the risky excitement of bomb duels, the joy of swimming while "Beachy Bill" was showering shrapnel over them, and the extortionate rates charged by the sailor on the beach for condensed milk and chocolates.

But a real "grouse"—never. Well, hardly ever. And when there was one, depend upon it there was some good reason for it. I remember one. It was when a man in Australia wrote to a friend at Anzac: "We're having a rather bad drought in this district; you're well out of it." The man at Anzac fairly lost his temper. He wrote back: "Come over here." And after painting a picture of a battle or two—a real growl, if ever there was one—he concluded: "It's nearly as bad as your drought, and you're 'well out of it'."

Later, I was told, these two men met on the bloodstained fields of Gallipoli.

CHAPTER 24

Reinforcements

At last the Second Australian Division arrived in Gallipoli, and their advent meant that we of the First Australian Division would get a well-earned relief—and "for this relief much thanks."

We had been waiting for some time for our comrades to come and take over the trenches, and it was good for our tired eyes when we saw General Holmes and his 5th Infantry Brigade landing on Gallipoli.

We note that nearly all the newcomers had the name of their home town printed in indelible ink on the front of their hats. So it felt just like a railway journey all over New South Wales to see the brigade marching by. There we saw Bathurst, Maitland, Goulburn, Glen Innes, Wellington, Dubbo, Kiama, Kempsey, Moree, Cootamundra, Albury, Hay, Dungog, Tamworth, Nowra, Narrandera, Yass, and scores of other towns and villages scattered over the length and breadth of New South Wales. The next thing we noted was that all the new-comers looked big and strong and fit. They looked just like our First Australian Division when it marched out of Mena.

General Legge and the Headquarters Staff of the Second Division had a lot of luck getting to Gallipoli at all, for the *Southland* was torpedoed with them on board. It is believed that an Austrian submarine did it. Our casualties were about twenty killed and fifteen drowned, Brigadier-General Linton dying after he was rescued from the water. It happened at about ten o'clock on the morning of September 2. The S.O.S. wireless signal was immediately sent off, and seven boats eventually steamed up to the rescue. The troops behaved magnificently, and were all put into the boats without much trouble. The firemen and stewards, however, got panicky, and three were shot before they sobered down.

But the *Southland* did not sink. So the skipper called for volunteers to take the ship back to Lemnos, and fifty Australians took on the job. General Legge and Staff stayed on board also. One soldier had a stroke of luck. He was blown unhurt into the air, and by the time he came down the water was in the hold, and he landed softly and safely.

The behaviour of our troops upon the *Southland* is to be numbered among the grand things of this war—one of the grandest. It has been likened to the *Birkenhead*.

When the Second Australian Division arrived how few of the old hands were left from the heroic band that landed on April 25! Just to show something of the wastage of war, here are some authentic figures. Of the 1,200 men in the 3rd Battalion who marched out of Kensington Racecourse, 100 were left. Eleven hundred were among the killed, wounded, missing and sick. Of the original sergeant's mess of the same battalion fifty-six left Kensington; five remained, and of these four were officers. The original G Company had 121 men—eight are left. Of the original 2nd Battalion, sixty remain out of 1,200. Of course, the majority of these are sick and wounded, and will rejoin their battalions. It is the immediate wastage that affects the army. That's why we want a continual stream of reinforcements.

Of the First Australian Division there remained on Anzac only the 2nd Light Horse Brigade, and the 3rd Infantry Brigade—plus, of course, the artillery and engineers. We were daily expecting to get our well-earned spell, and retire to the islands of the blessed in the Ægean Sea.

General Ryrie's brigade of Light Horsemen had their fair share of casualties. Of the original three regiments, Lieutenant-Colonel Cox's 6th, Lieutenant-Colonel Harris's 5th, and Lieutenant-Colonel Arnott's 7th, had 110 killed, 550 wounded and 1,050 sick with dysentery and enteric and other ills, or a total of 1,710 casualties. But the reinforcements kept us fairly up to strength.

Brigadier-General Ryrie, the brigade-major, Major Foster, and the staff captain, Captain Pollok, were all wounded. Of the fifty New South Wales officers of the brigade who landed on Gallipoli, the orderly-officer, Lieutenant Hogue, and the adjutant of the 6th Light Horse, Captain Somerville, were the only two who had not been killed, wounded or sick. A great many officers who had been sick and wounded, after a month or two in hospital returned to duty.

The landing of the 3rd Brigade, and the subsequent terrific three days' fighting on the heights of Gallipoli by the 1st, 2nd and 3rd Brigades made Wolfe's exploit on the Heights of Abraham sound like a picnic. The thrilling capture of Lone Pine by the 1st Brigade was one of the finest exploits of the war, while the splendid defence of that stronghold by the 2nd Infantry Brigade and the 2nd Light Horse Brigade against the repeated counter-attacks of the Turks was worthy of all praise. The magnificent charge of the 2nd Infantry Brigade down at Helles made the British and French troops thrill with pride. The charge of the 1st Light Horse Brigade at Walker's Ridge was a glorious sacrifice. Australians have every reason always to be proud of the first fights of her First Division.

CHAPTER 25

Shell Green

My dugout overlooked Shell Green.

From the comparative safety of this retreat I could sit and watch the pomp and circumstance of war, its pageantry and pathos.

To be sure there was little that was picturesque in war as we saw it in Gallipoli. There was no martial music. The "thin red line" had given place to drab khaki. There were no fiery war-horses with tossing manes and champing bits, no dashing cavalrymen with flashing sabres. There were no gun teams, spanking bays and blacks, for we had to manhandle the guns up and down the hills into action. The nearest approach to a pageant was when the British fleet flew along the Ægean waterway, and fired some reverberating salvos at the Turkish batteries.

Ashore all was strictly utilitarian; no ceremony, no display. It was midsummer, so we curtailed our trousers and wore shorts. Our shirts were sleeveless. Putties and leggings were mostly discarded. When out of the trenches shirts were usually considered superfluous. Our backs and arms and legs were so suntanned that the brownest of the beach surfers at Bondi would envy our complexions. So when on fatigues or off duty it was a tatterdemalion army that marched to and fro over Shell Green.

Humour and pathos were strangely intermingled. We saw after a skirmish a score of fine young Australians laid out for burial, wounds gaping and clothes blood-clotted. Our hearts were wrung with anguish for mothers and sisters and wives back in the great South Land, ignorant as yet of their bereavement. A minute later the antics of some humorist would set the camp roaring with laughter. *Anon* some of our chaps would be wounded, and carried in on stretchers; then some bolting mules or a wrecked dugout, or an explosion in the commissariat would set us laughing again. It is this saving grace of humour, as I have written before, that made life worth living in Gallipoli; but it also made the Gurkhas and the Tommies wonder what manner of men we were. The Englishmen regarded the Gallipoli campaign with great seriousness. The Indians appeared stoically indifferent. The Australians regard the whole show as a great adventure.

It's not hard to guess how Shell Green got its name. No gift for nomenclature is needed to find names for Hell Spit, Casualty Corner, The Bloody Angle, or Shell Green. The whole green is pitted with holes made by the enemy's shells. Some months ago these shells played havoc with our men. Some were killed as they lay in their dug-outs, others slaughtered on their way to and from the beach, some while in swimming. But we learned our lesson. We got to know the safety spots and the danger zones. Day after day the shells fell harmlessly, pock-marking the face of the earth, but doing us no ill. The Turks thought we had guns on Shell Green. So when our artillery got busy, the Turks blazed away, "searching" the area. But after four months' searching they failed to silence our guns. The remarks of our troopers as the shells landed were many and varied, but all were inspired by a quaint, unquenchable humour. When the quartermaster's store of the 4th Light Horse was wrecked, and four soldiers crawled uninjured from the *débris*, their mates called out, "Your luck's in. Get a ticket in Tatt.'s."

There are many graves on Shell Green—graves of Australian heroes. There's a little God's acre near the crest of the hill, overlooking the blue Ægean Sea. Sometimes towards evening the Turks tired of their fierce fusillade, and all seemed peaceful and quiet. The report of an odd sniper's rifle sounded more like the crack of a stock-whip. The sun sank in splendour on Samothrace, and the gloaming hour was sweet with meditation and thoughts of home. It darkened, and only the searchlights of the destroyers and the green streak of the hospital ship reminded us of war. We had our burials mostly in the evening. The *padre* came along, and a few of the dead soldier's friends straggled down from the trenches. The services were short but impressive. The shallow grave was filled in, and a rude cross marked the spot. Here's where we buried Colonel Harris, the loved leader of the 5th; Lieutenant Robson, the genial quartermaster of the 6th; Lieutenant Thorne, the brilliant Duntroon footballer, of the 7th; giant Gordon Flanagan, who was shot through the heart while asleep in his dugout; Tresilian, the dare-devil sergeant, who revelled in battle; and many more gallant horsemen of the 2nd Brigade, who will never more hear the *réveillé*.

Shells and bullets were not the only things that flew over Shell Green. Aeroplanes were frequent visitors. Mostly they were French or British, but now and then a German Taube streaked overhead, dropped a bomb or two, or a shower of darts, and then bolted for safety back to Turkish territory. So far we had not witnessed a duel in the heavens. It's about the one thing we missed. Several times we saw our airmen give chase to the Germans, but the latter never waited for a bout. One day we thought we were going to see an aerial scrap, and like rabbits from their burrows, the whole troglodyte population of Shell Green emerged from their dug-outs to witness the spectacle.

A Taube appeared over Suvla Bay, and a British airman took the air at Helles, and started in pursuit. The anti-aircraft guns of the Turks opened on our plane, and flecked the blue with a dozen shells, but scored no hit. Our gunners opened on the Taube, and made far better practice than the enemy, but could not bring the machine to earth. The two planes streaked across the sky like huge eagles, with outstretched wings. The Taube manoeuvred over the German guns, and our airman followed, despite the unfriendly greeting of the land-lubbers below. We on Anzac focussed our binoculars and strained our eyes till the fliers passed beyond the hills. Finally we heard the Taube had justified the maxim, "*Discretion is the better part of valour.*" Just as the aerial exhibition was over a couple of high explosives burst on Shell Green, and the "rabbits" bolted once more to their burrows.

It is the little incidents that relieve the monotony of war. I have seen some gallant deeds done here on Shell Green. One day a shell cut a telephone line between our observation post and a battery. It happened to be right on the most dangerous spot on the Green. But without a moment's hesitation a signaller sauntered out established the connexion, and sauntered back, despite the shrapnel. I saw Captain Evans, the little medical officer of the 7th, time and again streaking across the danger zone and tending men under fire. I have heard the cry, "Stretcher-bearers," and on the instant the devoted A.M.C. men have grabbed stretchers, and bolted to the rescue; this not once, but a hundred times. Some day I'll get a virgin vellum roll, a pen richly chased and jewelled, and in letters of gold I'll try to tell the people of Australia something of the heroism of these stretcher-bearers.

It was on Shell Green that the genial General Ryrie was injured. If he had been more careful of his own skin he would have got off scot-free. But a shell had just landed amongst the "rabbits," and the cry of

Brigadier-General G. Ryrie.

"Stretcher-bearers" told us that some of the boys had stopped a bit of shrapnel. Without a second's thought General Ryrie walked out on to the Green from headquarters with his brigade major and orderly officer. . . . "You know, Foster," he said to the former, "they could get us here too."

No sooner were the words out of his mouth than there was a crash. Shrapnel splinters and pellets zipped all round us. The cook's camp was a wreck. Pots and pans were perforated prettily. For a second I thought that no one was hit, for cook crawled out of the *débris* grinning. Then I heard the general in his cheery voice exclaim: "Holy Moses, they've got me where the chicken got the axe."

It was a close shave. The bullet entered the right side of the neck, penetrated a few inches, and stopped right on the sheath of the carotid artery. A fraction of an inch further and it would have been "Good night, nurse." . . . That night the old brigadier was taken off to the hospital ship and on to Alexandria. Colonel Cox of our 6th Light Horse Regiment took temporary command of our brigade.

CHAPTER 26

The Anzac V.C.'s

As there passes before my mind's eye a kaleidoscopic picture of the wildly hilarious fighting of the early days of Anzac, and the rough and tumble jumble of Lone Pine, I can't help thinking of the luck of the game. "Were honour to bestow her crowns on those who had a right to them, the skull up on the battlefield would often wear a diadem."

So many unknown heroes lie buried on Anzac. So many passed the crucial test of supreme trial and with strong arm and true heart performed prodigies of valour—but no one saw them. As a rule there was hardly time to take stock of everything. Time and again did individual Australians do great deeds, but the historians will never know of it. They are mostly too modest to talk of it. And the officers who might have reported and recommended are dead.

Take that wonderful landing on the fateful day, April 25, when Australia made such a gloriously picturesque *début*. How many men of Maclagan's gallant 3rd Brigade in that never-to-be-forgotten charge up the heights won the greatest military honour that the king can bestow. But so many officers were picked off; so many men really deserved the V.C. The only solution seemed to be the conferring of the coveted medal on the whole brigade. But there was no precedent for this. So none of them got it.

Our first Australian V.C. was young Jacka of the 4th Brigade. He was young and not of the splendid physique of most of the Australians, but he was greased lightning with the bayonet. It all happened on Courtney's Post. The Turks had been sapping in towards the front trench, and after a shower of bombs they swarmed in and captured the trench. But Lance-corporal Jacka, posted behind the traverse in the fire trench, blocked their advance. An officer and a few men hurried up and volunteers were immediately ready to eject the intruders.

Then while the officer and three men engaged in a bombing exchange with Abdul, Albert Jacka jumped from the front trench into the communication trench behind, ran round and took the Turks in the rear. He shot five of them and bayoneted two. The officer's party then charged and shot the four remaining Turks who tried to escape. They found Jacka leaning up against the side of the trench with flushed face, a bloody bayonet in the end of his rifle and an unlighted cigarette in his mouth.

The boys that took Lone Pine, who did that fine charge amid a shower of lead and shrapnel such as the war had not previously seen, got no V.C. for their valour. But the lads who held the hard-won post against all the subsequent counter-attacks did manage to secure a few. One of these was Captain Shout. But he never lived to wear the cross. For three long days and longer nights he participated in the furious hand-to-hand fighting in Lone Pine. Captain Sass and Lieutenant Howell Price both did great deeds in that thrilling time and each had several scalps to their credit. But Captain Shout with his bombing gang was ubiquitous. Laughing and cheering them on he time and again drove the Turks back, and then when he reached a point where the final sandbag barrier was to be erected, he tried to light three bombs at once and throw them amongst the crowding Turks. To throw a single bomb is a risky job. To throw three bombs simultaneously was a desperate expedient. One exploded prematurely, shattered both his hands, laid open his cheek and destroyed an eye, besides minor injuries. Conscious and still cheerful he was carried away. But he died shortly afterwards.

The heroic Seventh Battalion—victorious Victorians—participated in the great charge of the 2nd Australian Infantry Brigade down at Helles; the charge that made the French and English marvel at the dash of the young colonials. Then the Seventh managed to bag four V.C.'s in Lone Pine. The 2nd Light Horse Brigade and 2nd Infantry Brigade were holding the line against repeated counter-attacks, and it was then that Captain Fred Tubb, Lieutenant Symons, Corporal Dunstan and Corporal Burton won the V.C. On the night of August 8, while the British troops in the Suvla area were struggling to wrest the hills from the Turks, the Turks round Lone Pine were vainly endeavouring to recapture this stronghold from the Australians. On the right of the 7th Battalion things were particularly sultry, and early on the morning of the 9th some determined attacks by Abdul resulted in six of our officers and several men being killed and wounded. A bit of the front sap was lost, but Lieutenant Symons headed a charge, retook the sap, shot two of the Turks with his revolver and finally erected a barricade which defied all the attacks of the enemy. It was a bitter struggle and Abdul set fire to the overhead cover in the hope of driving back the Seventh. But the fire was extinguished and the position held for good.

It was give and take, attack and counter-attack all through August 9, that showed the qualities of pluck and determination which won the V.C. for Captain F. H. Tubb, Corporal Dunstan and Corporal Burton. Three times the enemy attacked with bombs, blew up our barricades, and swarmed into the trench, but each time Tubb and his companions returned to the assault, repulsed the invaders, rebuilt the barricades, and in spite of a shower of bombs held the post. Captain Tubb was wounded in the head and arm, but stuck to his job and baffled all Abdul's machinations.

Lance-corporal Keyzor was one of a band of heroes who did wonders in the hell-zone at the south-eastern corner of Lone Pine. It was a murder hole and after much slaughter we found that we could not hold the outer trench, while Abdul found that he also was unable to hold it. Finally it was abandoned as no man's land. But round about here there were lively times during August. As a bomb-thrower, Keyzor was pre-eminent. He was one of those who repeatedly caught the enemy's bombs and hurled them back before they could explode. It was here that Colonel Scobie was killed shortly afterwards, and here it was that for days and nights Keyzor moved amongst the showers of bombs with dead and dying all around, and threw bombs till every muscle ached and he could not lift his arm.

Young Hamilton was very young. But lots of these young Australians had old heads on their young shoulders. It was at Lone Pine where the 3rd Battalion was defending a section of the line against the repeated attacks of the Turks that young Hamilton won the coveted honour. He climbed on to the top of the parapet and with a few sandbags as a precarious shield against bombs and bullets he stayed there for five solid hours sniping merrily, potting off any stray Turks that showed up, and giving warning to the officer below each time the enemy started out to attack. There was plenty of shrapnel flying and the zip of bullets into the sandbags grew monotonous. But young Hamilton hung on.

It was away on the left of our line at Hill 60 that Lieutenant Throssell of the 10th Light Horse performed his great act of valour. There was one section of the enemy's line that obstinately defied the Australasian attack. At last the 3rd Light Horse Brigade received orders that the redoubt had to be taken. The brigadier sent the 10th Light Horse Regiment out to do the job. Just after midnight—August 28-29—the Westralians suddenly leaped on to the parapet and charged ahead. They were met with a hail of machine-gun and rifle fire and a shower of bombs, but nothing could stop those horseless horsemen. A brief *mêlée* on and in the Turkish trenches and the position was won. But holding it was a far more difficult matter. Lieutenant Throssell in charge of the digging party worked overtime putting the new line in a state of defence.

Soon the Turks massed for the inevitable counter-attack, and Throssell, with Captain Fry and a troop of the Light Horse, repulsed the first charge. But just as dawn was breaking the Turks came again with a shower of bombs as a prelude. The grenades were smothered as they fell or thrown back again, but Captain Fry paid the final penalty. One bomb rolled over the parapet into the trench, and spluttered. The men yelled "Let it rip." But the only safe thing to do was to smother the bomb or heave it out. The gallant captain chose the latter alternative, but the bomb exploded and killed him. The holding of this threatened elbow of the line devolved upon Throssell, who rose manfully to the occasion. With his rifle he shot half a dozen Turks and with his cheery example he heartened his command, and Abdul attacked in vain. Twice indeed they swarmed in and the Light Horsemen had to give ground. But only a few yards and a fresh barricade was immediately erected. Early in the afternoon Throssell was wounded in the shoulder. But he kept on. At four o'clock he got another bullet in the neck. He kept on. Then just after nightfall relief came and his superior officer sent him back to the field hospital.

There were other Australians who gained the V.C.—Captain Hawker of the Flying Corps, Corporal William Cosgrove of the Royal Munster Fusiliers, who did such a fine performance down at Helles, and others. But other historians will tell of their deeds. Corporal Bassett of the New Zealand Signallers won his V.C. for a daring exploit—laying a telephone wire right on to Chunuk Bair in broad daylight under a heavy fire. But Maori-land will do him full justice.

The 2nd Light Horse Brigade had a sultry time in Lone Pine during August. After the big attack early in August they complained that for twenty-four hours they did nothing but bury dead Turks. The stench was shocking—sickening. There was no time for decent burial.

Dozens of Turks were placed in the short communication trenches between the lines and covered up with earth, and the ends of the trench bagged up. Partly to kill the insufferable stench the boys smoked dozens and dozens of cigarettes. . . . Later on the boys had more than their share of the bombing. Sergeant Ryan won the D.C.M. But scores of the boys did big things that in lesser wars would have won distinction. Here they just were numbered with the unknown heroes. Every man on Lone Pine deserved special honour. If they had been Germans they would have been covered with iron crosses. As it is they are just satisfied that they were able to do their job. Anyhow, Australia won't forget Lone Pine.

Chapter 27

The Final Phase

Days dragged drearily on. Pessimism peeped into the trenches. Later in the solitude of the dugout pessimism stayed an unwelcome guest, and would not be banished. All the glorious optimism of April, the confidence of May, June and July had gone, and the dogged determination of August, September and October was fast petering out. Abdul had fringed the dominating hills with barbed-wire and bayonets, and in very surety Australia was "up against it."

Not that anyone dared talk pessimism. The croakers would have been squelched instanter. But deep down there was a feeling that unless heavy reinforcements arrived we could never break through to Constantinople. But at Anzac and Suvla the British hung on, desperately, heroically.

September's cold snap was forgotten in the unexpected warmth of October—just like an afterglow of summer. Then came the wintry winds of November—and the blizzard. . . . Of course we have snow in Australia. Kosciusko is all the year round covered with a soft white mantle. Down on Monaro it can be bleak and wintry. And the old Blue Mountains now and then enjoy a spell of sleet and snow. . . . But taking us by and large we are a warm-blooded race, we Australians. That is why we viewed the approach of winter with some concern. We knew Abdul could never, never, never break through our lines, and drive us—as Liman von Sanders had boasted—into the sea. But we were beginning to fear that we were a long, long way from Constantinople.

The blizzard swooped down on Anzac. Just like a shroud the white visitation settled on Gallipoli. It was cold as a Monaro gale. Soldiers crowded round the fires, and at night in the trenches it was terribly hard to keep awake. The cold was something to remember. We could keep our hands a bit warm by giving "five rounds rapid" and hugging the rifle barrel. Talk about cold feet; we had heard of "cold feet" when we were in Egypt. But this was the real thing. . . . How we invoked rich blessings on the heads of the Australian girls who had knitted us those warm socks! How we cursed the thieves along the lines of communication who pillaged and pilfered, while the men in the firing-line went begging! But through it all the indomitable cheerfulness of the Australian soldier would not be crushed. They laughed and joked when their teeth chattered, so that clear articulation was impossible.

To preserve some circulation they stamped their feet till exhaustion bade them cease. But the blizzard was inexorable. The cold permeated everywhere. We got just a glimpse of what the British army suffered in the Crimea.

Frost-bite was something to fear and dread. It was agonizing. Hundreds of men were carried down to the field hospitals and sent across to Lemnos. There were scores of amputations daily.... We had cursed the heat of July and the plague of flies, but now we prayed for summer again.

Now and then the English home papers blew in and we eagerly scanned the pages of the dailies for news of the war. We were astounded at the tone of the criticism hurled at the government. So much of it was Party criticism, captious criticism. So little of it was helpful constructive criticism. In Parliament and in the Press the critics were "agin the gov'ment" rather than against the Hun. We felt wonderfully proud of our Australian papers, the *Herald* and *Telegraph* and *Argus*. Also we were rather proud of the commendable restraint of our politicians. Not one word of captious criticism had there come from responsible Australian papers and people. We knew that mistakes had been made. We knew that it was a big gamble sending the fleet to hammer their way through without the aid of an army. But we did not slang-wang the government. In the dark hour when everybody was blaming everybody there was only one message from Australia. Press and politicians struck the same note. It was merely a reiteration of the prime minister's message that the last man and the last shilling in Australia were now and always at the disposal of the Empire.

Then came talk of evacuation. It staggered us. In the House of Commons and in the Press columns were devoted to discussing the Dardanelles question and evacuation was freely recommended. The Australians rose in wrath and exclaimed, "*We're d——d if we'll evacuate. We are going to see this game through.*" It was unthinkable that, having put our hands to the plough, we could turn back. The Turks and their German masters were kept well informed of the discussions at home and it made them tremendously cocky. England had practically admitted failure. The great Dardanelles expedition—the greatest crusade in the world—was an admitted fiasco. Then the Turks reasoned together. And they agreed that even "the fool English" would never talk so much about evacuation if it were even remotely likely. But it was worth an army corps to Abdul, and it did not make General Birdwood's task any easier.

Then Kitchener came. Many of us had seen him in Australia and South Africa. We had confidence that he would see the thing through. He landed on the beach and soon the word buzzed through the dugouts, up the gully, and along the firing line. "K. of K." was on Anzac and the boys off duty congregated to give him a rousing welcome. He went round the Anzac defences with General Birdwood, saw everything and then started in to weigh the pros and cons of a knotty problem.

Ever since the day of landing, we had discussed in an offhand way the possibility of "getting out." Not that we had ever considered it remotely possible that we should ever turn back. But just as a strategical and tactical exercise, we had figured out how it might be done. And it seemed that the job of getting out was fraught with more potentialities of disaster than the job of getting in. The landing on April 25 was responsible for some slaughter. The evacuation, we reckoned, would be carnage. At a most moderate computation 25 *per cent.* of the Australian and New Zealand Army Corps would have to be sacrificed to ensure the safe withdrawal of the remainder. But of course this was only a theoretical exercise. It was really outside the sphere of practical politics.

Then like a bomb came word that in very surety we were going to evacuate. In the House of Commons members had asked in an airy way why the troops were not withdrawn from Suvla and Anzac. To them, in their ignorance, it was merely a matter of embarking again and returning to Egypt or Salonica or France. So simple it seemed to those armchair strategists. They did not know that the beach at Anzac, our main *depôts*, and our headquarters were within a thousand yards of the main Turkish line; that the beach had been constantly shelled by "Beachy Bill" and other batteries for eight solid months on end.

However the powers that be had so ordained it and that was sufficient. The Australians had talked about "never retreating," but that was only a manifestation of the unconquerable spirit that animated them. They might talk, but they never yet disobeyed an order. It nearly broke their hearts to leave the spot where so many thousand gallant young Australians had found heroes' graves; but they knew how to obey orders. The only kick was for the honour of being the last to leave. So many wanted to be amongst the "die-hards."

It was to be a silent "getaway." Absolute secrecy was essential for its success. It sounds just like a wild bit of fiction. Just imagine the possibility of withdrawing an army of 90,000 men with artillery, stores, field hospitals, mules and horses, and all the vast impedimenta of war, right from under the nose of an active enemy, and all on a clear moonlight night. One single traitor could have queered the whole pitch. But British, Indians, New Zealanders and Australians were loyal to the core.

The final attack of the Turks on the right of our line had been repulsed by the 2nd Light Horse Brigade, though the enemy in determined fashion had pushed forward with sand-bags right to within a few yards of our trenches. There were half a dozen spots in the Anzac firing line where we and the Turks could hear each other talking; Quinn's Port, Lone Pine, The Neck, Apex, Turkish Despair, Chatham's Post. It would be fine fun sticking it out here while the army made its get-away. Men clamoured for the honour of being the last to leave...

It is the night of December 19; the fatal night which will see the evacuation of Anzac. Men talked cheerily, but thought hard. Had the Turks any idea of our projected departure? Two nights ago, a little after midnight, there was an unrehearsed incident. A fire broke out in a *depôt* near the North Beach. Soon the whole sky was reddened with the glare and the rugged outline of Anzac was brightly illuminated. Bully-beef and biscuits blazed merrily. Oil drums burst with terrific force. Then we wondered if the Turks would deduce anything from this. Would they guess it was a preliminary to the "get-away." It was hardly likely. The "fool English" would never burn the stores till the last minute. So the accidental fire did no harm. Maybe it did good. For during the past month the Anzacs had tried by all manner of tricks and subterfuges to induce Abdul to attack. But Abdul knew how costly a business it was attacking the Australians, and after a few abortive attempts he remained on the defensive....

Now all was normal. Down at Helles the British had, during the afternoon, made a big demonstration. The warships had joined in the fray and the bombardment of the Turkish lines was terrific. But on this last night there was nothing untoward happening. General Birdwood during the day had gone the rounds of the trenches and the boys yarned with him as of old. It was a good thing for us to have had a General like that—one who understood the gay devil-may-care Australian character. That's why the boys called him the "idol of Anzac."

Away to the northward at Suvla on the shoulder of Chocolate Hills the British divisions are getting ready to retire. On Hill 60, which saw so much sanguinary fighting, the stolid Indians are awaiting orders. This way a bit the New Zealand and Australian Division has started its first parties towards North Beach. On the right above Anzac and opposite Gaba Tepe the Australians were streaming away; all but the rearguard and the final "die-hards." Before the morning Anzac will have seen a great tragedy, or else the greatest bluff in history.... There is the usual desultory interchange of musketry at odd places along the line, now and then punctuated with the rattle of a maxim ... nothing abnormal. Down at Helles there is a fierce fusillade. This will help us.

Since dusk the first contingents had been steadily streaming down towards the North Beach and Anzac Cove. Quickly and silently they embarked in the waiting flotilla of small craft and streaked out to the transports. Like guardian angels the warships hovered around seeing to the security of the army. Up at Suvla we knew similar scenes were being enacted. Along the line the musketry played its usual accompaniment to the intermittent bombing. But the whole plan was working beautifully. The tension was gradually relaxing. There would be no 20 per cent. casualties as the pessimists foretold. Already from Suvla and Anzac over 60,000 soldiers had re-embarked without a single casualty.

Now and then there was a round of shrapnel sent by Beachy Bill on to the southern *depôt* at Brighton Beach. This clearly showed that the enemy suspected nothing. Yet it is bright moonlight.... It is midnight, and nearly all the men have embarked save the thin khaki line of "die-hards" in the trenches. An odd bomb or two is thrown by the Turks. The "die-hards" with insolent imperturbability heave a few bombs back and invite Abdul to come on.

If Abdul had entered our trenches then he would have found only a skeleton army waiting to fight a forlorn hope rearguard action. But all along the trenches he would have found other things. Cigarettes and jam and tobacco; all sorts of presents and Christmas boxes. Scores of the boys before leaving wrote little farewell messages to the Turks. Typical examples were these:—"*Au revoir*, Abdul. See you later on";

"Goodbye, Mahomet. Better luck next time"; "Abdul, you're a good clean fighter and we bear you no ill-will"; "Merry Christmas, Abdul; you're a good sport anyhow, but the Hun is a fair cow"; "So long, Abdul." And having told Abdul what he thought of him, the irresponsible Australian sauntered down to the beach and embarked! But many a silent tear was shed for the pals they had left behind, the quiet dead sleeping on Gallipoli. . . .

It didn't seem quite right to clear out and leave Australia's dead behind. Some of the boys voiced the thought of many, "Tread softly, boys, and don't let them hear us deserting them." Some of the padres planted wattle round about the graves on Shell Green and Shrapnel Valley and Hell Spit and Brown's Dip. . . .

By half-past one all were away but the "die-hards." Then from the Apex, after a final volley, streaked the first batch of the skeleton rearguard. There is a breach in the brave Anzac line at last. But Abdul does not know it yet. Soon the dare-devils at Quinn's Post heave a few bombs, then silently slink back, down the precipitous hill-side, and along the gully to the beach. From Courtney's and the Neck and the Pimple and Ryrie's Post and Chatham's all along the line came the "die-hards," full lick to the beach. But to their unutterable surprise there is no attack. They are not followed. The trenches that for eight long months defied the Turkish attacks are now open, not a solitary soldier left. But Abdul does not know it. There is still an intermittent fire from the Turkish trenches. They think our silence is some trick. . .

At half-past three on the morning of December 20 there was a burst of red flame and a roar like distant thunder. This was repeated shortly afterwards, and our two big mines on the Neck blew up. It was our last slap at the Turk. We cannot say what harm it did, but thinking the explosions were a prelude to attack the Turkish line all round Anzac burst into spiteful protest. There was a wild fusillade at our empty trenches, and on the transports the Australians smiled grimly. Shortly afterwards the Light Horsemen on the extreme right—Ryrie's lucky Second Brigade rearguard—entered the waiting cutters on Brighton Beach. Then the stores—such as we could not take away—burst into flame. Only two men were wounded.

Before dawn word came that the whole force had been safely taken off, together with many of the mules and horses and guns which it was thought would have to be abandoned. At dawn the Turkish batteries opened a wild bombardment of our trenches, all along the line. Marvellous to relate the enemy had not yet ascertained what had happened. But the silence soon told them the truth. Then they charged in irregular lines over the skyline at our empty trenches. The warships fired a few salvoes at the enemy swarming over the hills, and they hurriedly took cover in our old trenches. These were the last shots fired over Anzac at the Turks. Then the flotilla turned its back on Gallipoli and swung slowly and sadly westward.

So ended the great "getaway"; a feat quite unparalleled in the annals of war. Historians will pay tribute to Sir Charles Munro and the Fleet. We only take our hats off to General Birdwood and his staff and the staffs of the Australasian divisions. But deep down we know the wonderful work our navy did during the eight months of the Gallipoli campaign. The army may make mistakes, but the navy is all right.

As we swing off our last thought is not concerned with the bitterness of defeat. We think of our comrades quietly sleeping on Anzac. They gave their lives gladly, proudly, for Australia and the Empire. They showed the world that Australians could live and fight and die like Britishers. There are many sad hearts on the transports tonight. And there are very many breaking hearts back in dear old Australia. But old England has showered so many good gifts on her Colonies. The Colonies will not grudge this sacrifice for Empire.

Maybe our feelings are best expressed in the words of "Argent," written at the end of the most glorious failure in history:—

Anzac

Ah, well! we're gone! We're out of it now. We've something else to do.
But we all look back from the transport deck to the land-line far and blue:
Shore and valley are faded; fading are cliff and hill;
The land-line we called "Anzac" . . . and we'll call it "Anzac" still!

This last six months, I reckon, 'll be most of my life to me:
Trenches, and shells, and snipers, and the morning light on the sea,
Thirst in the broiling mid-day, shouts and gasping cries,
Big guns' talk from the water, and . . . flies, flies, flies, flies, flies!

And all of our trouble wasted! all of it gone for nix!
Still . . . we kept our end up—and some of the story sticks.
Fifty years on in Sydney they'll talk of our first big fight,
And even in little old, blind old England possibly someone might.

But, seeing we had to clear, for we couldn't get on no more,
I wish that, instead of last night, it had been the night before.
Yesterday poor Jim stopped one. Three of us buried Jim—

I know a woman in Sydney that thought the world of him.
She was his mother. I'll tell her—broken with grief and pride—
"Mother" was Jim's last whisper. That was all. And died.
Brightest and bravest and best of us all—none could help but to love him—
And now . . . he lies there under the hill, with a wooden cross above him.

That's where it gets me twisted. The rest of it I don't mind,
But it don't seem right for me to be off, and to leave old Jim behind.
Jim, just quietly sleeping; and hundreds and thousands more;
For graves and crosses are mighty thick from Quinn's Post down to the shore!

Better there than in France, though, with the Germans' dirty work:
I reckon the Turk respects us, as we respect the Turk;
Abdul's a good, clean fighter—we've fought him, and we know—
And we've left him a letter behind us to tell him we found him so.

Not just to say, precisely, "Goodbye," but "Au revoir"!
Somewhere or other we'll meet again, before the end of the war!
But I hope it'll be in a wider place, with a lot more room on the map,
And the airmen over the fight that day'll see a bit of a scrap!

Meanwhile, here's health to the Navy, that took us there, and away;
Lord! they're miracle-workers—and fresh ones every day!
My word! those Mids in the cutters! aren't they properly keen!
Don't ever say England's rotten—or not to us, who've seen!

Well! we're gone. We're out of it all! We've somewhere else to fight.
And we strain our eyes from the transport deck, but "Anzac" is out of sight!
Valley and shore are vanished; vanished are cliff and hill;
And we'll never go back to "Anzac" . . . But I think that some of us will!

GALLIPOLI

By L. H. Allen, in the *Sydney Morning Herald*.

1

Winter is here, and in the setting sun
York's [1] *giant bluff is kindled with the ray*

---

1. Mount York, in the Blue Mountains, New South Wales, where stands a monument erected in memory of three intrepid Australian explorers: Blaxland, Lawson, and Wentworth

That smites his gnarléd sides of red and dun:
And the spired obelisk that points the way
Where heroes looked, the first of English blood
To break the spell of Silence with a cry
Startling the ancient sleep in prophecy
Of you, my people of the Lion-brood.

2

Does his old vision watch that alien hill,
Embrowned and bleak, where strain upon the height,
Amid sharp silences that burn and chill,
Those heroes' sons, set in sterner fight
Than primeval war with solitude?
Lo now, the sullen cliff outjets in smoke.
And life is groaning death, blooded and broke!
So fell ye, brothers of the Lion-brood.

3

I weep the dead; they are no more, no more!
Oh, with what pain and rapture came to me
Full birth of love for dazzling-sanded shore,
For heaven of sapphire, and for scented tree!
Keen-eyed and all desire I feel my mood
Still fruitless, waiting gust of quickening breath—
And lo, on darkened wing the wind of death
Summoned austere the soul to nationhood.

4

Where cornfields smile in golden-fruited peace
There stalk the spirits of heroes firmly-thewed
As he that sailed their path to win the Fleece
For gods that still enchant our solitude.
I weep the dead; they are no more, no more!
Their sons that gather in the teeming grain
Walk sadlier than the men of hill and plain,
Themselves are harvest to the wrath of war.

5

I weep the dead; they are no more, no more!
When dusk descends on city and on plain,
Dim lights will shine from window and from door,
And some will guard the vigil of dull pain,
Yet, in the city or in solitude,

There is a burden in the starry air,
An oversong that cries, "The life is fair
That made its triumph nobler with its blood."

6

If English oaks should fret with shade their tomb,
Let them have burial here; for one would say
"I shall sleep soft if some once haunted room
Keep token of me when I take my way."
And one again, "The boon of quietude
Is sweet if that old corner of the stream
Where last I saw the creepered window gleam
Keep memory of my days of lustihood."

7

Some blossoming orchard-plot, some fencéd field,
Some placid strip of furrow-stainéd earth,
Or some grey coil of cottage smoke shall yield
Tribute to them that brought their kin to birth.
And this, in city or in lonely wood,
Shall be the guerdon of the death they died,
The cry of Folk made one in pangs of pride—
"They fell, not faithless to the Lion-brood."

.

The Cameliers

Contents

Foreword	169
The Soldier	171
The Sister	176
A Black Brother	181
The Coming of Flora	185
Romani—1	190
Romani—2	194
Eastward Ho	197
Maghdaba	201
In the Hospital	205
Battle of Rafa	210
The Ball—1	214
The Ball—2	219
The Bints' Retreat	224
Gaza	228
Mount Sinai	232
Some Cameliers	237
A Sandstorm Trek	242
Writing Home	247

Allenby—1	253
Allenby—2	257
Allenby—3	260
Allenby—4	263
Allenby—5	266
Red Triangle	269
Camel Races	274
Over the Jordan	281
Back to the Jordan	285
Kantara	289
Valley of the Jordan	293
Sister and Soldier	299
L'Envoi	304

To the Honourable
James Alexander Hogue
An Australian Patriot
This Little Record of the Deeds
—And Misdeeds—of the Imperial
Camel Corps in Egypt, Sinai, and
Palestine is Dedicated with Sincere
Filial Affection by
The Author

To My Camel

You're an ugly smellful creature:
You're a blot upon the plain:
I have seen Mohamed beat you,
And it gave me little pain.
You're spiteful and you're lazy,
You'd send a white man crazy,
But I reckon you're a daisy
When the Turks come out again.

Your head is most unsightly,
And so is your humpy back;
I hear you roaring nightly,
When you're loading for the track.
You're bow-legged and you're bandy,
But in this desert sandy
It's as well to have you handy:
You're a mighty useful hack.

You shake me something cruel
When you try to do a trot;
I've got to take my gruel.
But you make it very hot:
I've somehow got a notion
That your humpty-dumpty motion
Is worse than on the ocean,
It's a nasty way you've got.

It's a sun-scorched land, the East is.
So we need you when we trek:
My old prad a better beast is.
But he'd soon become a wreck:
You thirst a week unblinking,
And when I see you drinking,
You always set me thinking:
Lord, I wish I had your neck.

Foreword

This book will be placed before the public in the midst of worldwide jubilance consequent upon the termination of the bloodiest and most unjustifiable war in the history of mankind. Soon we trust the ban of the censor will be lifted and we shall be permitted to know more of those things which a curious public has been hungering for during the last four years. I do not refer to matters of ordinary gossip, but the revealing of all those circumstances leading up to great decisions, the explanations of misfortunes and the endless tales of individual heroism. Unfortunately, such subjects are shorn of much of their interest through delay in publication. The *Cameliers* is, therefore, issued at an opportune moment, following closely upon the triumphant progress of General Allenby's army in Palestine, with the sound of his victory still ringing in our ears, when we are better enabled to appreciate details.

The *Cameliers* presents a stirring picture of the arduous conditions of campaigning in that historical country in Egypt and the Sinai desert, of the inequality of numbers and equipment in the early days, of the gradual organisation of a magnificent mobile force, of hardship nobly endured, of courage and heroism daily manifested, and the final securing of the power to move forward culminating in the great sweep northwards which immediately preceded the surrender of Turkey.

The book is full of interest. It is well written, and appeals to the sympathy of all readers. Mr. Oliver Hogue is an Australian by birth and training. He is the son of Hon. James Hogue, one of the pioneers of Australian journalism, and who for many years was a well-known figure in the public life of his State. The son followed in the literary footsteps of his father, and has already contributed freely with his pen under the name of "Trooper Bluegum." Shortly after the outbreak of war he volunteered for service with the Australian Forces, and has undergone some years of continuous and arduous soldiering in Egypt and the East—an experience which fits him for a truthful reproduction of the life of a soldier in these sandy wastes.

I venture to commend this work of Trooper Bluegum not only to the general public as the attractive representation of aspects of one of the successful "side shows" of the Allies, but more especially to Australian readers as a record of the doings of the Light Horse Regiments and other Australian Units, who to their regret were unable to share in the horrors and glory of the Western Front, but have nevertheless proved themselves able in Palestine to maintain the high reputation won by the Australians as fighters in this great war.

C. S. Wade.

Sydney House,
11th November 1918.

CHAPTER 1

The Soldier

We hated the thought of 'em. We hated the sight of 'em. We hated the smell of 'em. We hated the shape of 'em. The very idea of association with such brutes was hateful to us—at first.

But the time was not far distant when we were to forget all our initial antipathies. Familiarity bred content. The law of compensation was in operation. A beast with so many obvious vices as a camel must have some compensating virtues. But it *did* take time to unearth them.

Those of us who were Light Horsemen loved our horses. It was a big wrench to go to Gallipoli without them. It was still harder to part with them finally when we joined the Imperial Camel Corps. For no Australian really loves a camel. It isn't done. All one can hope to do is to appreciate his good points and envy his thirst.

The good points manifested themselves sparingly, one at a time. The camel was strong. He was tractable—if properly handled. He could go thirsty for a week or more uncomplainingly. He could carry food for himself and his rider for many days in the wilderness. He was easily caught, and hobbled, and tethered. He gave little or no trouble at night. He would eat out of your hand—sometimes. Sometimes he tried to eat your hand.

Long before we saw our new mounts we knew all about them—or thought we did. The cognoscenti saw to that. In every camp somehow there seems to be a little coterie of 'know alls,' old soldiers to whom nothing is hidden in the heavens above or the earth beneath or the waters under the earth. In course of time we estimated these gentlemen at their true value, and found for the most part they had been kicked out of their units for worthlessness, or had deliberately chosen the soft and safe job at the details. But at first we listened openmouthed to their terrible tales of thrilling adventures and miraculous escapes: the buck-jumpers they had cowed, the ferocious Bedouins they had captured single-handed. Gladly we new chums bought them beer at the Canteen, and refilled their pint pots again and again that their tongues might be loosened and the worst be told. And at night, after 'Lights out,' as the wild wind off the Mokattam Hills wafted us the aroma of camel, we lay awake and thought apprehensively of the morrow. Towards morning we dreamed nasty dreams in which wild camels chased us, yet never caught us, though our feet seemed glued to the ground.

The boys of the I.C.C. looked back with a tolerant smile at those early days at Abbassia; the early morning parades, the mountains of equipment that were heaped upon us, the wild and woolly *shivoos* in Cairo in the evenings, the joy-rides round Heliopolis and Mattarieh, the realistic sham-fights on the Virgins' Breasts, the preliminary treks out to the desert in full marching order, with stragglers dotting the sand as far as the eye could reach, the strafes we got and never earned, the many more strafes we richly deserved but somehow escaped. We thought we were rather slow making the acquaintance of our camels, till one day a senior officer rode up and watched our company at mounted drill. We didn't know if he were a general or what, but we all bucked up a bit and performed the various evolutions with precision of Life Guards—almost. When we dismounted for 'smoko' the officer aforesaid cantered up and inquired, "How long have you chaps had camels?"

"Two weeks exactly," he was told.

Whereat he whistled, and confided to our O.C. that he had seen a company of Cameliers who, after two months' work, were not to be compared with us.

And in all humility be it said these adaptable young Australians took to camels like ducks to water. Admittedly their language, when a camel went mangoon, was simply shocking, and, I fear me, a few of them did drink a little more beer than was absolutely necessary. The captious critics will tell you this, and will dwell on the fact that a few thousand wild Australians on a couple of occasions tried to mop up Cairo and paint Alexandria crimson. Yet if you put these boyish follies in the scale, and against them set off their whole-souled patriotism, their imperturbable good-humour, their hardihood, their sturdy democracy, their supreme contempt of death and danger, then you see the Anzac in true perspective. His idiosyncrasies are forgotten, and he stands forth a virile and unique figure on the battlefields of Sinai.

It was not all plain sailing with those camels. Several men badly bitten went to hospital. A few were thrown hard on the gravel strewn plain. Others were kicked, and the padded foot of the camel is much harder than it looks. One unlucky officer achieved fame—or notoriety—by being knocked off his camel by an aeroplane. There was plenty of excitement when a mangoon beast broke loose and cleared the parade-ground. The Cameliers cheered and roared when a hapless gyppie fled before the onslaught of a mad camel. But they forgot to cheer when Stinker swung round and charged in their direction. It was *sauve qui peut* and devil take the hindmost. Then half a dozen men with a long rope, or one hero with an iron bar, was the only thing to stop the camel.

There was one man-killer there with a most unsavoury reputation. He had killed a few men and sent several to hospital. *Anon* he went on trek with an Anzac battalion, and after a spell of decent behaviour broke out again and threatened to slaughter a whole section.

He was laid out temporarily with a crack on the skull, but the rider was taking no more chances. Next day he loitered behind on the trek, blew the camel's brains out, and reported to the O.C. that the camel had died of a broken heart.

We were, while at Abbassia, lectured on camels. We studied their habits and habitat. We learned how, centuries ago, the Persian Camelry had routed the Lydian Cavalry, and how the Roman horses fled before the North African Cameliers. We inquired into the feeding of camels, and the reason for their prolonged abstinence and their wonderful thirst. Now and then we ate camels, though the obliging mess caterers assured us it was veal.

We were quite as careless as the average soldier, and no more moral.

So we were always losing saddles, or *fantasses*, or *dhurra* bags, or brushes, or head-ropes. And we had to make good the deficiencies.

But we never thieved—at least not within our own company lines.

True, it was no great crime to commandeer a saddle or a camel from headquarters. The commandment simply ran: "*Thou shalt not be caught.*" And it was an easy thing for an Australian to fake a brand and disguise a camel; we managed to get a few rather decent mounts from the H.Q. lines.

Grooming and ticking did get on our nerves. There were big ticks, little ticks, and middle-sized ticks. Camels newly arrived from the desert were swarming with ticks, and we had to slaughter them—the ticks I mean; and because the job offended our sense of the aesthetic we adopted the motto for the company: "*Infra dig camelorum, ora pro nobis*"; which being translated means, perhaps, "Lord, fancy coming to this."

Realising that all work and no play made the Anzac a dull boy, we indulged in the delightful pastime of buckshee riding. 'Buckshee' is the Australian's adaptation of '*baksheesh*.' For a while the scheme worked admirably. Ostensibly for the purpose 'of trying out' our camels, we got permission from the C.O. to take our camels off the lines on Sunday afternoons for short rides along the *wadis*. Then we grew bolder. We invited the nurses from the adjacent hospitals to ride to Mattarieh or the Gardens or Napoleon's Tower. And dozens of the boys held camel races on the desert. It was fine fun. All went swimmingly.

For six days of the week we laboured and did all our work, but on the seventh, perched on the top of our '*hooshtas*,' we were monarchs of all we surveyed. The only disadvantage was the proximity of telegraph wires, and the frequency with which we got caught under the chin and almost hanged for being so high up in the world.

Unhappily, 'buckshee' riding came to an end all too soon. I quote from *Barrak*, the official organ of the I.C.C.

"Rumours of impending strife reached us one morning at breakfast. A senior officer proceeding 'in the execution of his duty' from Cairo to Heliopolis, the previous afternoon, had seen every lamp-post outside every pub and *café*, from Abbassia onwards, garlanded and festooned with camels, while a seething crowd fought and jostled round six ships of the desert riding easily at their anchors outside Heliopolis House. Disciplinary action was taken, as the saying is, and buckshee camel riding came to an end."

Anon came the exodus. Goodbye to the flesh-pots of Egypt, the bints at the Barage, the carousals at the Kursaal, the fun on the *feluccas*, the games at Ghezira, the nights on the Nile—and the sweet smiles of the sisters.

A dozen times the rumour had run that we marched on the morrow. But rumour always was a lying jade. At last, however, it was dinkum. We were fully equipped—officially—and up to strength. In full marching order we formed up, and the camera fiends got very, very busy.

The general completed his inspection. A couple of magnificent camels from headquarters were unaccountably found in our lines, and these were reclaimed and culls given us in exchange. In a long column of humps we moved out into the desert.

At Abbassia all was peaceful again. The dust of our departure settled quietly on the empty huts, and Adjutant Barber breathed a sigh of intense relief as he turned to the G.O.C. and exclaimed, "Thank God they've gone."

Chapter 2

The Sister

"Sister!" cried the big, sunburnt bushman in the third bed.

The nurse rose from the little table in the centre of the ward and noiselessly glided across to the patient.

"Well, what's wrong now, Pat?"

"Sister, will you marry me?"

"Not today, Pat, thank you. I'm frightfully busy," answered sister, with a smile.

"If you die an old maid, you've only got yourself to blame," quoted the soldier.

"Oh well, I'll risk it."

"Then if you won't marry me, will you please have a look at this confounded ankle. Sure the bandage is too tight, or else my foot is swelling wisibly, as Sam Weller would say."

With a few deft movements she removed the offending bandage, exposing an ugly wound caused by a mauser bullet. Then in a minute or two Sister had bound up the ankle again, and the bushman did not know whether he should marvel most at her dexterity or the gentleness of her touch. "Oh, Sister darlint, I wisht I had a bullet in my other leg just for the sheer joy of watchin' ye."

The nurse tried hard not to smile as she straightened the bedclothes. "Anything else now?"

"Only my heart," said the patient resignedly.

She ignored this, for every one of her eleven patients seemed to be suffering from the same affection. Glancing round the ward as she turned her back towards the table, she caught sight of a signal of distress from the far corner.

"Well, Billjim, what's the matter with you this morning?"

Of course his name was not Billjim. That is the curious composite cognomen that has been used indiscriminately of late, and serves as a label for any of the Anzacs. But by general consent the other ten patients in Ward B4 had christened this wiry young colonial 'Billjim.' Perhaps it was because his physiognomy was curiously like unto the Australian youth depicted by that consummate art1st Norman Lindsay. Perhaps it was on account of his devil-may-care disposition, or his extraordinarily elastic vocabulary, or his inveterate cigarette smoking, or his lack of reverence for staff officers, clergymen, *medicoes*, or silk hats. Whatever the reason, no one in the ward challenged his exclusive right to the honoured name of Billjim. To be sure the board next his bed, with the zigzag lines and the hieroglyphics, had at the top "Private Eagleton James, 1st Battn., A.I.F." But only the M.O. troubled about his official name.

"Say, what about that letter you promised to write to my bit of skirt. Sister?" he now demanded.

"It won't be too long, will it?" This in view of a host of other calls on sister's time.

"Lor' lumme, I ain't written since I left Gallip," he replied in an aggrieved tone.

So, seating herself at the foot of his bed with pencil and pad in readiness, sister turned to Billjim and invited him to begin.

"Come closer, Sister. I don't want that redheaded, freckled-faced coot in No. 8 to hear my love letters."

"Oh, he's asleep, I'm sure."

Loud snoring suddenly sounding from the adjacent bed only partly reassured Billjim, but without more ado he began:

"My dearest Liz.—Got that?—I hope this finds you well, as it leaves me at present.—Got that?"

Sister looked at his right arm in a sling, and thought of the shrapnel pellets in his shoulder, but she only smiled. The wounded swain proceeded:

"I'm in the 14th A.G.H.; that means Australian General Hospital.—Got that?—And they treat you bosker. I got a couple of lumps of shrapnel in my shoulder from Beachy Bill, but it ain't nothin' to cable home about.—Got that?—Why didn't you answer my letter from Lone Pine?—Got that?—I guess I'll be back into the scrum in a couple of weeks.—Got that?"

Sister smiled again. She knew better. But she scribbled on.

"We didn't do too bad over there considering.—Got that?—Every time we took a trench there was more trenches behind, and whenever we breasted a hill there was more hills ahead.—Got that?—But they wouldn't send old Ian nearly enough men, considerin' Winston Churchill had sent the navy on ahead to warn Abdul we was comin'."

"Here," exclaimed Sister, "you cannot go on criticising the High Command like that, you know."

"Who's criticisin' 'em?"

"You are, of course."

"Well," replied Billjim doggedly, "what's generals for if they ain't to be criticised? What's the good of learnin' history?"

This was a poser for the amanuensis, so she meekly resumed her task. Billjim fired away, and in queer staccato phrases told his own plain tale of the glorious landing of the Anzacs on that never-to-be-forgotten morning of 25th April. There were incidents of splendid heroism and stoical endurance, yet he just kept on with no more excitement than he would have shown in describing a cricket-match or a wallaby drive. It never appeared to him as anything extraordinary. But when he described the wild charge at Lone Pine and Walker's Ridge, in the face of a veritable hail of lead. Sister forgot to write, and just sat there exclaiming, "Wonderful! Wonderful!"

"Oh, that ain't nothin'," deprecated the unimaginative warrior. "You ought to 'a seen Dally Messenger playing for Easts the season before last. O' course he wasn't any good at all. Oh no."

The epistle was finished at last. There was a blotch on one sheet where he had described thirty young Australians laid out in Brown's Dip for burial. He knew not that the blotch was caused by sister's tears. Scanning the letter critically, he remarked, "You might put at the end, 'Please excuse bad writin'.'"

There was a sound of stifled mirth in No. 8 bed, but sister ignored it, and did as she was bid.

"You can just sign it 'Jim,' now, and fill the rest of the sheet in with crosses," he added in most matter-of-fact tones.

A few minutes afterwards the medical officer entered, and sister needs must accompany him on his rounds. Captain Evans was quite a brilliant young *medico*, and knew his job, but he had the fatal gift of 'swank,' which the Australians could not tolerate. Besides, he was head over ears in love with sister, and did not seem to care who knew it. The Australian Eleven resented this, for they held that Sister Livingstone was their own exclusive property.

"Good morning, Sister," he greeted. "How is the Australian Eleven today—eh, what?" And he went the round of the ward, glancing at the charts, questioning here and there, attending to a few of the more serious cases, and, on the whole, behaving most affably. Then, as he concluded his tour of duty, he said to sister, quite loud enough for several of the boys to hear, "I'm frightfully bucked today, Sister. Six serious cases in Ward 3 have recovered, and are well on the road to convalescence. And we had almost given them up."

Sister was about to murmur the usual congratulatory platitudes, when she heard Billjim say, in a stage whisper to No. 8, "That's 'cos the doctor's always playing golf lately. It gives the fellows a chance."

At the entrance to the ward the doctor turned and whispered, "What about dinner at Shepheard's tonight, Sister? The music will be excellent."

"I ought to write home to my old dad," she answered, half consenting.

"There's no Australian mail for over a week."

"Very well," agreed sister, smiling. "Thanks awfully."

As the medical officer left the ward another case entered, or rather was carried in on a stretcher. One arm was swathed in lint. His face was drawn and haggard as if with pain. He was no light weight, and the stretcher-bearers who carried him upstairs were only too glad to give their burden over to the safe keeping of the ministering angel of B4. The newcomer eyed the sister hungrily, as if he had not seen a lady for years. And once, when the sister went to the other end of the ward for another pillow, Billjim heard the stranger exclaim, "God bless the Turk that shot me." But not a word did he say to sister. His wound was dressed and bandaged anew; his old Light Horse uniform, torn and bloodstained, was taken away. With a sigh of great content he lay back in a nice clean bed, the first he had slept in for months and months. His name was entered in the hospital records, "Sergeant Robert Blaine, 7th A.L.H. Regiment, age 30," together with various details as to his religion, service, wounds, etc. And when all these preliminaries were satisfactorily accomplished. Sister stood smiling before him and asked, "Is there anything else I can do for you?"

He looked up at her sweet face with a concentrated attention that was rather embarrassing. The sun shining through the open window touched her golden hair till it seemed to the soldier that a halo had framed the most beautiful face he had ever seen. Frankly and, fearlessly her deep blue eyes looked down on him awaiting an answer. But she had to repeat her question before he roused himself. "Well, anything else, Sergeant?"

He shook his head slowly, and instead of answering her question said deliberately, "Do you know, I've been looking for you for thirty years."

"Oh, Sergeant Blaine, you must not start saying such silly things."

"Yet I dare swear it was the sanest thing I have ever said in all my life," he maintained.

And the irrepressible Billjim sat up in his bed and called out to No.3, "Say, Pat, you're an 'also ran'."

During the day sister rather avoided the big man in No. 12, and in the evening went cheerily forth with the doctor to join the gay throng in Cairo. But several times when the music was playing softly, she found her thoughts winging back to the hospital, and she heard a deep, musical voice saying, "*I've been looking for you for thirty years.*"

Chapter 3
A Black Brother

German agents had been rather busy out on the Tripoli frontier amongst the Senussi, with the result that several thousand tribesmen, armed with Turkish rifles and buoyed up with ridiculous hopes based on the alleged helplessness of Egypt, swooped down on Dakla and the Kharga Oasis. In course of time they were driven back to their base and smashed up by the Western Frontier Force.

But the German agents were quite satisfied. That little manoeuvre cost the Egyptian Government at least a million sterling. Also it brought some Scottish Yeomanry, Egyptian Cavalry, half a flight of the Royal Flying Corps, some armoured motor-cars, and a company of Australian Cameliers right across Egypt from the Sinai front, and kept them there for six months all through a scorching sun.,

Australians know what heat is. Bourke, Cloncurry, Oodnadatta, and Marble Bar are not so very far behind Cairo when it comes to real dinkum scorching weather. Still the hardy Cameliers, who had experienced a blazing drought in Central Australia, were quite prepared to accord the palm to the Sahara. They trekked for days and days and weeks and weeks. Time and again their meagre supply of water gave out, and with leathery tongues, blistered faces, and cracked, bleeding lips they staggered back to camp again. Several times it looked like a tragedy; once it was very, very nearly one.

A patrol following up the Senussi had gone just beyond the safety radius. Finally, water gave out. Two of the strongest men, after swallowing the last drop of water, made into Kharga, arriving almost dead with thirst. Water was hurriedly sent out to the patrol. When the rescuers got there, none of the patrol could speak. All their tongues were swollen up and their lips scorched and blackened. All had to be sent to the hospital for a time. A month later they were all well and out on the desert again.

There was one pitiful tragedy enacted out on those scorching sands. An airman with his mechanic went out and never returned. The Cameliers were hurried off to scour the Sahara in search of them. There had been two 'planes out. One struck engine trouble and made a forced landing. The other flew back to Kharga, after telling the pilot in the damaged machine to stay where he was till assistance arrived. Knowing—approximately—where the 'plane was stranded, the camel patrol started out. On the second day they found the tracks of the landing and the take off. The bird had flown. But not back to Kharga. Other 'planes joined in the search. Still there was no trace of the missing airmen.

The weather was blazing hot—the hottest our men had ever experienced. With blistered faces and scorched hands the Cameliers kept going. If the poor pilot had only stayed where he first landed all would have been well. Water convoys moved out to replenish the meagre supplies in the *fantasses*. Motorcars joined in the search. But what a tiny spot a 'plane is on thousands of square miles of desert! On the seventh day the scouts espied a white speck on the rim of the earth. They had long given up hopes of finding the airmen alive. Off they trotted and reached the 'plane. They found the pilot, Lieut. Ridley, and Mechanic Garside, both dead, but stood aghast when they saw the pilot had a bullet wound in his head. A bully-beef tin was there and a couple of biscuits. But the water had been finished days ago. Near by was a notebook, and in it Garside's diary. It told of the forced landing, the attempt to fly back, the petrol giving out, and the husbanding of the scanty water supply. Then this entry:

"Lt. Ridley shot himself at 10 o'clock on Sunday morning."

Death was certain for both. One might last another day or two on the water; so, to give his mechanic another faint chance to live, the young officer had gone West. "He was a very gallant gentleman."

When first the I.C.C. lobbed into Kharga they got the greatest surprise of their life. The oasis had been evacuated when the Senussi swooped down, so the Cameliers did not know whether to expect an ovation or a fusillade. So they went warily. Natives gathered round in friendly fashion, throwing the usual '*Saieeda*' at the visitors, when a cheerful voice yelled out, "Hullo, Australia; what are you doing out here?" Rather nonplussed, they pulled up and looked round, but every face that wasn't brown was black as ebony. There was no sign of a white man anywhere. Then they espied a big African striding forward with a grin that exposed more teeth than Roosevelt at his fiercest.

"Who are you?" demanded the section officer.

"My name's Bluegum. I come from Kalgoorlie. I've not seen an Australian for ten years," replied the black.

It took some time to satisfy the Cameliers that old Bluegum was dinkum. "Oh, I'm an Australian all right," he said, with a laugh. "Any of you boys from the West?"

There happened to be several of the boys from Perth and Broome and the Kimberley and the Goldfields, and they crowded round old Bluegum and put the third degree on him good and hard. But he was trumps all right, and proved a very valuable ally indeed. He showed the patrol the best place to camp, where to get water and grain, and bought at very reasonable prices vegetables and fruit for the hungry and thirsty men. Probably he made a good ten or twenty *per cent*, for himself out of the transaction, but *Maleesch!* the boys didn't mind.

There was one episode in connection with the operations round Kharga and Dakla that never was mentioned in any official dispatch. Maybe it was just as well. It was not a particularly creditable episode—though a most natural one. It was midsummer, the hottest, thirstiest summer the Anzacs had ever experienced. The company had gone out after the Senussi, who were reported by aeroplane to be moving on Kharga. Orders were given to rendezvous at a certain spot called Hell's Gates, where *fantasses* were to be filled. One section remained behind, with orders to join up during the night.

Unfortunately, or fortunately, there was no officer in charge of this section. But a canteen had been started at Kharga. And it was frightfully thirsty weather. Try as they would, the boys could not assuage their thirst. They bought bottles of whisky and put them in their saddlebags. They mopped up unlimited beer. They waxed merry. They saw two blades of grass where one had grown before. They saw twice as many 'planes as were really on the oasis. They sang "Australia will be there." They saw two suns fiery red sinking into the west. The section sergeant returning from a visit to the outpost found his section hopeless. They loved him, and told him so. They sang to him that he was a jolly good fellow, even if there was a war on.

Sergeant Blaine was something of a philosopher. He thought hard. Then he grinned and exclaimed, "*Maleesch.*" In the midst of their cacophony he roared, "Silence. 'Saddle up,'" and they saddled.

Ordinarily a section of the I.C.C. can saddle up in a quarter of an hour and move off with five days' grain, water, and rations into the wilderness. In the competitions without packs or *cacholets* it has been done in five minutes. On this memorable occasion it took the section nearly an hour. Men were continually tripping over their gear. Several fell asleep leaning on their camels. The sun had disappeared before they were mounted. Several fell off their mounts and miraculously broke no bones. Eventually the section moved off in a column of humps, singing, "The Long, Long Trail." The sober ones in the lead knew the track. The camels behind just naturally followed. Still more fell off, and as their camels went on they had to walk—or stagger.

Half a dozen slightly inebriated cameliers in a bunch saw, a few miles from Kharga, a camel train coming in. They yelled out, "Senussis, charge the blighters." Without waiting for orders they whipped up their patient camels, yelled like demons, and charged full tilt at the caravan. It happened to be a convoy of transport camels returning from the water-dump. The fiery cameliers were terribly disappointed.

An aeroplane passed over, flying low, for the pilot could not make out the meaning of the scene below. A scared rider cried out, "Taube," and blazed away.

Back along the track were empty bottles, full men, riderless camels, and much flotsam and jetsam. The head of the section was trotting happily to the rendezvous. At the rear came the patient sergeant coaxing the crazy ones, helping the lazy ones on with a stick.

And back at headquarters the staff were puzzled to get the following cryptic message from the aeroplane pilot:

Blaine's section last seen going for Hell's Gates, hell for leather.

CHAPTER 4

The Coming of Flora

This is the why and the wherefore of the coming to Egypt of Sister Flora Aird Andrews Livingstone.

A crazed Serbian killed an Austrian archduke. This incident brought on Armageddon. It set Central Europe ablaze, and gave Germany the cue to launch out on a swash-buckling expedition with a view to making good her ambition of dominating Europe—and, incidentally, the world.

Now the Huns might have crushed France and Russia—very probably they would have done so—but the German powers that be made the unpardonable error of tearing up a scrap of paper, and ravaging Belgium with a ferocity and ruthlessness unbelievable in this twentieth century. That brought old England out of her splendid isolation, and her contemptible little army crossed the Channel, to perform such miracles against overwhelming odds that all the world wondered.

Britain having stripped for the fray, Australia simply couldn't keep out of it. Mr. Joseph Cook, the Commonwealth Prime Minister, offered 20,000 men; but this little division was to increase, until the great South Land with its insignificant population sent about 500,000 soldiers—every man a volunteer—to fight in the cause of freedom.

It was September 1914—September and springtime, when the Australian bush decks herself in all her glory. The Hunter Valley, garden of sunny New South Wales, lay like a fairer Garden of Eden between the enveloping hills. The old river ran lie a trail of silver laughter past the happy homesteads. Magpies carolled merrily, all the feathered songsters joined in the bushland melody. Golden wattle bloomed in rich profusion from the watershed to the Pacific, and filled the balmy air with the scent of honeydew. On the rich river flats, and in amongst the foot-hills, hares and paddy-melons fed unmolested, while higher up the mountain rocks wallabies hopped hither and thither undisturbed by the hunters. Even the foxes and dingoes in their lairs enjoyed a period of peace, for the bush boys were already wending their way to the metropolis to embark on the great adventure. Every little farm, every homestead, every sheep and cattle station sent its quota. Sturdy youths from the towns and valleys casually remarked that they would go on a walking tour to Berlin, took train to Sydney, and enlisted in the 1st Infantry Brigade. Station lads mounted their favourite hacks, and with a cheery 'So long' took the long trail eastward to the Light Horse camp. And the heroic Australian mothers and sisters and sweethearts choked back their tears and bade them go.

Colonel Livingstone's fighting days were done. He was barely sixty years of age, but a shell in South Africa had taken off his right arm. So he lived the peaceful, prosperous life of an Australian squatter, watching his flocks and herds increase and multiply. And now that the dogs of war were again let loose he sighed to think that he had no son left to give the Empire. His only son had been killed at Eland's River, and, now a widower, all his love and ambition centred in his daughter Flora.

Barely a year had passed since she had completed her training as a nurse at Prince Alfred Hospital, and had come back to the old home to be the joy of her old father's life and the sunshine of his home. She was twenty-six years old, but looked twenty-one. Being born on the 29th of February 1888, she playfully persisted that as she had only enjoyed about half a dozen birthdays, she was really only six years old. This was her excuse for any escapade. Suitors for her hand, and incidentally for the colonel's broad acres, had come to Langlands, stayed awhile, but had not conquered. Smilingly she saw them come; sadly she watched them depart. When the Polo Carnival came to Muswellbrook, she was the most radiant figure on the ground. At the dance she was the *belle* of the ball. Yet ever she had remained heart-whole and happy.

Day after day the old colonel and his daughter had watched the young men, singly or in twos and threes, riding gaily along the river road that led to war and glory. From the verandah of Langlands they waved a cheery God-speed to the light-hearted volunteers. But the old man sighed and shook his head. So when the freshness of September's spring had merged into the heat of October, Flora reckoned it was time to say what had long been in her mind.

The sun had set behind the western hills, which were still sharply silhouetted against the rose-red of the afterglow. All was peaceful and quiet, save for the occasional cry of a curlew or a *mopoke*, or the jingle of a bullock bell down the creek. The colonel was enjoying his after-dinner cigar, and it was just at that time Flora well knew his heart was warmest and his purse-strings loosest. So she sat on the arm of his big chair and gently ruffled the few grey hairs left on his kind old head. This had been her mode of attack when she wanted a trip to the Melbourne Cup, or a late model automobile, or a new hunter, or a ball dress, and it had never yet failed her, not even when she had wanted to take up nursing in Sydney.

"Daddy," she said, nestling closer, "it must be a fine thing to give a son to fight for the king."

He thought of Eland's River, and nodded his head sadly.

"I chanced on a little verse today. Daddy. It's the most beautifully loyal verse ever written, I think. It's just the proud lament of an auld Scots wife:

I had three sons. I now hae nane,
I bred them toiling sairly.
But I wad gie them a' again.
To live an' dee wi' Chairlie.

"There, isn't that fine, Daddy?"

Again the colonel nodded his head.

"Did you see in the *Herald* that four sons of Parson Howell-Price and the five sons of Mrs. Leane had all enlisted? I think that's just wonderful. Daddy."

"They won't all come back," said the colonel sadly.

"True; but you'd far rather have your son play the man and never return than play the craven and live at Langlands; and you'd far rather your little daughter did her bit for Australia than loaf at home living on the fat of the land."

The old man stiffened, sat bolt upright, and exclaimed, "My son I gave loyally for the Empire, though it nearly broke my heart; but not my daughter—not my daughter."

It was very late before the wilful girl won her way and the old man was induced to make the great sacrifice. But finally he capitulated. Next day Flora sent in her application for a position on the staff of one of the Australian War Hospitals. She did not get away with the first batch. That was the proud privilege of the Senior Army Nursing Sisters. Neither did she get away with the second batch. But every period of waiting has its end, so early in 1915 Sister Flora Livingstone found herself on the mail boat in Sydney harbour, looking back with tearful eyes, and waving farewell to a tall, grey-haired, one-armed old gentleman who stood on the circular quay wharf and blew his nose vigorously when anyone chanced to look in his direction.

Swinging through the heads she had a last long look at the red roofs of Mosman as the steamer breasted the waves of the blue Pacific. Sydney was left behind, then Melbourne Adelaide, and Fremantle. With no *Emden* [1] to cause any trouble, the liner crossed the Indian Ocean, looked in at Colombo, and in the fulness of time entered the Suez Canal. On the right were Moses' Well and Sinai, and Flora was glad she had not forgotten all her Old Testament history.

Picturesque Tewfik and smellful Suez were passed, and then in turn Kubri, Kabrit, and so on to Ismailia, the one really pleasant place on the Canal. Flora saw the trenches and defences all along the Canal, waved cheerily and impartially at the Gurkhas and Indian lancers and Territorials, and cooee-ed delightedly whenever she saw an Australian. With a wide expanse of desert on either side the boat steamed on past Ferdan and Kantara, and eventually anchored off Port Said.

Here the nursing sisters disembarked, spent a while and some money in the bazaars, paying about double the value of the articles, and then took train for Cairo.

Now it so happened that just as they arrived at the main station at Cairo the 1st Australian Division was entraining for Alexandria, there to embark for Gallipoli. And as she saw that heroic band marching in platoons and battalions and brigades, the soul of Flora Livingstone was stirred as never before. They were giants, these men, tall, sun-tanned, and wiry, alert, clean-limbed, and sturdy—whole platoons averaging about six feet—whole battalions with not an undersized man amongst them. There was an English officer near her on the platform, newly arrived from France, and she almost embraced him when he said to a civilian standing by, "That's the finest body of men in the whole Allied Armies." And they were her own lads from the Sunny South. How proud she was of them! How much prouder she was to be ere a few short weeks had passed and the world resounded with their praises! And when the 1st, 2nd, 3rd, and 4th Battalions marched in—her very own brigade from sunny New South Wales—a lump came into her

---

1. *The Kaiser's Raider!* (*The Emden* and *The Ayesha, being the Adventures of the Landing Squad*, two classics of war at sea) by Hellmuth von Mücke is also published by Leonaur.

throat and tears streamed down her face.

The trains moved out. Discipline was relaxed. The boys seeing the Australian nurses cheered till the vast building echoed with their shouts. Unable to control her emotion, Flora held out her arms to them and cried, "Oh, I love you; I love you all! I'll nurse you and serve you till I drop. Oh, how I love you all!"

In this wise came Sister Livingstone to Egypt, and thus she plighted her troth and swore to serve for the duration of the war—and four months afterward.

CHAPTER 5

Romani—1

Romani was one of the decisive battles of the war. It settled finally the pretensions of the German-led Turks in the direction of Egypt. Prior to August 1916, the enemy had always assumed the offensive, while the British devoted their energies to the defence of the Suez Canal and Egypt. After Romani the desert campaign took on a new aspect. The British assumed the offensive. Steadily the invader was pushed back and back, till at Rafa he was driven for good and all beyond the bounds of Sinai.

The Australians in Sinai knew what thirst meant during the summer of 1916. May, June, and July had witnessed terrific heat—heat that Anglo-Egyptians of long standing declared to be the record. Soldiers in hospital at Tel el Kebir, recovering slowly from various dysenteric diseases, were stricken down by the excessive heat and died. Out east of the Canal the thirsty garrison toiled early and late, building redoubts and filling millions of sand-bags. In those enervating days there was but one joke out in the sandy waste. Said one Billjim to his mate, "What did you do in the Great War, Daddy?" And his comrade wearily replied, "I helped to bag Sinai, my boy."

The building of trenches was a hopeless task. Shovelling sand was like unto shovelling water. Fast as the sand was scooped out it trickled in again. Then, when a trench had been boarded up and wired and sand-bagged, a stifling *khamseen* would blow up, and the swirling sand would fall in the trenched again. The magnitude of the task can be estimated when it is remembered that during the desert campaign, which ended at Rafa, there were used 30,000,000 sand-bags, 2,000,000 square feet of timber, 50,000 rolls of wire netting, and 7000 tons of barbed wire. In addition, 220 41 miles of macadamised roads were constructed, 359 miles of railway, and 300 miles of water-pipes.

Briefly, it was *some* job.

Romani changed all this—at least the prosaic, defensive, sit-tight part. Henceforth the defence of Egypt rested with the attacking desert column. Abdul was too busy looking west and running east to think of threatening the Canal.

Romani was preceded by two interesting interludes—the one picturesquely victorious, the other even more picturesque, but quite a regrettable incident. At Duiedar the Scotties held an outpost. In the dark the Turks crept up, and at dawn attacked in greatly superior force. But the Scotties fought magnificently, and in spite of many casualties beat off their assailants, and held the line till the Anzac Mounteds came up and drove off the enemy. The other interlude was the surprising of some Yeomanry who were routed and sent in full retreat to Kantara, where one breathless officer arrived in his pyjamas!

After that, the Cavalry and Camelry and Light Horse and Mounted Rifles patrolled the front unceasingly, while the airmen did a daily reconnaissance. The movements of the enemy were thus carefully noted and the element of surprise eliminated. So we knew in July that a considerable force of Turks was making steadily towards Romani. We did not know, however, how perfect had been the preparations of the German Staff, how rough roads had been constructed over the soft sand for the passage of artillery, how ammunition and stores had been sent ahead and hidden in the palm groves; how plans of all our defences had been made from photos by German airmen, and how old wells all along the old caravan route had been reopened and put in working order. Their telephonic signal communications were perfect. It is doubtful, however, if the Hun really thought he could break through to Kantara. The most he could hope for was to make a big feint for Egypt, and so keep as many British troops as possible in Sinai and prevent their being sent to France.

During July the enemy arrangements were completed, and in August he advanced to the attack. Patrols of the 1st Light Horse Brigade met the Turkish patrols, and on 3rd August this brigade found itself opposing the determined attack of the main army. Brigadier-General Meredith therefore threw his regiments right in the path of the invader, blocking his advance and forcing him to deploy. The superior mobility of the Australians enabled them to choose excellent positions from which to fight rear-guard actions, and while they inflicted considerable losses on the enemy, they got off very lightly. Thus the enemy was enticed into the maze of sand-dunes, where his heavily laden infantry floundered and had all the ginger taken out of their attack. Still, by sheer force of numbers the Turks won through on to Mount Meredith, Wellington Ridge, and Mount Royston.

By daylight on 4th August the 2nd Light Horse Brigade, with Brigadier-General Royston in temporary command, swung up to the battle line, and the two brigades, fighting side by side, continued to hold up the advance. But the Turkish infantry were now helped very materially by German gunners and machine gunners. Their artillery was splendidly served, shell after shell exploding over the ridges lined by the defenders, or in the *wadis* where the led horses were waiting. The Taubes participated in the attack, spotting for their artillery, bombing our horses and trenches, and then flying back to a specially prepared landing-place a few miles east and taking on more bombs for our annoyance. Our airmen on inferior machines did heroic stunts, but admitted themselves hopelessly out-manoeuvred and out-flown.

On our left flank towards Muhamediya the Scottish infantry barred the way. Knowing the ranges, they were able to inflict considerable damage on the Turks. Enjoying the comparative security of trenches with formidable barbed wire entanglements in front, Abdul could not get near them, and their losses were slight.

Down south the Queenslanders effectually blocked any out-flanking of our right wing. The Fighting Fifth had a very strenuous time. It was just such a fight as poor Colonel Hubert Harris—who was killed on Gallipoli—would have loved. But Lieut.-Colonel Wilson handled the Fifth with consummate skill. A few thousand Turks swinging round to attack Romani from the south found only a regiment of Light Horse in their way. But these bushmen were ubiquitous. Everywhere that Abdul went the Fifth were sure to go. Always there was a fringe of emu plumes on the crest of every hill. The superior numbers of the enemy availed him not. His casualties increased every hour, but his goal ever receded. The boys of the Australian Light Horse have a wonderful admiration for General Royston. He is essentially a cavalry general, like Jeb Stewart. He has been fighting Zulus or Boers or Huns ever since his sixteenth year.

He commanded Australians in South Africa. Coming to Sinai, he commanded first the 12th A.L.H. Regiment, then the 2nd Brigade, and finally the 3rd Light Horse Brigade, and always the men loved him for his fighting fearlessness. At Romani he was a ball of inexhaustible energy. One after another his horses knocked up, but he seemed to be made of green-hide and whalebone. And he bore a charmed life. Bullets and shrapnel fell thick and fast all round him. His A.D.C. and several orderlies were wounded, but Fighting Jack galloped on unscathed—always where the fighting was thickest.

The New Zealand Mounted Rifles, a brigade of Yeomanry, and a brigade of Territorial Infantry now came into the fight. The sorely-tried Light Horsemen had been hard at it for nearly forty-eight hours without a spell. Their horses were knocked up and starving. The men were hard put to it to keep awake. They had fought a wonderful rear-guard action, holding up and inflicting heavy casualties on an enemy five times their strength, and taking all the sting out of the offensive. But still the German Staff persevered with the attack. On came the Turks, yelling, "*Allah* finish Australia," "*Allah* finish Australia"—a rather unique battle-cry, which tickled the Anzacs immensely.

From the Scottish redoubts on the left to the Camelry on the right the action now became general. The Turks pushed on till their vanguard was right in sight of Romani. Here near ancient Pelusium, where the Persian hosts of Cambyses routed the Egyptians centuries before, another invader was to meet with a far different fate. But as the Turkish vanguard pushed along the *wadi* towards the railway no one dared prophesy what would happen. The German guns having the range to a yard, fired a never-ending hail of shrapnel on our front line, our horse lines, and, on the redoubts. They had tons of ammunition. The Light Horse captured a whole camel train of ammunition, but this never affected the enemy's fire. Our artillery having less definite objects to concentrate on and with constantly varying ranges, yet did splendid work.

The Ayrshire battery in particular won the whole-souled admiration of the Anzacs. Every time a likely target showed up the Lowlanders smashed it instantly. Once some German machine guns, cleverly posted, were inflicting considerable damage on the Australians. The Ayrshires vouchsafed the Huns three shells, which landed precisely on the spot, wrecking the guns and slaughtering the teams. One silent and twisted gun barrel sticking in the air told the tale. *Anon* a camel team bringing up ammunition was sighted. A few shells were sent in their direction, and after the dust had subsided an Australian in a pained voice expostulated to the gunner, "Look, Scottie, there's one of them camels making off home."

CHAPTER 6

Romani—2

The battle waged with increased vigour all along the line, Romani in the centre being the main objective. It was at Romani that the Turks made their final thrust. Along the *wadi*, out of sight of the gunners, came an irresistible wedge of Turkish infantry. It was a spear thrust right at the heart of our position. For a while it threatened seriously. No thin line of khaki horsemen could block that rush. Abdul had staked his all on one desperate charge.

That rush might have won the day but for the New Zealanders. As the Turks came on, yelling, "*Allah* finish Australia," the Mounted Rifles saw their chance. With a blood-curdling yell the Maorilanders charged with the bayonet, and cut their way clean through the attacking column, cleaving it in two. Auckland, Canterbury, Wellington, and Otago won the day The head was sawn oft the spear. The Turkish column, bisected neatly, faltered, and the rear half retreated. Had the first half possessed a clever leader, had they any zest for the fight, they might have made things merry. But just as they realised they were cut off, the New Zealanders were upon them with the bayonet, yelling like demons. Nothing could withstand that charge. The Turks dropped their rifles and called for quarter. The victorious "*Allah* finish Australia" died on their lips, and they and their German officers cried "*Kamerad*," "Finish war," "Australia good." In the vicinity of Mount Royston the New Zealanders bagged 500 prisoners.

As the enemy wavered the British fine advanced. Round Katib Gannit there was some stiff fighting, till the Light Horsemen manoeuvred the Turks into a hopeless position. Rifle and machine-gun fire concentrated on them, and when the Light Horse charged 400 Turks surrendered.

Round about Romani were performed many deeds of valour that

some chronicler may perhaps redeem from oblivion. One heroic incident stands out because of the peculiar circumstances connected therewith. During April and May, when the Australian infantry left Egypt for France, quite a number of Light Horsemen, hearing 'the call of Stoush,' and thinking that Sinai would not provide them with sufficient excitement, stowed away on the transports and mingled with the infantry. Several managed to elude the vigilance of the Military Police at Marseilles and got right up to the front line, where in due course the majority of them were killed or wounded. Several, however, were caught on the transports or at Marseilles, and in time were returned crestfallen to Egypt.

Amongst these was Curran of the 7th A.L.H. Technically he had deserted, so he was placed under arrest. And he was under arrest when Abdul swooped down on Romani. It was against his nature to miss a scrap, but his rifle had been taken from him. So he escaped from the guard and started out on his own as a stretcher-bearer. Right out to the front line he went, entirely indifferent to the death-dealing hail that spattered in the sand. Slightly wounded men he gave water to drink, and cheered them on their way in with jest and joke. The badly wounded he helped or carried in himself. Fourteen times he braved the bullets, and each time brought in a wounded man. But his good luck petered out. When next he essayed to carry out his errand of mercy, he was killed. He had shown the '*greater love*.' He had laid down his life not only for his country but for his friends.

Romani was now fought and won. Scottish and English Territorials, Australian and New Zealand horsemen. Cavalry and Camelry, now pushed on to complete the overthrow of the enemy. The German gunners, so accurate at known ranges, lost their sting as the British line swept forward. They shortened their range again and again till it was time to make a get-away. The machine gunners tried in vain to hold up the pursuit. Parties of Turkish infantry, tired out and dispirited with their long march, their incessant fighting, and their final defeat, surrendered all along the line. About 20,000 with several guns and a big quota of machine guns had started out from El Arish. About 18,000 had come into action between Katia and Romani. Of these, by the time the pursuit was finally held up, 5000 were captured; over 1200 were killed; about 4500 had been wounded. In honour of their 'Victory' (?) the Turks struck a Romani medal.

The Anzac Mounted Division enjoyed a brief rest for the sake of their horses, and the pursuit was resumed. Yeomanry and Camelry co-operated in the hunt. The 3rd Light Horse Brigade, having accounted for an isolated body of the enemy to the southward, made a belated arrival on the scene, and joined in the chase. But round about Katia the defeated Turks were rallied. Strong rear-guards with many machine guns were thrown across the line of our advance. In spite of gallant attacks and splendid charges on to adventurous rear-parties, the Turks would no longer be thrown into disorder. The rear-guard was harried, but the main body was not hurried. Every inch of the way back was fiercely contested. After a few days of hard fighting the pursuit eased up, and Abdul marched back to Bir el Abd.

Romani is claimed to be largely an Anzac victory, for the Anzac Mounted Division, under General Chauvel, bore the brunt of the attack, and had almost a monopoly of the casualties. Of the total casualties the Yeomanry had 2 *per cent.*, the British infantry and artillery 10 *per cent.,* and the Anzacs 87 *per cent.*

Amongst the 5000 prisoners captured were a number of German officers and men. One of these officers was talking to a group of Australian Light Horse officers when a long and wiry trooper, with characteristic disregard for the conventions, butted in and exclaimed' "Say, old Hun, what do you think of the Australians now?"

And the German officer replied, "They are splendid fighters. Still, I do not think they are any better than they think they are." Which, all things considered, was one to the Hun.

That trooper's ruffled feelings were, however, mollified when he read in the English papers Mr. W. T. Massey's [1] tribute that the Anzac Mounted Division was the cream of the Overseas Forces.

---

1. An excellent trilogy of the Great War in the Middle East by W. T. Massey in two volumes, *The Great War in the Middle East*: 1 and 2 is also published by Leonaur.

CHAPTER 7

Eastward Ho

Someday the war historians will get busy over the Sinai Campaign. For difficulties encountered and hardships endured, it must rank as one of the most interesting campaigns ever carried to a successful issue.

From the first skirmishes east of the Canal—not, of course, including the original abortive attacks of the Turks at the beginning of 1915—to the capture of Rafa, the bulk of the patrols and the brunt of the fighting fell on the Anzacs. Yet it was not till well into 1917 that the people of Australia realised what a heroic part had been played in that campaign by the Australian Light Horse, New Zealand Mounted Rifles, and Imperial Camel Corps. Owing to some oversight of the Commonwealth Government, no Australian Press Representative had been detailed for the task of informing Australian fathers and mothers how heroically their sons had fought and died.

Thus day after day, when the mails arrived from the Antipodes, sun-scorched troopers out on the desert or wounded men in hospital were sickened by letters from their loved ones saying, "We never hear anything about the Light Horse," or, "You're lucky you're not in France," or, "I suppose you hardly know there's a war on there." The climax came when a badly-wounded Light Horseman in the 14th Australian General Hospital received a pair of socks from the Red Cross. Inside Was a message from some well-meaning but very cruel young lady, and the message read: "I hope these sox go to some Australian hero in France, but not to any of the cold-footed Light Horse." That trooper cried like a kid.

In 1916 the G.O.C., A.I.F., in Egypt and Sinai, General Sir Harry Chauvel, seeing the totally inadequate reports of the battles which were being cabled out to Australia, cabled to the Defence Department, recommending that a War Correspondent be sent to keep the people in touch with operations in Sinai, and to compile the war records of the A.I.F. regiments. But for some inscrutable reason nothing was done.

So the meagre reports of the doings of the Light Horsemen continued to percolate through the home papers and the cables to Australia. Romani was billed as a great British victory in which, incidentally, the Australians and New Zealanders participated. But in 1917 a paragraph in the Sydney *Bulletin* told astonished readers that during the fighting round Katia and Romani the Anzacs had suffered over 87 *per cent,* of the total casualties. The published reports of the battle, and the subsequent rewards and decorations, never gave a hint of such disproportionate losses. If the Light Horse did any particularly good work, the cables in the English papers—zealously copied and condensed for Australian consumption—referred to "Our Mounted Troops" or "The Victorious Desert Column." And later on, at the second battle of Gaza, when the Imperial Camel Corps (1st Anzac Battalion) was the only unit to reach its objective and capture the Turkish redoubts, the cables told Australian readers that "The Camel Corps did good work carrying water for the Light Horse."

There are lone graves left on the league-long track from Romani to El Arish. Day after day the Light Horse and Camel patrols pushed eastward, ever eastward. Every now and then there were skirmishes with the Turkish patrols, and Abdul is no slouch as a scout and sniper. And following the track blazed by the Anzacs came the British infantry and the pipe line and the iron horse. There was heavy fighting round the Katia Oasis, amongst the palms, for the German staff had selected the rear-guard halting-places with consummate skill, and the Light Horse being the attacking party suffered many casualties. The Turkish defence of the Katia line was so stubborn and so successful that the main Turkish Army, which fled in disorder from Romani, was able to continue the retreat to El Arish in comparative ease.

There is a fine story waiting to be written by some New Zealander who was with the Mounted Rifles during the strenuous months from June 1916 to January 1917. English staff officers, competent critics, have declared that the New Zealanders were the pick of the whole E.E.F., and I've heard Australians gladly endorse that verdict. Australians and New Zealanders fought side by side all the time, and as the scorching heat of summer gave place to the bitter cold of winter, they pushed steadily on, always in the van. ... On the occasion of the second trek to Palestine of the 1st Anzac Battalion I.C.C, I saw three graves on the scrubby sand-hills near Bir el Abd. They were not very far apart. Rough wooden crosses marked the sites. I rode across to investigate, for I had many Light Horsemen comrades killed in Sinai. These, however, proved to be three troopers of the Otago Mounted Rifles—Ryan, Mahoney, and McCarthy; three gallant Irish Colonial crusaders.

After suffering a fair share of casualties at Romani, the Cameliers moved eastward with the Desert Column. Day after day the patrols pushed on, and the railway construction followed apace. The Hun 'planes kept busy bombing the Desert Column and the dumps and the railway. Our 'planes went up daily, and had fine sport with enemy fliers. Whatever there is sporting or chivalrous in the German Army seems to have risen to the Flying Corps. Dare-devil Hun airmen, after bombing the Light Horse bivouacs and the railhead workers, dropped cheeky messages on the Australians. At this period the bombing of our dumps and working parties was a regular occurrence. 'Archies' being rather scarce, the only thing to do was to dive for a dugout.

On one occasion a Light Horseman was watching a gang of E.L.C. natives at work, when they suddenly downed tools and dashed for a big trench near which he was standing. Intuitively the trooper guessed there was a Taube above, so he dived for the trench, landing a half-second ahead of the gyppies, who piled themselves on top of him. As the last native landed in the trench there was a deafening explosion and a wild chorus of yells. The lucky horseman scrambled from underneath the writhing mass without a scratch, but several of the gyppies were badly wounded and a few killed outright. Familiarity with bombs bred contempt, and soon the sight of dozens of men streaking for the shelter of a dugout provoked naught but a mild interest or simple mirth.

One incident provided the comic relief which kept railhead laughing for a week. An A.S.C. officer was superintending the stacking of some *dhurra*, incidentally yarning with an Australian and at the same time keeping one eye on a black dot in the sky overhead. Suddenly there was a warning whistle, and the pair dived for the shelter of a dugout, making a dead heat of it, while the Australian's dog came third. Hardly were they settled before there was a sound of scrambling, and a frightened native, being too far from his own dugout, and risking anything rather than remain in the open, flung himself headlong into the dugout. The sagacious dog resenting this intrusion, snapped at the native, nipping him painfully on the fleshiest part of his body.

But at the precise instant the dog bit, the aeroplane bomb exploded, and the poor gyppie, thinking he was mortally wounded, grabbed the injured part and ran howling to the Field Ambulance.

Time came when railhead and pipehead and roadhead had been pushed far enough eastward for the G.O.C. to reckon he was within striking distance of El Arish—and El Arish is the half-way house to Jerusalem. For several days the enemy 'planes had been over reconnoitring and bombing, so when all was ready for the final dash on El Arish, our 'planes were kept very busy keeping the enemy airmen away.

For long the Turks had made El Arish their base for operations against Egypt. Its strategical advantages were many. Surrounded by a natural barrier in the shape of rolling billows of sand, the approach of attacking forces was made very difficult. It looked absolutely impassable for artillery; yet our guns got through. With its hills and palm groves it might have been stubbornly defended, but at the last moment the German staff, having a wholesome respect for the encircling manoeuvres of the Desert Column, decided on evacuation. So just when the British were about to strike, the airmen came in with the news that the Turks were leaving. It was therefore decided to send the Camelry and Cavalry on ahead to make sure, and to capture the town. So on top of a hard day's march the Desert Column moved off again at midnight for El Arish.

Over the sand-dunes they trekked, a moving mass of mounted men—but silently, and with no tell-tale pipes or cigarettes to warn Abdul of their approach. Masaid, a few miles west of El Arish, had been strongly entrenched and held, but the advance guard found here only empty trenches. On went the column over precipitous sand-banks, so steep that one wondered how the camels and horses didn't topple over. When nearing the town just at dawn, the column divided and surrounded the town on the west, south, and east sides—to the north being the blue Mediterranean. But the bird had flown.

The ancient town with its mosque and mud-built houses was all astir. For over two years the Turks had held sway there. But when the Light Horsemen cantered into view, the Bedouins came out to greet them. And they showed as much jubilation as a Bedouin ever shows—which is not a great deal. So the main army followed on, horse, foot, artillery, and camelry, and camped beneath the palms on the banks of the Wadi el Arish. They rested. But the hard-worked Desert Column had a very brief respite. Hardly had they settled in their new bivouac before they were once more hurried off to mop up Maghdaba.

CHAPTER 8

Maghdaba

The Battle of Maghdaba was one of the most brilliant and picturesque little battles in the whole war. It was rather presumptuous of the Anzac Mounted Division to think that it could manage the job.

On the face of it, no student of war would believe that a small body of dismounted cavalry and camelry, armed only with rifle and bayonet, could charge across open country and capture a strong natural fortress, heavily entrenched, defended by a resolute soldiery scarcely inferior in strength, and armed with artillery, machine guns, and bombs. And this on the top of a 20-mile night march over unknown country. Yet that is exactly what the Anzacs did.

The Turks having found discretion the better part of valour, retired eastward from El Arish, leaving the half-way house to Palestine to the British.

But blocking the further progress of our army towards Sinai were the two strongly entrenched and well-garrisoned posts of Rafa and Maghdaba, and because of the absence of water on the way and the difficulty of transport the Turks felt fairly secure at Maghdaba.

After an all-night trek down the Wadi el Arish, the Anzac Mounted Division, plus the Cameliers, came at dawn in sight of Maghdaba. It was a weird and wonderful stunt, that march in the silent stillness of the night. Like a column of spectres the Cameliers glided noiselessly down the *wadi* bed. Now and then, however, from the ranks of the Light Horsemen came the clang of a stirrup iron or the clink of snaffle bars. Riding near the Bing Boys one could see against their swarthy faces the gleam of white teeth or the sparkle of black eyes. Not a light was shown. There was no smoking. It is a terrible act of self-denial for the Australian to go without a smoke for any length of time. It was a long, slow, sleepy, silent ride. Abdul therefore got the surprise of his life when, with the breaking day, the Light Horse patrols came circling round his stronghold.

There was hurry and hustle and excitement, then, amongst the men of Maghdaba. The supports were hurriedly thrown into the trenches and redoubts. The guns behind the hills were mounted, and soon their shells began to play upon the manoeuvring horsemen. The 6th Light Horse came under a salvo of shrapnel. It looked as if dozens of saddles must be emptied, but not a man was hit. The regiment manoeuvred as on parade, and swung clear of the danger-zone. The Cameliers—three companies of Australians and one of New Zealanders—dismounted out of artillery range, and in a long drab line moved forward gaily to the attack. On the right the 2nd Light Horse Brigade swung up, dismounted, and, while the horses moved back to safety, the troopers joined up with the Cameliers and pressed on. The enemy artillery, Krupp and mountain guns, having kept the horses at a distance, now concentrated on the long line of approaching riflemen. Knowing the ranges, they made good practice, but the continually moving line necessitated a shortening range, and the fire was not very deadly.

The Bing Boys (Hong-Kong and Singapore Mountain Battery) now took a hand. In double-quick time they barracked their camels, put their mountain guns together, and quickly finding the range, devoted their attention to the Turkish redoubts. Our Royal Horse Artillery next took up the running, and from behind a convenient rise engaged in some counter battery work at the expense of the Turkish gunners. The action became general, and the fusillade of musketry all along the line was punctuated by the roar of the artillery. Nearer and nearer crept the long khaki line to the Turkish redoubts, and a steady contest began for the desired superiority of fire. The enemy machine guns were well served, but on the whole their musketry was very second rate.

Word of the dash on Maghdaba had reached the enemy headquarters, and a strong mounted force was sent to relieve the garrison. But the New Zealanders swung round to the north-east, held up the relief, and, attacking vigorously, sent them back in disorder to the frontier. Maghdaba was now almost surrounded, but the advantage of position lay with the defenders. They were all under cover in excellently prepared trenches, while the Anzacs were attacking in the open. But the latter's marksmanship at long ranges was far superior. The crests of the redoubts were lashed with bullets, so that the Turks feared to raise their heads, and their fire grew erratic. Nearer and nearer drew the attacking force. Hotter and hotter grew the fire. Horsemen, Yeomanry, and Cameliers, now fired with the spirit of emulation, made a race of it. Soon they were within striking distance of the enemy. A rattle ran along the line, and a glint of steel shimmering in the sun told Abdul that the bayonets were out. A cheer sounded, and was carried from end to end of the line. The whistles sounded the 'Charge,' and the attackers sprang forward. Faster sounded the Turkish fire, but it was wild, mostly whistling harmlessly overhead. The British never troubled any longer to reply. The bayonet was to settle the whole matter.

The line now broke up as the cheering soldiery faced straight at the various redoubts. There was a wild final charge, some hot work with the bayonet, and soon white flags began to show up in the redoubts. One after another the scattered post garrisons surrendered. Each redoubt was, however, commanded by the one farther on. But the day was already won. Small parties of Turks were flying in all directions, and wild-eyed Anzacs, too tired to chase them, swore lustily and blazed away a few parting shots. Away east, Yeomanry and Mounted Rifles were rounding up the fugitives, and only a few hundred got away. The last redoubt was captured, and the victors charged for the German guns and finished the fight.

Back on the plain were dozens of still khaki figures. Here and there were stretcher-bearers carrying in the wounded. At the dressing-stations the doctors and medical orderlies were working furiously. Parties were told off to bury the dead. Our losses, considering the lack of cover during the attack, were surprisingly few. Five officers had been killed and 17 wounded. Seven other ranks were killed and 117 wounded.

It was at this stage, while all hands were busy bringing in the prisoners and the wounded, that one camel went mangoon. Breaking away from the line and tearing the nose-peg free, it started out to mop up the earth. Every Camelier that crossed its path had to flee for his life. Huge stones were hurled at the brute, but it grew madder and madder, and nothing could stop it. Then the Camelier *medico* sauntered into view, and the enraged beast charged fair at him. There were wild yells of warning, and the doc made the run of his life. He turned and doubled round and about, dodging like a tricky rugby three-quarter, but the camel, ignoring all others, followed hard in his wake. The crowd divided their time between cheering on the doc and heaving bricks at the camel. At last the *medico* saw in a heap of forage a haven of rest. The Cameliers were now taking pot-shots at the camel, which, bleeding from half a dozen wounds, still floundered at the heels of its quarry. Then to the surprise of all and the intense relief of the *doctor*, the camel stopped, and started feeding away at the *dhurra*.

The Maghdaba garrison was wiped out. Comparatively few escaped. Over 1300 prisoners were bagged, including 45 officers. Four mountain guns and three Krupp guns, with a big store of ammunition, rifles, and machine guns, were gathered in. And when these were got ready the victorious cavalcade started off back to El Arish. More reinforcements appeared out East, but the Light Horse shepherded the column home, and the Turks dared not attack.

Chapter 9

In the Hospital

It was night. All the lights in B4 were out except the shaded globe on sister's table. All was quiet save when, now and then, some weary soldier groaned, or maybe fighting his battles over again in his sleep, gave forth some incoherent ejaculation.

Without, the full Egyptian moon shed a silvery light on old Cairo and the Nile, while the age-old Mokattam Hills loomed black and Sphinx-like to eastward. A gentle breeze filtered through the windows. Sister Livingstone sat at the table. It was her turn for night duty, and, having seen all her patients comfortably settled for the night, she was revelling in the newly arrived Australian mail. Strange how welcome the most trivial home news becomes when one is in a far country. How the soldiers, and the sisters too, just long for news from home.

Sister had finished reading her mail, and now, staring into space, was thinking dreamily of sunny New South Wales and the old homestead in the Hunter River Valley. She was thinking of old times—the dances, the polo carnivals, the shooting excursions in the mountains, and the picnic races.

Suddenly she was roused from her reverie. In the distance there sounded a long, tremulous note rising high and shrill, then dying away to a soft, plaintive cry. It was the cry of the curlew, that sad, mournful bush note that no Australian, once hearing, ever forgets.

Again the cry was repeated, nearer it seemed, yet so softly that she seemed to hear but the echo of it.

Rising softly she tiptoed towards the door. Passing No. 7 bed an aggrieved voice in a stage whisper cried, "O' course I don't want any attention at all. I'm only a silkworm."

"What's up, Billjim, old chap?" said sister, going to his side.

"Oh, nothing at all; just dying o' thirst."

Smiling, sister brought him a drink, and when she had turned and smoothed his pillow, he looked up with a grin and said, "O' course you don't want to kiss me goodnight. Sister."

"Oh, I daren't, Billjim; the rest of the Australian Eleven would be jealous."

"But I wouldn't tell. What sort of a knark do you take me for?"

"Walls have ears," she replied sententiously, "and the night has a thousand eyes."

Glancing round the ward to see that all was well, sister again moved towards the door, and looked forth into the night. She was still wondering whence came the cry of the curlew, when she saw a beckoning hand at the end of the verandah. It was Blaine, the big sergeant, who always slept in the open. Born and bred in the bush, he said the walls of houses and hospitals seemed to cramp and stifle him. He was smiling as sister came up. She expostulated gently, "It's nearly midnight, and time you were asleep."

"You promised to write home to poor Mrs. Giltinan tonight. Sister, and I promised to tell you why George died."

"Why he died?" she reiterated in a surprised voice.

"Well, how he died."

"Very well," she acquiesced, seating herself at the bedside. "I'm afraid I was dreaming when I heard that curlew. It brought such a flood of bushland memories with it. But I didn't know there were any curlews about here."

"There aren't," said the soldier, with a grin.

"What, you did it?"

"Well, you see, Sister, I peeped through the window, and you looked so awfully sweet with the light shining on your pretty angel face that I simply had to bring you out to make sure if you really were an angel."

"'*It's a lee, but it's a bonnie, bonnie lee,*'" she quoted.

"Oh, you've been reading J. M. Barrie," he said.

Sister nodded, and was silent for a while.

"On such a night as this, a couple of thousand years ago," he said quietly, "Antony and Cleopatra glided down this same old Nile, with the same moon floating aloft, and the same old pyramids standing sentinel."

"Suppose you tell me about Giltinan instead of Cleopatra," sister suggested.

"Righto," said the patient, pocketing the gentle rebuke. "But mind I can only give the facts. You will have to decide how much or how little you will tell poor George's mother."

Sister nodded, and Robert Blaine proceeded:

"George Giltinan was one of the very best lads in my troop, and perhaps the crack shot of the 7th Light Horse. At the range, once he'd got his sighters right, he frequently registered a possible, and you could safely back him to get a three-inch group at 200. One day we were out on the Petrified Forest and he winged a hawk at 900 yards. But the most wonderful thing was that at night-time he was a deadly shot. Well, you know that on Gallipoli the Turkish trenches were anything from 10 yards to 100 yards from ours, except on the flat opposite Gaba Tepe. Here the navy dominated the position, and there was a stretch of No-Man's-Land about 1000 yards wide. We patrolled this area every night, and had some exciting skirmishes with the Turkish patrols. Now one night I had a dozen men out. We were about 500 yards in front, and Giltinan was with me. He was a fine fellow, as hefty a lad as you could want for a rough and tumble, a great footballer, and as strong as a horse. 'Birdie' wanted a prisoner, and we were dead set on getting one. Now just a little after midnight we were lying doggo, when I saw, dimly outlined ahead, a short, stout figure with a forage cap on. It could be nothing else but a Turk, yet there was something curiously familiar about it. I heard a movement on my left, and cried out as loudly as I dared, 'Don't shoot, George;' but it was too late. Even as I spoke his rifle went off, and the figure in front, with a cry that rings in my ears even now, threw up his arms and fell."

"Who was it?" asked sister.

"Well, Giltinan thought it was a Turk—so did we all, but I couldn't get over the feeling that it was someone that I knew. So, taking George and another chap with me, I went forward to investigate. We had gone about 30 yards when I heard a voice say, 'That you, Bob?' It was poor Captain Wood, lying on his back with a bullet wound in his chest. He had evidently been doing some reconnaissance on his own. As I bent over him he gasped, 'Better leave me, Blaine, old chap. I think I'm a goner. Go on. *Imshee.*'

"'Oh, you're worth a dozen dead men yet,' I answered to reassure him; but his face was deathly white, and I feared he spoke truly. Giltinan never spoke once while we carried the captain in. The latter just remarked, 'Bit of bad luck, wasn't it? *Maleesch.*' The M.O. bound up his wound, and reported to the colonel that poor Wood could hardly survive the night. I went into the dressing-station to see him before turning in. 'Goodbye, Bob, old chap. Don't tell me who fired, but he was a d——d good shot, wasn't he?' So they carried him down to the beach and off to the hospital ship *Gascon*. A week later we heard that he was dead."

"Cruel luck," murmured sister.

"Poor Giltinan never spoke to a soul for a. week. All the boys wondered what had come over him. Only a couple of us knew. He volunteered for all the dare-devil patrols. When there was a stunt on he exposed himself recklessly. He seemed just itching to get killed, but, as often happens with men who are tired of living, he bore a charmed life. He got two bullets through his tunic, yet himself went scatheless. One night he was out fixing barbed wire, and a machine gun opened and put a few shots round him, and one pierced his hat. 'You're a rotten shot,' he cried in derision to Abdul, then sauntered back over the parapet. He grew thin and gaunt and haggard. The doc asked him if he was sick, and he replied that he was better than he was ever likely to be again. Some of our non-com.'s were killed and wounded, and the troop officer wanted to make Giltinan a corporal, but he said he had enough stripes on his conscience without having any on his arm.

"One night I was asleep, and Giltinan was in the next dugout. Suddenly I was awaked by him rushing into my 'possie' wild-eyed and dishevelled. 'Listen,' he cried fiercely.

"'*Rat-at-tat, tat, rat-at-tat.*'

"'Why,' I laughed, 'that's only Abdul with his machine gun. He's been at it every night for weeks and we can't locate him.'

"'Yes, but hark what he's saying,' persisted the wild-eyed warrior.

"Once again there sounded the familiar barking of the maxim, '*Rat-at-tat, tat, rat-at-tat.*'

"'There,' he demanded; 'did you get it that time? "Giltinan is a guilty man." "Giltinan is a guilty man." That thing has been haunting me days and nights for months, and I can't stand it any longer.'

"I tried to laugh away his fears, but he was obdurate. At last I seemed to share his hallucination, and it appeared that the maxim was ticking out, 'Giltinan is a guilty man.' At last poor George could bear it no longer. 'I won't stand it,' he cried, and rushed out into the night.

"I feared for his reason, so, slipping into my boots, I followed fast after him. There was a bit of a moon, and I could just see him grab his rifle and rush up the communication trench to the front line. When I reached the fire trench I saw him standing on the parapet and blazing away in the direction of the maddening maxim.

"'Come down, Giltinan,' I roared. But he only laughed the wild laugh of a maniac, and ramming another five cartridges into his magazine he once more blazed away. The Turkish trenches opposite were soon spitting, fire and bullets began to zip all round him.

"At last the boys couldn't stand it. Someone shouted, 'Grab him.' Four of us made for the parapet, but before we could clamber over, a commanding voice cried, 'Stop.' It was Major Cameron. 'I can't risk four good men over one madman,' and I suppose he was right.

"The whole Turkish line was now blazing away at Giltinan, who was firing and laughing and yelling like mad. It was a miracle how he escaped. We yelled at him to come back, and our line opened fire to counteract to some extent the Turkish fusillade. But it couldn't last. The wild laugh on Giltinan's lips suddenly changed to a choking gasp, and he fell back into our trench.

"The next day we buried him, and—such is the irony of fate—a few hours later we received word that Captain Wood was not dead, but out of danger and doing well in the hospital at Alexandria."

CHAPTER 10

Battle of Rafa

In the days of trench warfare, when battles last for weeks and months, it is pleasant to dwell on battles like Romani and Maghdaba, for they only lasted a few hours. There was no long-drawn-out agony of stalemate, and there was no doubt as to who won. As the Australians expressed it, 'they were dinkum scraps.'

Another victory, sudden, brilliant, and decisive, which history must place to the credit of Sir Harry Chauvel and the victorious Desert Column, was that at Rafa. After their splendid fight at Maghdaba, they returned for a brief respite at El Arish, then made a sudden dash on Rafa. The fight was fiercely contested—the Turks in their well fortified stronghold, the British on the open desert—but as at Maghdaba the victorious Desert Column performed wonders. The entire Turkish garrison was killed, wounded, or carried off in triumph to El Arish.

Rafa is on the extreme north-east corner of Sinai, just within the Egyptian boundary, and therefore just on the border of Palestine. It was the last Turkish stronghold on the eastern frontier, and as it was only about 30 miles from El Arish, it constituted a menace to the Egyptian outpost, so Sir Archibald Murray decided to treat it to the same medicine that had been meted out to Maghdaba.

Marching out of El Arish on the evening of 8th January, the Desert Column's striking force was composed of a portion of the Anzac Mounted Division, some companies of the Imperial Camel Corps, some Yeomanry, British Territorial Artillery, the Hong-Kong and Singapore Mountain Battery, and aeroplanes. The bulk of the force consisted of Anzacs, and their performance justified the title conferred on them after Romani as the "Cream of the Overseas Forces."

The enemy made the same mistake that they made at Maghdaba. They thought it impossible for a mobile force strong enough to attack

Rafa to move up from El Arish before Turkish reinforcements could arrive. Yet the Flying Column did a 30-mile night march over the desert, and within twenty-four hours had the battle fought and won. Turkish relieving columns were hurried up from Shellal and Khan Yunis, in all nearly 4000 strong, but the New Zealanders held them off till the stronghold was captured and the remnant of the garrison safely on the road to El Arish. The only effect of the abortive attempt to relieve Rafa was to encourage the garrison to a fiercer resistance, and so add to the toll of their casualties.

Leaving El Arish at four o'clock on the afternoon of 8th January, the Desert Column reached Sheikh Zoweid in five hours, and bivouacked till half-past one in the morning. The moonlight march was then resumed, and by dawn our patrols had come into touch with the enemy at Magruntain. Here the main Turkish force was entrenched, the site being a couple of miles from Rafa. German engineers and gunners had worked zealously to make the stronghold impregnable. There were several lines of trenches. In odd vantage posts were cleverly concealed rifle-pits. Posted round the central position were six large, well-constructed redoubts. Krupp mountain guns and well-trained German machine gunners afforded additional strength to the Turkish regulars who constituted the garrison. To add to the difficulties of the British the attack had to be made in the open, our ground lacking any cover whatever. As the attackers were operating 30 miles from their base, the Turks—like they did at Maghdaba—thought they could beat off all attacks till lack of supplies, shells, and especially water, compelled the Desert Column to swing back, disgruntled and discouraged, on El Arish. Once again the Turks miscalculated the quality of the Anzacs and the punch of the Camelry.

The defences of Rafa were so constructed as to withstand attack from all quarters; and this was well, for the attack came from all sides at once. In the dim light of dawn the garrison could be seen hurrying and scurrying in all directions, proof positive that the rapid advance of the British had taken them unawares. Having captured and isolated an Arab encampment five miles to the southward, the New Zealanders pushed on and captured the town of Rafa. This done, they swung round and attacked the Magruntain position from the rear.

This manoeuvre cut the Turks off from Palestine, prevented any reinforcement reaching them, and blocked their retreat. The British artillery then, aided and abetted by the aerial scouts, pounded away at the Turkish redoubts, and engaged in a duel with the German gunners. Under cover of a very strenuous bombardment the attack developed, and was pushed home with the utmost gallantry.

Companies of the 1st (Anzac), 2nd (British), and 3rd (Anzac) Battalions of the Imperial Camel Corps, swinging in from the southwest, came under artillery fire from the German gunners behind El Magruntain. But camels can't be stampeded or even excited by shell fire. In fine precision the Cameliers swung away, dismounted, and in a huge segment of a circle advanced on the main Turkish redoubts. On their left the English and Scots Yeomanry dismounted, linked up, and pushed forward, their left resting on the sand-hills overlooking the Mediterranean. The New Zealanders, working wide, like a sheep-dog rounding up a big flock, executed a fine encircling movement, and, dismounting, attacked the position from the north-east. Abdul now found himself fighting for dear life, attacked from all sides, while a hail of shrapnel came from the British guns.

The Krupp guns worked manfully, but soon a couple of them were put out of action. The German machine gunners, as at Romani and Maghdaba, handled their guns with great skill, but the rain of shells soon discounted their efficiency. On the other hand, the British machine guns swept up and down the Turkish trenches, and prevented the garrison firing too freely at the attackers in the open. So with the Hong-Kong battery in support of the Camelry, and the Territorial gunners covering the advance of the Anzacs, the attack was pushed steadily on to the objective.

Aloft our airmen were busy, while the Taubes, splendidly handled, strove hard to prevent our aerial scouts from directing the fire of our artillery. There were thrilling air combats, but for the most part, those down below were too busy with their own affairs. Behind the lines the stretcher-bearers did wonderful work. Entirely indifferent to the bullets, which zipped into the sand all round, they rescued the wounded and carried them back to the safety of the ambulances.

The enemy air scouts kept their headquarters well informed as to the strength of the British attack. So with a view to preventing a repetition of the Maghdaba defeat, strong reinforcements were hurried up from Sheikh Neiran and Beersheba. These were the party held up by the New Zealanders. Had these reinforcements pushed on with vigour they might have changed the fortunes of the day. But the New Zealanders, as they approached, poured in a heavy fire from rifles and machine guns. So Abdul, probably overestimating the strength of the Maorilanders, gave over the attempt to relieve Rafa.

Meanwhile the accurate and well-sustained fire of our guns, maxims, and rifles at length achieved a superiority of fire over the garrison, which enabled the attackers to approach, by well-timed advances, nearer and nearer the Turkish trenches. The cordon tightened. An ever-closing circle menaced the defenders. When within striking distance, a glitter of steel flashed all round the circle. The British bayonets were getting ready for the final rush.

Nearer and nearer they came, and then, with a final shout, charged straight at the enemy. Abdul stuck it until the gleaming bayonets were about 30 yards from his trenches, when discretion triumphed over valour, and up went the hands in surrender. By five o'clock the whole garrison had surrendered, and had been hurried back towards El Arish. About 300 enemy dead were buried, nearly 500 wounded men were cared for, and over 1600 un wounded prisoners were led away. They included 30 Turkish officers with their commander, the whole of the 603rd German Machinegun Company, and some German officers, one of whom was caught riding in the town of Rafa. Our booty included 4 Krupp guns, 7 machine guns, 1600 rifles, 45,000 rounds of ammunition, 83 camels, and other warlike stores.

Our own casualties were heavier than at Maghdaba, but light considering the open ground over which they attacked. There were four officers and 68 men killed, and 31 officers and 384 men wounded. At this cost the last Turkish stronghold in Sinai was captured. The Sinai Campaign was over. The next phase of the war in the East would be in Turkish territory—in Palestine.

The Cameliers now jogged on back to El Arish for a well-earned spell. They missed several well-known faces round the fire at night. The officers grieved over the loss of Captain George Smith, Captain MacCullum, and Lieut. Linforth. But soldiers don't grieve long. It might be their turn next. Sergeant Blaine bolted down to Cairo for a holiday. All the way down he was thinking of a little angel in the 14th Australian General Hospital.

CHAPTER 11

The Ball—1

Sergeant Blaine, up in Cairo for a week's Christmas leave, made his first call at the Bints' Retreat. Flora was unfeignedly glad to see him. But he was far happier at seeing her.

"I've got a whole week's holiday, Fair Lady," he said, "and I hereby dedicate every minute to you."

Sister curtsied prettily in acknowledgment, then shaking her head, she said:

"It can't be done, sir."

"In the bright lexicon of youth," he said, "there is no such word as can't."

"In this old hospital," she retorted, "there seems to be nothing else. We can't go out or talk with anyone unless he be an officer. We can't dance. We can't stay out later than ten o'clock. Oh, Bob, if you could only see the list of 'thou shalt nots'! Then there is the Christmas Eve Dance at Shepheard's Hotel, and I can't go."

"Do you remember what the Irishman said to the Yankee guide at Niagara Falls? Well, the Yankee pointed down at the seething waters, and said grandiloquently that five million gallons of water rolled down there every second. The Irishman just looked over and said, 'Well! what's to hinder?'"

Sister laughed and said, "Oh, but there are several things to hinder me."

"Namely?"

"Well, matron for one; and, anyhow, I'm in disgrace."

He whistled in mock seriousness.

"Oh, it's no joke," she persisted. "Some old cat told Matron that I had tea at Groppe's with some private soldiers. I said they were not private soldiers; they were 'Gentlemen of the Australian Light Horse.'

But she couldn't see it. Then I went to Maadi to some awfully nice friends, and time simply flew, and I was an hour late in getting in. So I'm in the bad books, and no leave for a month."

"Then what's the good of my holiday?" he demanded.

"Oh, I'd risk anything to go to that ball," she cried, ignoring his query.

"Do you really mean that?"

"Yes," she said decisively. "I'm sick to death of this discipline. That proves I'm an Anzac. I want to discard this old uniform and wear pretty clothes and have a real good time again."

"Are you prepared to take the risk?"

"I just am," she asserted.

"Righto, we'll do it."

"We?"

"Why, of course," he replied. "I couldn't let you risk it on your own. Besides, I'll have to arrange for escort, introductions, and a host of things. Now, is Matron going?"

"Yes, with the P.M.O. and Sister Smith."

"Good; that simplifies matters. They can't come here and find you out."

"But she'll be there—"

"And will fail to recognise you," he added. "Now, will you trust me to see the whole thing through?"

"Shake," she said.

✶✶✶✶✶✶

The principal medical officer's car drew up at the entrance to the Bints' Retreat. matron and Sister Smith and the P.M.O. and Captain Evans entered, and just as they were moving off, Sister Livingstone hurried up with a big bouquet of flowers for matron. "It's from the Australian Eleven, Matron, and they wish you a very happy Christmas."

"Oh, thank you, Sister Livingstone. I'm sorry you'll miss the ball."

"*Maleesch*," cried sister, turning back to the hospital.

"I do wish you were coming," cried Captain Evans.

"Never mind. My turn next. Be sure to dance with my sister, and tell her I'll be in to see her tomorrow."

No sooner had the car moved off than sister dashed into the Bints' Retreat. Sisters Douglas and Peters, sworn to secrecy, hurriedly dressed her in all her finery. Her fine silk dress that had remained so long at the bottom of her cabin trunk, her gorgeous ostrich feather fan, diamond-clasped osprey, and beautiful necklet, ear-rings, and bracelet, and brooch that her indulgent parent had given her—all were put on in record time. Both the sisters kissed her and wished her luck.

"Oh, you look ravishing," cried Sister Peters, as she threw a big cloak over Flora and hurried out.

A beautiful closed-in motorcar, timing her exit to a second, glided up noiselessly. The door opened and she sprang in, and the car shot off like a Bristol fighter. A strong arm deftly surrounded her with rugs—for Cairo is very cold in midwinter.

"Oh, Bob," she cried, "I'm deliriously happy."

"You're going to be the *belle* of the ball tonight. Honey. All is going swimmingly. All that you have to remember is that you are Miss Mary Livingstone, sister of Flora; you arrived in Suez yesterday, came on to Cairo, and are leaving tomorrow to catch the boat again at Port Said. You are two years younger than Flora, and you are awfully sorry that she could not come to the ball. So that's that."

"And you?" she queried.

"Oh, I'm just Robert Smith, an Australian journalist. I've got a weak heart or cold feet. That's why I didn't enlist."

"It all seems plausible enough, but I wish we could have arrived before Matron."

"We will," he said, with a grin. "It was essential that she should see you back at the hospital as she left. That absolutely killed any suspicions she might have had. Then I closed the railway gates just as they came along, and the poor old doc honked for five minutes before the old gatekeeper arrived."

"Yes," she replied, "that's great, but they are still five minutes ahead of us."

"Oh, but they are going to have an accident," he said prophetically. And as he spoke the lights flashed on a car stopped at the side of the Heliopolis Road, with the chauffeur sprawled beneath.

"Good for Jimmy!" cried Blaine as they flew past. "Now, as old Midgley used to say, 'We've got 'em stone cold.'"

"Bob," cried Flora, "I think you're wonderful. But suppose we had an accident?"

"Look behind," he said.

She looked through the window, and saw the light of another car a chain or so behind.

"Now I'm sure we'll win through."

Shepheard's Hotel, known to tourists all over the world, was a blaze of splendour. A brilliant throng crowded the hall, the *piazza*, and the corridors. The youth and beauty of Cairo were engaged in high revelry. The uniforms of the officers, though mostly khaki, added to the gaiety of the scene. Big Nubian waiters in baggy breeches and gold-laced coats hurried hither and yon, providing the necessary Eastern colouring to the picture. As Flora emerged from the cloak-room, Blaine, who had never before seen her except in her nurse's uniform, was entranced with her loveliness. The excitement of the venture had given an added colour to her cheeks and a brighter sparkle to her eyes. She moved with an easy grace that denoted perfect health and the joy of living. As she hesitated near the hall she found her way barred by a tall, bronzed gentleman in immaculate evening-dress.

"Bob!" she gasped. "I hardly knew you. You do look fine."

"There aren't enough beautiful adjectives in the English language," he said, "to describe how wonderful you are. Honey."

Then the orchestra gave forth the enticing strains of "Blue Danube," and they waltzed away to paradise.

"Oh, Flora," he whispered passionately, "you're the most beautiful thing God ever made."

"Please, Bob," she pleaded, "I'm so happy; but don't give me any more to think of tonight. It might spoil everything. But you do dance divinely."

He vouchsafed only the gentlest pressure of her hand in acknowledgment of the compliment. He had a curious fear that he might suddenly clasp her in his arms before the whole crowd.

All dancers have experienced the psychology of the ballroom. There is always a *belle* of the ball. One girl or one couple in an incredibly short time become the cynosure of all eyes. It may be a certain skill in the execution of the newfangled Tango or an audacious display of silken hose that catches the eye. Sometimes, as in this case, it is sheer physical beauty. Flora and Bob had hardly thrice circled the room before they instinctively felt that nearly everyone was looking at them. They were certainly the handsomest couple there, if not exactly the best dancers. A perfect waltzer, Blaine had never found time to master the intricacies of the later-day dances. Sister was the best dancer on the Hunter River. So in the gay throng these two danced, deliriously happy—Blaine, however, frowning as he realised the unexpected social success his partner had instantly made. He had foreseen and provided for every contingency save this.

As the music ceased, many eyes followed them towards the gardens.

Blaine realised that no one in the crowd knew them, and every girl in the hall was demanding, "Who is she?" which was not exactly what he desired. So he kept his eyes working overtime till he sighted his good friends of Maadi. He took Flora across the lawn, and presenting her to Mr. and Mrs. Hart, said:

"Permit me to present Miss Mary Livingstone of Sydney. She has just landed in Cairo, and goes on, *via* Port Said, to London tomorrow."

To Mrs. Hart he said:

"Your duty as chaperon is no sinecure, for the whole army in Egypt will be besieging you soon."

CHAPTER 12

The Ball—2

Blaine had taken the precaution to shave his moustache and wear *pince-nez*, so in his dress-suit he was pretty confident that none of the Light Horse or Camel Corps officers would recognise him. He hurried through the hall and out into Sharia Kamel just in time to see the P.M.O.'s party drive up. After they had entered the hotel he went across to the chauffeur and pressed a note into his hand.

"Jimmy, old sport," he cried, "you're a brick."

Jimmy Eagleton stared for a second, blew a long but subdued whistle, and then exclaimed:

"Well, I'm blowed! If you just don't beat the band, Blainey. O' course you won't get court-martialled at all."

"I'll risk that, Jimmy. Now what time is the car ordered for?"

"Eleven-thirty."

"Good! Now do you think you could arrange for your lights to peter out on the way home?"

"It'll cost another hundred disasters *baksheesh*," said Jimmy.

"Righto," agreed Blaine. "You see, sister must be here and matron must see her here when matron leaves. Yet we've got to be back at least a quarter of an hour ahead. I've got Pat to halt you and take your name near the old barracks. That will give us five minutes. Then, if all goes well—tomorrow night at the National."

Hurrying in, Blaine found Flora the centre of a gallant throng of Australian and New Zealand and British officers. Even though he had previously booked three waltzes and two two-steps, he could not resist a pang of jealousy as the officers clamoured for the honour.

Mrs. Hart was keenly enjoying the situation, being tremendously proud of her *protégé*. Flora was in the seventh heaven. She had just danced with General Cox, and gallant old 'Fighting Charlie' had paid her some very pretty compliments, then brought all the Light Horse officers along.

As the music suddenly burst into the lively strains of the "Frog Puddles Two-Step," Blaine with difficulty insinuated his way to the front and bore her off in triumph. They were entering the ballroom when they encountered General Cox and the matron's party. Blaine gently pressed her hand as it rested on his arm, and whispered, "Bluff hard, Honey." The introductions followed.

"Oh, Matron, I am pleased to meet you," said Flora. "My sister has often written nice things of you. I'm so sorry she could not come tonight, but you will let her come in tomorrow to see me, won't you?"

Matron was surprised into an assent, when the P.M.O. remarked:

"You are startlingly like your sister. Miss Livingstone."

"May we see you after this dance?" interrupted Blaine. "I hate to lose a second of this music." And they whirled away with joyous abandon.

"Beautifully done. You've got matron thinking hard, and poor Sister Smith is gasping."

As the hospital quartet gazed after the pair. Matron remarked:

"The resemblance is wonderful, but I think this girl is a little bit taller and slighter than her sister."

"And much prettier," interpolated Sister Smith.

Captain Evans smiled enigmatically, and then vouchsafed:

"No two sisters were ever so extraordinarily alike."

Heedless of the comment, Blaine and Flora threaded their way amongst the dancers as happy as a pair of school children on holiday. He had passed the forbidden notice-board which said, "Out of Bounds for N.C.O.'s and Men," and for a brief while again he tasted the joys of the life he had known. Pretty *Cairenes*, who had condescendingly given him a cup of tea in a canteen some months before, now smiled frankly on him and said he danced beautifully. Field officers and generals, whom he had punctiliously saluted that morning, were now inviting him to partake of iced coffee cocktails. He grinned sardonically at the farce of it all. As an Australian soldier, an original Nineteen-fourteener, wounded on Gallipoli and at Romani, he dared not enter these hallowed precincts. But as an alleged slacker, a mere civilian, he came unchallenged. And Flora, curiously enough, voiced the sentiments he only thought.

"Isn't it curious," she said. "As a nurse, doing my little bit for Old England, I'm forbidden to dance, and I must go home early. But as a civvie slacker, I can dance the red stars to their death."

As the music ceased with a snap, not dying away like a waltz, but suddenly, with exaggerated syncopation, the dancers all crowded, laughing and chatting gaily, into the vestibule and thence to the gardens. The trees and palms were all hung with coloured lights and Chinese lanterns. The fountain splashed musically. The lawn and paths were dotted with dancers, two and two, revelling in the cold night air after the heated dance hall. Now and then Blaine and Flora, in darkened corners, stumbled across couples very close together. Still, it was Christmas time, and kissing goes by favour; and Cairo is the world's playground.

"I wonder who is my next partner," suddenly exclaimed Flora, as the seductive strains of the "*Barcarolle*" percolated through the doors and out into the still night air. Halting under a lamp she glanced at her programme. "Brown. Now who is Brown?"

"That's my pagan name," Blaine admitted guiltily. "You see, I couldn't sprawl Smith all over your programme, could I?"

"Young man," she admonished, "you're incorrigible. If you don't get on in this world, it won't be for want of push. Still, I'm so deliriously happy tonight, I can't refuse you anything; and anyway I'd hate to waste the '*Barcarolle*' on a stranger. It's a gorgeous waltz."

Blaine always remembered that waltz as the most perfect soul-satisfying dance in all his life. "Flora," he cried, as they swung to the very poetry of motion, "you're perfect. I've never till this minute prayed for a night that's a thousand years long. If I'm court-martialled and shot at dawn tomorrow, it's been well worth it. Tonight's the night."

And Flora's heart was beating so joyously that she dared not voice her reply.

At the door going out they encountered matron again and Sister Smith.

"We are having a little midnight supper," said Bob; "I do hope your quartet will join us."

"Thanks so much, Mr. Smith," replied matron, "but we have to be back at the hospital before twelve."

"Oh, here's the colonel," cried Flora. "Surely he can give himself permission to remain out late on Christmas Eve."

"I'm sorry it cannot be done," said the P.M.O., smiling.

Flora just then was claimed by a gallant camelier and whisked off for a foxtrot.

And as Blaine watched her perfect grace and radiant beauty he found himself building beautiful castles in the air. . . .

"Bob, you're in love."

He turned and encountered Mr. Hart smiling at his side. Curiously enough he never troubled to deny the soft impeachment. He only ejaculated, "My God, isn't she just perfect!"

"Here, you want a drink," asserted the matter-of-fact friend. "Come on."

On the way to the bar he chuckled and said, "It's the best joke Cairo has seen since the Anzacs scandalised the good folk by putting a nose-bag on the charger of Soliman Pasha's statue. Mrs. Hart has received a dozen pressing invitations for Flora, and hundreds of inquiries about her. And she's come to the end of her tether. She's told wonderful tales of how Flora fought bushrangers and escaped from wild natives and rode buckjumpers. Oh, the Gyppie *Mail* will be quite readable tomorrow."

The four of them, Mr. and Mrs. Hart, Flora and Bob, were out on the *piazza*, where a dainty little supper had been laid Filling his glass Mr. Hart raised it aloft and gave the toast:

"To the *belle* of the ball."

Shortly afterwards the P.M.O., the matron, Captain Evans, and Sister Smith emerged. Flora hastened to bid them goodnight, while Bob signalled to the waiter for his car. The party had scarcely moved off in the hospital car before the four conspirators had hurried forth into Bob's automobile. He and Mr. Hart sat in front, while in the roomy, enclosed *tonneau*. Flora and Mrs. Hart got busy.

"You've got about a quarter of an hour to change," Blaine told Flora as the car glided after the P.M.O.'s machine.

"Well," exclaimed matron as they moved off, "I could never have believed such a resemblance possible."

"It certainly is unique," concurred the P.M.O.

Captain Evans in his seat in front smiled grimly. As the car swung round the broad way and approached the railway station, a native policeman halted them and drew attention to their dim lights. Jimmy jumped out and took a shocking time fixing them up. Suddenly Captain Evans laughed.

"Say, Colonel, did you ever read *Dr. Jekyll and Mr. Hyde?*"

"Yes; why?"

"Oh, nothing," replied Evans. "I was just thinking."

Shortly after midnight matron and Sister Smith entered the ward where was housed the Australian Eleven. They found Sister Livingstone seated at the little table writing in the ward-book.

"How are all your patients, Sister?" asked matron.

"Oh, they are all doing nicely," replied Flora in the bored tones of the night-duty nurse. "I hope you enjoyed the ball. Did you meet my little sister? Isn't she pretty?"

CHAPTER 13

The Bints' Retreat

Amongst the Egyptian words destined to be incorporated in the Australian language, the most popular are *'baksheesh'* and *'maleesch.'* Neither of these has an exact equivalent in our own tongue. Even as *'baksheesh'* is the first word that the gyppie baby learns to lisp, so was it the first word to fall on the ears of the Australians in Egypt. No child in the land of the Pharaohs is too young to accost strangers with the plea for *baksheesh*, and no decrepit old derelict too old to do the same. Blessed word—like unto Mesopotamia—it is with the Egyptian from the cradle to the grave; it permeates everywhere; it puts the finishing touch on every commercial transaction, no matter how trifling or how great.

And *maleesch* is more blessed still. It expresses, oh, so wonderfully, the spineless, emasculated spirit of resignation which is the foundation of the *fellahin's* philosophy. A subject race, prey to all the warlike nations of the earth for centuries, exclaims at each change of masters, *'Maleesch.'* The plagues of Egypt come and go, and the *fellah*, with imperturbable stoicism, says, *'Maleesch.'* He is knocked down by a motorcar, *'Maleesch.'* He dies, and the neighbouring *fellahin* cry,

'Maleesch.' And the word cannot be translated into English. The nearest approach is, 'What matter.' So in days to come Australian settlers, viewing the devastation brought by fires and floods and drought, will grin and exclaim, *'Maleesch.'* There are other words curious and expressive adorning the Anzac's vocabulary, but the only other necessary to mention here is ' bint.' A bint is, in short, a girl. So we will not be surprised if some day an Australian on London Bridge greets a countrywoman with the cheery ejaculation,

'*Saieeda, Bint.*'

Which brings us to the fact that the nurses' quarters of the hospital were always known as the 'Bints' Retreat.' Things had been very lively out East of Suez, and the hospital trains had been working overtime. And back in the hospitals of Cairo were thousands of soldiers wounded and maimed and stricken and blinded. Here was all the hideous aftermath of battle.

Sister Livingstone had been toiling with only the briefest respite for several days, and was now in her little cubicle in the 'Bints' Retreat' resting. She had been too tired to accept kind invitations of Captain Evans and others to dinner at Shepheard's. The doctor had been very assiduous in his attentions to sister for a long time now, but his suit had made but little headway. When the nurses in friendly raillery—maybe rivalry—chided Flora about the doctor, she laughingly replied that she loved every single soldier in the A.I.F. If she had a preference she hardly knew it herself, though every week she received a cheery letter from a big sergeant in the Cameliers, and once a month she wrote a gracious letter in reply.

Lately she had also received from him the first few copies of the Cameliers' Journal *Barrak*, a quaint little paper edited somewhere in Wadi Ghuzzie, and written by men of the I.C.C. all over Egypt and Sinai and Southern Palestine. Sergeant Blaine had interpolated explanatory paragraphs throughout the pages wherever there was a reference he thought Sister might not understand. So she turned the leaves idly, smiling proudly at the devil-may-care spirit of the soldiers, which made them make light of all their hardships and see only the cheerful side of everything. The heterogeneous nature of the I.C.C. was well shown by a skit by Corporal 'Cuss' called 'Abbassia.'

From the farthest isles of Orkney,
From the edge of the Sudan,
From the flats of Murrumbidgee,
Or the purlieus of Japan,
From amid the waving pampas.
Or the banks of Windermere,
They have gathered, gathered, gathered
To the huts of Abbassia.

He whose single thought was salmon
Met the rogue who poached for pearls,
And the Billjim made a cobber
Of the darling of the girls:
The guardsman and the terrier,

The plutocrat and peer—
All are jumbled up together
In the huts of Abbassia.

If you seek for information
On polo, maps, or gin,
Beer, beauty, or ballistics.
You can find it all within:
If you seek the heat of battle,
Or you're finding life too drear—
Go and join 'The Curse of Egypt'
In the huts of Abbassia.

The Light Horseman considers himself a cut above the infantryman and several cuts above the Camelier. Of course neither the infantryman nor the Camelier endorses this view, though the Light Horsemen who have joined the I.C.C., when they do get up to Cairo for a holiday, like to put on their old leggings and spurs just for old times' sake. Hence "*The Cameliers' Lament.*"

When we lob in from the desert with a thirst that's worth a crown.
Heavy laden with piastres, and the mood to paint the town,
Having left our smellful camels somewhere east of El Arish,
Then the world is full of sunshine, and we've just one little wish—
For feathers and leggings and spurs.
Feathers and leggings and spurs.

On the desert we're 'Camels'; we're rough, rude, and coarse men,
But when up on leave we're once more 'Light Horsemen,'
With feathers and leggings and spurs.

We mooch up to the Kit Store, Abbassia, like a thief,
Like a sneaking, crawling Gyppi who has pinched some bully beef:
Shorts and puttees are discarded and we don our breeks again.
We fling away our jamboks and we swish a little cane.
Oh, feathers and leggings and spurs.
Feathers and leggings and spurs.

Out East with the 'Hooshters' we're rough, rude, and coarse men.
But round about Cairo we're 'Pukka Light Horsemen,'
With feathers and leggings and spurs.

Our boots are brightly polished, like the old-time Kiwi Lancers,
We join the gentle soirée and we mingle with the dancers,
Till a maiden, gently 'sniffing,' knocks us all into a lump,

> *By disdainfully exclaiming, "Camels do give me the hump,"*
> *Tho' plumed and booted and spurred,*
> *Plumed and booted and spurred.*
>
> *Once you join Camels you're smellful and coarse men:*
> *Goodbye to the swank of the Kiwi Light Horsemen,*
> *All plumed and booted and spurred.*

The lines by Captain Morgan, however, seemed to sum up finely the unique qualities of the I.C.C.:

> *I.C.C.*
> *Known from the 'beer' in Shepheard's Bar*
> *To the 'U' in unsurveyed;*
> *Silent under a watching star*
> *Or by our dust betrayed.*
> *Where Kharga blossoms 'mid western rock.*
> *Or Sollum fronts on the shore,*
> *By river bank or 'mid grazing flock,*
> *The Imperial Camel Corps.*
> *When the mounted troops on Rafa dash.*
> *Or lost in the drifting sand;*
> *Where successive waves of battle clash.*
> *Or the lonely outposts stand;*
> *Any and every job we know.*
> *Used as a transport corps.*
> *Shelled and bombed by friend and foe,*
> *The Ikonas of the war.*

CHAPTER 14

Gaza

There were three battles round about Gaza. The first and second were costly defeats, involving a loss to the Egyptian Expeditionary Force of at least twelve thousand men in killed and wounded. The enemy losses are variously estimated, but from the nature of the conflict they must have been less than ours.

So the victorious Desert Column after its uninterrupted series of successes from Romani to Rafa was at last brought to a standstill, and the German general commanding the Turkish forces was able to send this delightful message to the British commander:

I have defeated you in the field, but you have beaten me in the *communiqué*.

The enemy had taken up a strong defensive position with Gaza as its culminating point, the right flank resting on the Mediterranean and the left on Beersheba. General Murray made his dispositions with a view to (1) preventing the threatened withdrawal of the Turks from the Beersheba side, (2) capturing the Wadi Ghuzzie so as to protect the advance of the railway from Rafa, and (3) seizing Gaza by a *coup de main* and cutting off the garrison. It was in this third and vital objective the British failed.

As usual, the Anzac Mounted Division opened the ball, swinging east and north and heading for Beit Durdis. In their wake came the Imperial Mounted Division and the Imperial Camel Corps. Crossing the Wadi Ghuzzie the Cavalry and Camelry pushed on round the left wing of the Turkish Army. The rapid move of the Light Horse took the enemy by surprise, and a squadron of the 7th Light Horse captured the commander of one of the Turkish divisions. The dumbfounded general heard a wild Colonial yell, his carriage was surrounded, and a stentorian voice cried, "Here, give us your ——— sword."

Great enterprises hang on little incidents. A fall of rain or a passing mist may decide the fate of a nation. It is the opinion of several British generals that had there been no mist on the morning of 26th March the first Battle of Gaza would have been won. Be that as it may, the whole plan of our operations was very seriously retarded by a heavy mist which enveloped the whole countryside. Spreading like a pall over the battlefield before dawn, it did not clear off till eight o'clock.

While General Chetwode's Desert Column was mopping up the country north-east of Gaza the infantry moved forward from the south. The 53rd Division (Major-General Dallas) pushed in, and after dogged fighting captured the Ali Muntar Ridge. The 54th Division held Sheikh Abbas, while for some reason or other the 52nd Division was kept back in reserve. In the late afternoon the situation was full of possibilities of victory, though the Cavalry and Camelry on the right were strenuously withstanding the onslaught of a continuous stream of Turkish reinforcements. However, during the night the Anzacs were withdrawn; the 53rd Division being thus 'in the air' were compelled to retire, likewise the 54th Division, and by daylight the army—beaten when victory was just within its grasp—had fallen back to the west of the Wadi Ghuzzie. It is estimated that the Turks lost 8000 and the British 4000. The enemy *communiqué* gives different figures entirely. But our captures were about 950 Turks and Germans, with two Austrian guns gallantly captured and held by the New Zealanders.

Preparations were immediately made for a second attack. But the enemy had been reinforced till there were five divisions of infantry, one of cavalry, and a full complement of artillery ready to dispute the possession of Gaza. The hills were lined with trenches and redoubts. Machine guns dotted the entire front. In view of the fact that the Turks had constructed trenches and wire entanglements on the fine south and east towards Beersheba, Sir Archibald Murray presumed that any encircling movement by the mounted divisions was out of the question. In this conviction his strategy differed from that subsequently and successfully pursued by General Allenby.

The second Battle of Gaza therefore began on 17th April by the capture of the Sheikh Abbas-Mansura Ridge to the south and south-east of Gaza. Tanks were thrown into the fight, but as there was no element of surprise in their projection they were not an unqualified success. Three of them lumbering along in full view of the enemy artillery were pounded with shells and put out of action. However, the first objective, the Sheikh Abbas-Mansura Ridge, was captured without many casualties. Then came two days' further preparation and the final assault. The guns of two British monitors and the French battleship *Requin* made excellent practice on the Gaza defences and also got busy amongst the Turks assembling for counter-attacks. Three British Infantry Divisions—one Welsh, one Scots, and one English—were launched in the main attack. The 53rd Division, in the face of a tremendous fusillade from rifles and machine guns, charged and captured Samson's Ridge and Delilah's Neck on the south side of the town. The 52nd and 54th Divisions were given the herculean task of securing the Ali Muntar Ridge and redoubts and the Khirbet Sihan line of trenches, east of the town; while Sheikh Abbas and the redoubts farther east were the objective of the Cameliers.

Abdul had not wasted the respite given him since 26th March. In twenty-four days the German engineers had transformed the hillside into a citadel. With great gallantry the 54th and 52nd and Anzac Cameliers charged the formidable line of trenches. This was the signal for the enemy artillery, which opened a terrific bombardment of the attacking line. They searched the whole area with wonderful precision. Shrapnel seemed to tear up every inch of the ground. Though facing a veritable avalanche of shells without a vestige of cover, the long khaki line never wavered. But the path they had trod was dotted with still, crumpled-up figures. Then as the line neared the hill it seemed as if hell were let loose among them. Mingling with the roar of the artillery now came the incessant rattle of dozens of maxims. The charging line melted away like wheat before the scythe. Successive waves pushed on, but Outpost Hill was a hornet's nest of machine guns. This redoubt effectually held up the 52nd and incidentally exposed the 54th to a devastating enfilade fire from the east.

But two companies of Anzac Camelry on the right would not be denied. Leaving a trail of casualties behind, they charged right into the Turkish redoubt and bayoneted the few Turks who had not fled. But the infantry on their left could not advance. The right was 'in the air.' They were immediately shelled by the enemy batteries and a counterattack followed. But the heroic remnant with well-directed rifle fire held off their assailants. One spot of the main objective had been gained. But without reinforcements it could never be held. From flank and front came the enemy rifle and machine-gun fire. Then, that their cup of joy might be filled to overflowing, they became a target for their own gunners. Five messengers were sent back to say that the redoubt had been captured, but not one got through. Finally, when their ammunition had been exhausted and every officer killed and wounded except Lieut. Archie Campbell, and 75 *per cent*, of their number casualties, the Cameliers decided to make a get-away. About thirty unwounded men returned to the battalion.

Meantime about a dozen of their comrades in the next redoubt were less fortunate. They had fired their last cartridge when a Turkish counter-attack ten times their strength swarmed over, and after a fierce bayonet melee took the remnant prisoners. As they were being lined up and marched off, two troopers of No. 3 Company, Kelly and Storey, decided that Stamboul was no good to them.

"How about it, Bert?"

"Righto, Kelly. Let her go."

Then, before their captors could guess their intention, the pair leaped the parapet and ran like startled hares towards the Wadi Ghuzzie. The Turkish line suddenly began to spit fire all along. Machine guns took up the chase. Bullets zipped all around the adventurous pair, but by some freak of good fortune neither was hit. Amid the wild cheers of their comrades they fell exhausted into the *wadi*, Kelly boasting bullet holes through his hat.

It now became a matter of throwing in the reserves—74th Division—and risking all on a further assault, or digging in. Already there had been about 8000 casualties. The G.O.C. Eastern Force and the divisional commanders advised against a resumption. So the army dug in, and the second Battle of Gaza had been fought and lost.

CHAPTER 15

Mount Sinai

Way back in the centre of Sinai, where the mountains rise gaunt and rugged from the shining sands, where gazelle and ibex roam almost unmolested by the hunter, where the summer sun scorches like a furnace and the winter rains lie frozen in the rock holes at dawn; here, where the Bedouin is monarch of all he surveys, went the Pilgrim Patrol.

Small scouting patrols, starting out from Ayun Mousa for a few days' scouring of the hills, had not been entirely immune from attack. Several had been sniped from the ranges. An English officer and some Yeomanry had been killed. The Bedouin will not fight, but he does practise the ambuscade. So the Pilgrim Patrol was fairly strong, 50 Anzac Cameliers, with a couple of machine-guns; enough to account for several hundred Bedouins should they prove troublesome—which they did not; enough to mop up any Turkish patrols that might be encountered—which they were not.

Now in the centre of the Sinai Peninsula, hidden away in the *wadis*, leading the same nomadic life that they did thousands of years ago, live several thousands of Bedouin Arabs. These are divided into the three inevitable groups—sympathetic, apathetic, antipathetic—and the greatest of these is antipathetic. Most of the men of the tribe follow their *sheikh*, who may be influenced by fear or gold, as the case may be. Some are loyally pro-British; others having heard the musical clink of German gold have sided with the Turks. The remainder, following the spineless example of Mr. Facing-both-ways, sit at ease and watch the way the cat jumps.

Thus it transpired that in the early days of the war, when the Turks overran Sinai, even to the bounds of the Red Sea, the bulk of the Bedouins saw the Crescent in the ascendant. Abu Zenima was captured. Tor was invested. El Arish and Nekhl were in the hands of the enemy. Hundreds of Turkish rifles, with abundant ammunition, were distributed amongst the Bedouins. It took many weary months and many hot fights finally to drive the invader back into Palestine. But in the fastnesses of the mountains the Bedouins remained, and, of course, the Turkish rifles remained with them. But the fiery Crescent waned. Cameliers and. Light Horse patrols scoured the desert sands and the *wadis* and the oases till the Bedouin saw the game was up Most of them swore allegiance, and handed in their rifles. Many hid their rifles underground, and with protestations of loyalty greeted the Anzacs who invaded their villages. Smoke signals gave warning more readily than the telegraph. And away in the centre of Southern Sinai were still hundreds of Bedouins with Turkish rifles ready to snipe at a few adventurous scouts, or fawn with Uriah-Heep humility on a strong patrol. Hence the three weeks' stunt of the Pilgrim Patrol.

Australians are now aware that the Camel Corps can exist for days at a time on the desert without the aid of wells or the A.S.C. In winter it is no hardship for the camels to go for over a week without a drink, especially if there is any herbage about. So the three weeks' trek of the Pilgrim Patrol necessitated merely the prearrangement of depots at two particular points for replenishing the tucker bags, grain sacks, and water *fantasses*, which done, the party, following in Moses' footsteps, went forth into the wilderness.

It does not serve any purpose here to detail the number of Bedouin villages visited and rifles confiscated, nor record the tribes which came into Abu Zenima and Tor to swear allegiance. Rather is it the intention to describe the visit to far-famed Jebel Mousa, or Mount Sinai, where back at the dawn of history Moses gave to the Children of Israel those Ten Commandments which have become the code of ethics for the civilised world. It was because of the pilgrimage to Jebel Mousa, and the visit to the famous old convent of St. Katharine, that this particular patrol won the sobriquet of the Pilgrim Patrol.

There is some difference of opinion amongst learned archaeologists as to which is the actual mountain where Moses received the Law. Four peaks in Sinai are mentioned, and each has some claim to consideration. But the general consensus of erudite opinion leads to the belief that either Jebel Serbal or Jebel Mousa is the actual spot. The Pilgrim Patrol—making no claim whatever to erudition—endorses without prejudice the claims of Jebel Mousa (Mount of Moses) for three potent reasons:

1. The ancient Greek Church, convinced that Jebel Mousa was where Moses received the Law, here 1600 years ago established the famous monastery.

2. Round Jebel Mousa are wells and *wadis* and several thousand acres of green pastureland, admirably adapted for the camping-ground of the Children of Israel.

3. The vicinity of Jebel Serbal is rocky and barren, with no possible place for the Israelites to have camped to receive the Law.

The road to Jebel Mousa, through the *wadis* and over the hills, is so exceedingly rough and rugged that one marvels how camels in full marching order could possibly have negotiated it. There is a very narrow opening, just like a crack in the face of the mountains, and it is here that the Wadi Isleh escapes from the gargantuan grip of the hills and debouches on to the Plain of Oda. Into this picturesque defile, with mountains towering up thousands of feet on either side like frowning bastions, went the patrol. How many centuries of rain and wind and flood had it taken to carve that passage through the granite rocks?

It was the season of the winter rains. A couple of thunderstorms had drenched the Cameliers. Here and there the resultant slime on the bed of the *wadi* had produced such a precarious foothold that the camels at times slithered and slipped like novices on skates, flopping in the mud, throwing their riders into the mire, to the huge delight of all except the actual performers. The Wadi Isleh here and there opened out to the width of a decent river. *Anon* it closed in to a narrow gorge of barely sufficient space to allow the passage of the camels. Here it was smooth as the sands of Manly Beach. *Anon* the path was strewn with rocks and boulders, forbidding enough to bar progress until an improvised road had been constructed. In places the limpid waters, rippling lazily along the bed of the *wadi*, would suddenly disappear into the receptive sand. Farther along it would bubble up merrily like a spring, and continue its interrupted course towards the sea. Here and there were clumps of date palms, or stunted trees or wells, or Bedouin encampments. Charcoal-burning is the Bedouins' only industry, and many were encountered with their patient camels or donkeys heavily laden with charcoal, making for Tor, whence it is shipped to Suez.

Leaving the comparatively good going of the *wadi* bed, the ill-defined track led over rough, boulder-strewn plateaus down into other *wadis*, over more hills, down mountain paths offering a most precarious foothold, till in the fullness of time the patrol camped under the lee of the famous Jebel Mousa. Here was the quaint old monastery founded, so tradition hath it, by Constantine the Great in the early part of the fourth century, and completed by Justinian later on. Considering its sacred associations, and its rich literary and artistic treasures, this is surely one of the most interesting spots on the face of the earth. Incidentally it may be mentioned that although the records go back for hundreds of years, there is no record of any Australians having visited there, so the Pilgrim Patrol has the unique distinction of being the first Australians to set foot on Mount Sinai.

The adherents of the Monastery of St. Katharine are mostly Russians and Greeks, and Father Polycarpus and the priests under his authority graciously showed us through the old chapel, with its wonderful old paintings, quaint mosaics, gorgeous vestments, its gems and jewels, sacred relics, ancient effigies, and priceless works of art. The library contains some of the oldest Greek, Arabic, and Syrian Bibles and manuscripts, and it is available for inspection by scholars and scientists; but the distance from civilisation renders the cost of the pilgrimage almost prohibitive. The beautiful effigy of St. Katharine merits a special notice. The lower part of the body is encased in a dress of solid silver. The bodice is beaten gold. The face is of coloured enamel, while on the head is a crown of gold blazing with precious stones. In a specially-made, richly-chased casket is kept the mummified head of St. Katharine wearing a golden tiara inset with gems.

In an anteroom adjoining the altar is the reputed spot where Moses saw the burning bush. The Biblical story was vividly brought to mind by old Father Polycarpus saying, "Take your boots from off your feet, for you stand on holy ground." A beaten brass table, wonderfully decorated, marks the spot. In the little chamber are many old paintings of scenes recorded in Genesis and Exodus, some beautiful mosaics and inlaid mother-of-pearl work. And near by, growing vigorously by the chapel wall, was a bush not unlike a brier, which we were assured was a lineal descendant of the actual burning bush of Moses.

There is a charnel-house adjoining the convent, and here, stacked in a gruesome pile, are the skeletons of the priests who throughout the centuries lived and died at Mount Sinai. Oh a chair at the door was the uncanny spectacle of old Stephanus the doorkeeper, propped up in the attitude in which he was killed many years ago. In a corner were several other skeletons, and on inquiry we were graciously informed that these were the remains of *visitors* who had died there.

As the Cameliers saddled up and once more trekked out into the wilderness, followed by the benediction of old Father Polycarpus, the convent bells pealed out a joyous message. But some of our irrepressibles reckoned it was because, they were so mighty glad the rough unshaven Anzacs had departed in peace.

When we first saw the Mount it was shrouded in a snow-white mantle of cloud, even as it was when Moses of old ascended to receive the Ten Commandments. The height of Jebel Mousa is about 6000 ft. above sea-level, and when the patrol bivouacked there it was so bitterly cold that the water in our canvas water-bags froze solid, while a sheet of ice had to be broken through before the men could dip at the convent well. After an all too brief sojourn at this absorbingly interesting spot the patrol made across the flat where it is almost certain the Israelites camped, and trekked northward over more hills, along the sandy beds of more *wadis*, past many other spots of Biblical interest, till, still following in the footsteps of the Israelites, they crossed the border at Rafa and camped once more in Palestine.

Chapter 16

Some Cameliers

In the silence of the night sister sat writing. The ward was in semi-darkness save for her little table where a shaded globe directed the light on her paper. She wrote:

I have just been making the acquaintance of the Cameliers, Daddy. They have Guest Nights up at the officers' mess every week, and it's great fun. And they are a fine devil-may-care lot of officers. Quite a lot are old original nineteen-fourteeners, and what exciting adventures and hairbreadth escapes they could tell—if they only would. But they won't talk—at least about themselves. Some of them, with set lines round their eyes and a sprinkling of grey hairs on young heads, bear mute testimony to the nerve-wrecking Gallipoli days. Others are later arrivals from Australia. Quite a lot of them have risen from the ranks. In the old days 'risen from the ranks' had a distinctive significance, as you know, but amongst the rank and file of our 1st Division were hundreds of men of good old Australian families, whose education and professional or business standing were much better than many who, instead of enlisting at the outset, hung back for the Officers' Training Schools.

As a matter of fact,—here's a confession. Daddy dear,—the camelier I am most interested in is only a sergeant. And the curious thing is that his section officer is a man from the same office, much junior to my camelier, and in every way his inferior. But that is the fortune of war.

Oh, Daddy, I've met the general. He's awfully nice, and he looks too young to be a general. He surely has command of the most interesting and truly Imperial force in the whole army. For in the Imperial Camel Corps are Australians, New Zealanders, Indians, and South Africans, besides men from every part of the old country. More than half the whole I.C.C. are Australians, and of the original companies all were Gallipoli men. I sat next to the general at mess. He's got a breastful of medals. He comes from the Duke of Cornwall's Light Infantry, and is still under forty years of age. His military career began in the South African War and continued through the Somali Campaign of 1903-4, where he won the V.C, and the Soudan Campaign of 1910. He joined the Egyptian Army in 1905, and won his Military Cross in the Soudan in 1914. In January 1916 he went to Abbassia to raise and command four companies of Camelry. But the I.C.C. has grown and grown to its present dimensions.

There were several other distinguished cameliers present at the last Guest Night, for the Camel Brigade was spelling at Rafa.

I met Colonel Langley, a Melbournian, who is about the only colonel I know who plays rugby with his battalion team. He also possesses a voice. Colonel De Lancy Forth, also a Victorian, has seen quite a lot of service and looks a typical British cavalry officer. Perhaps the most popular of all the senior officers is Colonel Mills, from sunny New South Wales. His men swear by him, and he in turn has a wonderful faith in, and appreciation of, the Australian camelier. 'They'll do me' is a favourite expression of his, summing up his confidence in the boys.

Some English officers also were gathered round the festive board. Everyone in the Camel Corps knows Captain Barber. He holds autocratic sway amongst the details at Abbassia and fills all newcomers with feelings of dread. But his bark is far worse than his bite. A little while back Captain Barber was presented with the Order of the Nile decoration, which event prompted Captain Morgan to perpetuate the following effusion:

CAPTAIN JAS. BARBER, O.N.

There was joy among the waiters, there was joy in Shepheard's Bar,
And the gloomy cocktail-mixer just contrived to raise a smile,
For the crowd kept growing deeper till it stretched both near and far.
When Barber got the Order of the Nile.
His regiment never knew him, but there's plenty more who do,
In the Horse and Guns and Camelry and Foot,
And they were very lucky who could see the evening through

And not receive the Order of the Boot.
There's rumour that he's getting yet a decoration higher
To recompense his service to the State.
He's merited the Ribbon of the Star of Stana Schwaya
For his lifelike imitation—Harry Tate.
There are various decorations: there's the Order of the Bath,
Very comforting when evening shadows lag;
And that frequent hard-earned honour—which is often for the Staff—
The Ethiopian Gold-Embroidered Bag.
I've seen 'em all distributed—and sometimes seen 'em earned;
But I shan't forget for quite a goodish while
That evening—or the morning when my head thereafter burned—
When Barber got the Order of the Nile.

Major Buxton, Earl Winterton, Captain Tredennick, and Lieutenant Newson represented the English companies, while there was a host of Australian officers whose names I'll never remember. I know there were four Lieutenant Matthews, and they were differentiated as Camel Matt, Irish Matt, English Matt, and Sailor Matt. Then there were 'Fairy' and 'Togo' and 'Sporto' and 'Chum' and 'Cash' and 'Goldie' and 'Gulliver' and 'Buck' and 'Sandy' and 'Doc' and 'Nick' and 'Dusty' and 'Dickie' and 'Kess' and 'J. P.' and 'Robo' and 'Heppie,' and, as the social scribes say, 'others too numerous to mention.' There were singing and elocutionary efforts, and the gramophone filled in the gaps. Of course, Heppie recited. It was positively his last public appearance in Abbassia, for the next day he was out on the desert trying his camel's paces, when an aeroplane swooped down and knocked him flying, while his startled camel started for the skyline. Heppie is now down in the officers' ward with a broken arm and other injuries, but he's as full of heart as a lion.

Oh, Daddy, do you know Colonel Todd? He's one of the livest officers in the whole of the A.I.F., and a real genial soul. He commands the 10th Light Horse Regiment, which has seen probably more fighting than any unit in the whole E.E.F. Well, he was there, and so was Colonel J. M. Arnott, who at Moascar has done wonderful work for the A.I.F. Mrs. Arnott also was there. She has been doing a lot of generous self-sacrificing work for the Red Cross here in Cairo. With her were Mrs. Featherstonhaugh, Mrs. Davies, and Miss Rentoul. The Anzacs in

Egypt owe a deep debt of gratitude to these four ladies for all they have done to lighten the soldier's burden. Every sick and wounded Light Horseman or Camelier landing in at the hospital is met by one of these ladies and given a bag of comforts from home.

Does it interest you, Daddy, this idle chatting about the folk I meet over here? Or would you prefer that I should retail the latest stories I glean from the wounded soldiers just in from the firing line? Some of these stories you would hardly believe, even though your Little Flora absolutely vouches for them.

"For instance, in the 1st Battalion there was one young camelier who was a frightfully keen photographer. Scores of times he risked his life taking snaps during scraps. At Maghdaba, just as the front line—first wave, they called it—was getting ready to charge the redoubt, this wild harum-scarum yelled out to the officer, 'Half a mo!' and he rushed forward on his own, 20 yards or so, and fixed his camera. 'Righto!' he cried; and as the yelling Cameliers came on he got a fine picture. Also he got a bullet in the leg which put him out of action for a couple of months.

But one of the most picturesque pictures of the campaign was when the Cameliers got into the Turkish trenches in the second Battle of Gaza. They were the only unit in the British line to gain their objective. And they stuck to them in spite of repeated counter-attacks by the Turks, in the face of a hail of shells, and a devastating enfilade fire from machine guns. With the right not having come up, and the left held up after sustaining terrible casualties, the poor Cameliers were 'in the air.'

Abdul kept on attacking till sheer weight of numbers enabled him to fall on the last thirteen sundowners and capture them. As the unlucky baker's dozen were starting off as prisoners an adventurous pair ducked past the guards, leaped the parapet, and with bullets flying thick and fast around them, did a marathon for our trenches, 600 yards distant. As their cobbers rose in the trenches to cheer them in, they yelled frantically for beer and a ticket in Tatt's.

Digging in amidst a shower of bullets and shrapnel opposite Gaza, one Anzac cavalier exclaimed, 'My Gord, I wish I was an ant.' Another scratching with his bayonet and scooping out with his hands at a tiny funkhole, cried plaintively, ' Oh, why did I cut my nails this morning!' A third, as he gazed ruefully at a gaping wound in his shoulder, soliloquised, 'Cripes, it must ha' been an axe that stopped me, not a bullet.' Another, toppling over with a bullet in his knee, remarked judicially and without a trace of animosity, 'One to you, Abdul.' Many and varied are the exclamations of Billjim in the heat of battle; but on the eight hours' train-journey back to Kantara the crowds of wounded cried unanimously for 'Water, water, water!'

Chapter 17

A Sandstorm Trek

After the two costly and abortive attacks on Gaza the I.C.C. settled down to the humdrum of trench warfare. They camped in and about the Wadi Ghuzzie, with the British infantry on their left and the cavalry on their right flank. There was but little excitement except the daily visits of the Hun 'planes, and in course of time even these daily strafes lost their savour.

The camels were eating their heads off, so the G.O.C. decided to give them something to do. One day when the enemy 'plane scouts had come and gone, and darkness had loomed up over the *wadi*, the Camel Brigade saddled up, and under cover of night moved back to Rafa. Few who participated in that trek will ever forget it. Early in the evening a blinding sandstorm swung up from Sinai. The west wind, charged with desert sand swept over the land with the force of a hurricane. The Cameliers coming back from the east got the full force of the storm in their teeth. The swirling sand lashed their faces. The poor camels instinctively swung round and had to be whipped forward. Surplus gear was ruthlessly jettisoned. The wind howled and played an Aeolian dirge on the wires. At last, when every man's temper was ragged and every soldier's eyes, nose, mouth, and ears were full of grit, the cavalcade halted and bivouacked for the night.

Next morning early the unwashed, unshaven, bleary-eyed brigade resumed their trek and camped at Rafa. Here the camp had been so laid out that the battalions, and signallers, and gunners, and ambulance, and veterinarians, and headquarters were so far from each other that the enemy bombs could not possibly hit more than one unit at a time, and there was far more green sward to aim at than camel camps; which was fortunate, for the Taubes came over and bombed us, entirely ignoring the protecting fire of our 'Archies' and the salvos of the Bing Boys. However, *Allah* was kind, and the bombs for the most part ploughed up the innocent earth, and only managed to put on the casualty list one native and two camels.

A day or two later we started out for the Wadi Abiad. The scheme of the commander-in-chief was to smash up the railway line southeast of Beersheba, for the Turks were notoriously short of rolling-stock and rails. The victorious Desert Column was, of course, selected for the job. Major-General Chauvel was in charge of operations, and he took his cavalry and Light Horse and made a strong demonstration against Beersheba. The Turkish defences were shelled; the railway bridge north of the town was destroyed, and two enemy brigades of cavalry that came up were driven back home again. Under cover of this demonstration the special party of Light Horsemen and Engineers started on the railway line and made the whole length a wreck from Sadaj to Asluj. Fine stone bridges and culverts were blown up, and not a single rail left intact.

Meanwhile the Cameliers, without haste, without pause, had trekked southwards to El Auja. They travelled all night, and at dawn reached the Wadi Abiad, where they breakfasted. A long line of skirmishers then moved southwards over the line, scattered several Turkish patrols, and settled down ready for any attack, while the demolition party coming behind played havoc with the railway. For over an hour there sounded a continuous roar of detonations. Big railway bridges with solid stone and concrete pillars and arches all crashed and crumbled to ruin. Such is the waste and destruction incidental to the prosecution of war.

In the afternoon we drew off, and moved back to the Wadi Abiad to bivouac. Our aeroplane, which had kept us advised of Abdul's movements, landed near the old police posts of El Auja, but striking a bit of rough ground had the bad luck to bend the axle and break some minor parts. The pilot was unable to effect repairs without a forge and wires and special tools. It looked as if the machine would have to be destroyed to prevent it falling into the hands of the enemy. When the airman had about come to this decision, a couple of Cameliers sauntered up, had a look at the wreck, and reckoned they could patch it up somehow. The pilot was incredulous, but he said, "Go ahead." So they made a fire, heated and straightened the axle—using lumps of railway line for an anvil. They commandeered some telegraph wire, and soon had the aeroplane in working order again. The airman was delighted. So he got aboard again, waved a 'cheerio,' and flew back to Rafa. Later on a special letter of thanks came from the flight commander to the bush carpenter who had effected the repairs, and they wondered why he should have made a fuss over such a Little thing.

The Cameliers having had two nights in the saddle were mighty tired, so for the few hours vouchsafed them they slept without even taking their boots off. Before dawn we were on trek again, heading north for home. Here and there were Bedouin villages, and we tried to buy eggs and poultry and sheep; but the Bedouins did not want to trade with us. The boys cast covetous eyes on the sheep, but orders were that the property of the inhabitants was to be respected. So we thought of our bully beef and biscuits, and let the sheep pass unmolested—for the most part.

I say for the most part, for that night, as I munched my bully and biscuit, I detected a most savoury odour proceeding from our company lines. It was tantalising, aggravating in the extreme. I was fed up with bully beef anyhow. A few minutes later my section sergeant came along, dumped a delicious piece of roast lamb on my plate, and departed without a single word. I had learnt that pleasant mystery should simply be endured, so forbore to ask of sergeant where the mutton was procured. I just took a pinch of salt and pepper and waded in.

We had a couple of hours' sleep that night—and had earned them. Then once more it was saddle up before dawn and trek onward. We had left the sandy country behind us, and the going was excellent. The camels knew they were going home. The men were too sleepy to care. There had been a few shots fired at our rear-guard, but nobody worried. In due course we arrived back at Rafa. The usual 'furfy' had preceded us. It had been rumoured that we had been cut off and annihilated. We were hungry but happy at the prospect of a good night's sleep. So we gave our camels a drink—the first for five days—and were preparing to settle down for the night when orders came that we were to saddle up and trek back to Gaza.

Oh, what a roar was there, my countrymen. Tired troopers, having had scarcely any sleep for several days, lay all about the Hues oblivious to everything. And here were they rudely awakened and ordered to saddle up. They grumbled and swore, and some fell asleep over the job. However, just at nightfall once more the league-long column straggled out of Rafa towards Gaza. No one cared now whither we were bound. Men were falling asleep, as they rode, and then falling off their camels. Several woke up next morning, only to find that their camels were gone on without them. Several times the column halted to rest the camels. Each time we dismounted and walked about and tried to remain awake. We trod on sleeping Cameliers, but they took no notice. We fell against our camels and slept. The camels didn't mind; they were too tired to care. We were rudely awakened as the camels rose up to follow the column.

That journey was one long nightmare. It seemed interminable. But at last, somewhere about three in the morning we heard someone say, "Rest for one hour." We just tumbled over where we were and slept.

It was dawn, with a rosy glow showing over the Eastern hills, when we were roused again. The larks were singing the morning hymn of praise. The poppies glowed red like drops of blood in the grass. Along the *wadi* thin spirals of smoke ascended heavenward. Evidently nothing startling had happened since we left. Away to the north was dimly heard the rumbling of artillery fire. We went back into our old dug-outs in the Wadi Ghuzzie and slept and slept and slept. About midday someone called, "Mess orderlies." But no orderlies responded. No one woke to eat any dinner. Nobody cared.

From my dugout I could see a Taube sailing overhead with bursts of shrapnel all around. It never interested me in the slightest. For some inexplicable reason I was thinking of the *Ancient Mariner*.

O sleep it is a gentle thing,
Beloved from Pole to Pole.
To Mary Queen the praise be given,
She sent the blessed sleep from Heaven,
That slid into my soul.

I do not know if the lines are correct, but that is how, twenty years after I first had learnt them, the lines came again into my memory.

Nature's sweet restorer . . . sleep. . . .

This demolition stunt of the Camelry formed the subject of the following parody on Mandalay published in *Barrak*:

Demolitions

Where the Turco-Gyppie frontier swings down south towards Akaba,
Where there ain't no Ten Commandments, and there ain't no motor-car,
Where the Camel Column straggles like a league-long desert snake,
There's a weeping Bedouin maiden, and she cries,
"For Allah's sake.

Don't come back to Abiad,
Oh, the shocking time we had.
When your wild-eyed Camel soldiers smashed our railway awful bad.
On the road down Abiad,
Poor old Enver Pasha's mad,
And at dawn he swears like thunder, from Asluj to Abiad."
'Er petticoat—she 'ad none, and 'er dress was chocolat' tint.
We never knew her proper—she was just a Bedouin bint—
But we missed 'er baa-baa lambie when the Anzacs hurried by.
And all the long-night marches we could hear her plaintive cry:
"Don't come back to Abiad,
For the Turks are ragin' mad;
And tho' my lamb tastes better than the bully beef you've had,
Don't come back to Abiad.
Now you've gone I'm mighty glad, For you rather wrecked El Auja when you trekked down Abiad."

Ship me somewhere west of Suez, where a bloke can get a sleep;
Where there ain't no blank Fray Bentos, and yer needn't pinch a sheep;
For my camel's getting dopey, and I cannot keep awake;
My bleary eyes are closing, and I pray, "For Heaven's sake,
Don't go back to Abiad,
For I need a snooze so bad;
Men are falling off their camels with a bump that sends them mad,
On the road to Abiad.
Oh, my humpy, grumpy prad,
You have brought me scathless, sleeping, from the Wadi Abiad."

Chapter 18

Writing Home

Colonel Livingstone sat on the verandah of the old homestead, smoking his morning cigar and gazing across the fertile fields of Langlands. But his thoughts were far away—with the Hunter River boys in France and Sinai, but more particularly with his daughter in Egypt.

He seemed to live solely that he might read her letters, and Flora, knowing how lonely her old father must be, never let a week go by without writing home. Ever and anon the cowboy cantering along the river road with the mail-bag roused the old soldier from his reverie. A mail had arrived at Sydney from Egypt a few days before, so he knew there would be a letter from Flora.

"My dear old Daddy,—I'm fit and well, so don't worry your dear old head about your wayward springoff. And I've been sent down to the officers' ward, which is nicer in some ways. For instance, I've only been here a week, yet I've had three offers of marriage, four dinners at Shepheard's, and a trip on the Nile in a *felucca*. And I've got one dear little patient all to myself. He's just a mere boy; came in the other day with a shrapnel wound in his arm—stopped one while flying over Abdul's 'Archies.' He's in the Australian Flying Corps, and they are all heroes. I used to think the Australian Light Horse were the pick of the whole empire army, but I guess the airmen are a bit above them. Anyhow, about 80 *per cent*, of the Australian airmen in Sinai and Palestine are ex-Light Horsemen.

Do you know, Daddy, these knight-errants of the clouds have fought in every battle on this front since Romani. Oh, I do wish I could write a book about them! They've won about fifteen Military Crosses and a V.C, already. And they never think they are doing anything heroic. To them it's all a gorgeous adventure.

I suppose the unimaginative censor will cut this out, though the enemy knows it better than we do, but during the Sinai Campaign our poor boys had to do long reconnaissance patrols in old buses that could only do 60 miles per hour. The boys called them buses; the proper name is 2E.B.C. and 2E.B.E. My patient told me. Yet the Turks had beautiful fast Fokkers, and Albatross Scouts; and D.3's which were twice as fast and miles better fighting 'planes. But our boys never hesitated, and went up day after day. Sometimes they managed even in their old buses to drive Fritz off, but often they were chased home to Rafa or Sheikh Narran. Some never came back. (That's a blot and not a tear, Daddy.)

These cavalry of the clouds are all frightfully loyal to each other, and they risk anything rather than let their pals get into trouble. That was why M'Namara won his V.C. Dug Rutherford had to come to earth, through engine trouble, in the Turkish lines. The enemy cavalry were near, but M'Namara never hesitated. He zoomed down and had a look, then he alighted to take Rutherford up. But he struck a bad landing and broke his machine. He was wounded at the time, but he helped to fix the old machine and they both got in. Mac took the air, and they both got away just as the Turks came up. It was awfully lucky.

But oh, Daddy, it's sad to think of the splendid young fellows that have been killed, and for every one of them some mother or sister or sweetheart is breaking her heart. Already the Australian Flying Squadron has lost Steele and Jack Potts and Gerry Stone and Bowd,—we all loved Harry Bowd,—Paget, Searle, Harvey, Oxenham, Farquhar, Adams, and Muir. Muir was just splendid, and did some wonderful stunts before he was killed.

This is not a cheerful letter, is it, Daddy? But I must buck up. They do such comical things too, at times, these supermen. One chap was anxious to become a pilot. He went to Heliopolis to learn, and was landing after his first solus, when he crashed into the hangar and smashed his machine. The irate flight commander dashed out and yelled, 'You clumsy animal. That's the last time you'll fly here.' The culprit grinned, threw his cap, gloves, and overcoat to the mechanic, and said, 'Sir, I could have told you that.' Then he stalked off and went back to the Light Horse.

My airman tells me that the pilots and observers 'chiack' each other when they make a dud landing or anything. For instance, their champion bomber tried several times to blow up a Turkish pontoon over the Jordan, and though he got near it he just failed. He was very depressed with his failure, but the last straw was when an unofficial *communiqué* stated that when the Turks saw Haig's Horror coming to bomb it they rushed to the bridge for *safety!*

The officer in the next bed to my airman is a mining engineer, and he has been thousands of feet down big mines, and he has done a lot of sapping and tunnelling in this war. I asked him why he didn't join the Flying Corps; and he exclaimed emphatically, 'I'll go down, down as far as you like, but up? Not one blanky inch'...And I feel like that myself sometimes when I hear of the airmen's exploits.

Oh, I ought to tell you, Daddy, that whatever good sports there are in the German Army seem to have gravitated to the Flying Corps. There is one chap named 'Filmy.' He's their star pilot. He has brought down several English and Australian airmen. One day after one of our chaps had been brought down 'Filmy' flew over our aerodrome, fired a Very light to show he had a message, dived down through our machines—which of course never attacked him—and dropped a message saying Vautin was all right, and that the Australian airmen were real good sports, and he hoped to meet some of them after the war.

I must stop, Daddy; I could write for hours and hours about the boys. The main thing is that since our airmen got the new Bristol Fighter Machines they have easily maintained the supremacy of the air. Frequently one or two of our boys will attack and disperse several Hun machines.

I've not told you much about the Camel Corps this time, have I? Well, now listen: 'I'm a bit fond of a big sun-tanned camelier, somewhere in Palestine. So there.'—

    Your affectionate daughter,   Flora.

It was a curious coincidence that just as the old colonel finished reading his daughter's letter he picked up the *Sydney Morning Herald,* and in it read the following account by a camelier of the doings of the Australian airmen in Sinai and Palestine:

Airmen, birdmen, fliers, pilots, observers, kings of the air—heroes all:

We ordinary soldiers of *terra firma*, horse, foot, artillery, and camelry—we salute you!

In the good old days when the world was wide our fathers fought on land and sea. Today Armageddon is so vast that men needs must fight above the land and under the water as well, and those who still follow the prosaic paths on land and sea look up and wonder or look down and ponder.

I have flown. For a brief space, one glorious hour—or maybe less—I shared in the kingship of the air. I have mounted up with wings like an eagle, and breathed the rarefied air of the high places. Tomorrow, and the next day, and the next, I will ride a camel, breathe dust, live in sand, drink lukewarm water, and eat bully beef and biscuits. But today I have been aloft and looked down on the dwellers on the earth.

The first phase is just like a wild rush in an automobile. The 'plane streaked across the ground at about twenty or thirty miles an hour, and aimed straight at a huge hangar. It looked absolutely certain that we must crash into the building. Then it seemed a miracle happened, and we leapt into space. The pilot had just touched a lever, and the machine, spurning the ground, cleared the hangar and floated away into the rosy dawn. Farther and farther receded the earth. Trees dwindled till they became little smudges. Trenches thinned until they looked like irregular lines disfiguring the landscape. The horizon momentarily widened. For miles and miles the vast panorama stretched away and below—green fields, golden sands, blue shimmering waters, one great cyclopean picture. The tents of the soldiers looked like Little whitey-brown drops of paint. The blankets laid out on the ground to air were just like tiny black, brown, and grey patches, one-eighth the size of a pocket-handkerchief. 'Way out in the open is a long string of little grey ants—at least they look like ants; in reality they are camels. How the airmen must look down on the poor Cameliers!

We circled and banked; flew before the breeze at anything over a hundred miles an hour. Facing the wind again the 'plane throbbed and quivered; swerving and swooping as we encountered various air currents or pockets. Then the whirring engine suddenly ceased. We poised like an eagle with outstretched wings. *Anon*, the 'plane tilted forward, and with incredible velocity we rushed earthwards. The distant horizon dropped out of sight. Bigger and bigger grew the tents and the camels and the trenches. A little toy train some miles off assumed quite respectable dimensions. Up, up, up came the earth to meet us. Soon we could distinguish the Lilliputian soldiers. A breathless swoop, one final exhilarating rush through the air, and we were once more safe on *terra firma*.

Let it be at once admitted that this was no daredevil flight over the enemy's lines, with its attendant dangers from 'Archies' and Taubes. It was just a simple 'joy ride' right back in the safety of our own territory. But the experience only served to heighten the admiration I had always felt for our intrepid airmen. Some days before, I had been the guest of the Australian Flying Squadron at Rafa. It had been good day after day watching those courageous pilots taking their machines out, executing fancy flights overhead, and then streaking east for the daily duel with the Hun. Now it was fine to see them at close quarters, when the day's work was over, happy and care-free as a party of schoolboys. Indeed, the first thing noticed was the extreme youth of the majority of the airmen. They seemed all to be within the enviable twenty to twenty-five period. There was not a middle-aged man amongst the lot of them, and hardly a man over thirty. They were really just a party of big boys engaged in a great game.

Each day brought its attendant excitement: a flight over Abdul's hues, a brief and thrilling duel with a Hun, a bombing expedition anywhere between Gaza and Jerusalem; perhaps a forced landing on account of engine troubles, or maybe a hilarious rush to funkholes when the Hun airmen paid the return visit. Then when the day's 'strafe' was over the airmen lounged about the mess, reading or smoking or sleeping. And at night they fought their battles over again—not in a spirit of bravado, but that all might know all that was going on, and profit by the experience of the day. The airmen have a jargon of their own, and it takes the uninitiated some time to gauge the import of their vernacular. And some of their exploits are enough to make one's hair stand on end. A few of the more spectacular deeds now and then find their way into the cable columns of the papers. But for the most part very little is heard of the airmen's doings.

There seems to be such a lot of luck—good and bad—in the air fighting. A bullet in the petrol tank, a mishap with the engine, makes all the difference between plus and minus. The other day our Cameliers saw a thrilling duel aloft. A Hun and a Briton entered the lists. They were only a few thousand feet up, but being close together the 'Archies' could not open fire. So Turks and Anzacs looked on. The pilots circled and manoeuvred for position. At last the red and blue circle managed to get over the Taube, which promptly bolted. Then like an eagle the Briton swooped, blazing away with his machine gun at the flying Hun. It looked a certainty that the German must be riddled with bullets and brought crashing down. Then luck stepped in. The unexpected happened. Something went wrong with the British 'plane. The wings buckled, and like a wounded bird it swerved, dipped, then crashed to earth a shapeless mass. The report should have been: 'We brought down one enemy 'plane today.' Alas, it read: 'One of ours failed to return."

CHAPTER 19

Allenby—1

When Sir Edmund Allenby arrived in Egypt at the end of June 1917, things were anything but bright. The British Army, twice hurled back with heavy slaughter from the heights of Gaza, had taken up a position extending for 22 miles from the Mediterranean Sea opposite Gaza to Gamlie. The midsummer sun seemed to focus all his rays on the Wadi Ghuzzie, and the tired infantry sweated and swore and prayed to get back to France.

Out towards Beersheba and Hareira the Light Horse and Cameliers played poker and two-up, and when a newcomer grumbled about the heat they grinned and shrugged their shoulders, and exclaimed "*Maleesch!*" So to relieve the monotony the Hun 'planes came over on moonlight nights and bombed the bivouacs. Incidentally they deliberately bombed the hospitals and killed several of our wounded. And when the medical officers lit flares to show up the Red Cross, the Huns swooped down and loosed off a few thousand rounds from machine guns. Oh, there is nothing half-hearted about the Hun. He is as thorough as Stafford. It was not a cheerful prospect for the new commander-in-chief. The enemy occupied an almost impregnable position stretching from Gaza to Beersheba. Gaza itself, with its protecting redoubts, had been converted into a fortress. Earthworks and redoubts at intervals along the Beersheba Road commanded all approaches. On a front of about 30 miles Marshal von Falkenhayn had disposed an army of 200,000 men, including German and Austrian gunners, machine gunners, and cavalry.

But it was not long before a new spirit of optimism animated our whole army. Allenby's genius, his enthusiasm, his energy permeated everywhere. The Expeditionary Force settled down manfully to prepare for the strenuous days ahead. The soldiers knew that when all was ready Allenby would strike, but not an hour before; and when he did strike they knew he would strike hard.

The 1st Battalion I.C.C, having borne the brunt of the Sinai Campaign, Romani, Rafa, and Maghdaba, and having been badly cut up in the second battle of Gaza, were now sent down to the Suez Canal for a few months' spell. The 4th Battalion, heartily sick of the scorching sands of Sinai, were brought up to the Wadi Ghuzzie in their stead. Later on there was a change in the command of the 4th. The commanding officer returned to Australia. The 4th hailed with unfeigned delight the news that Lieut.-Colonel Mills was to command. Lieut. Colonel Mills won the whole-souled devotion of his men, and he in turn had implicit confidence in them. "They'll do me," he had exclaimed with pride at his first battalion parade. And the men, reciprocating, said, "He'll do us." Which was very satisfactory all round.

When summer had done its worst, and the cool winter nights were freshening up the men, there was a general stir which presaged a renewal of the conflict. Abdul knew the blow was coming, but he could not guess when or where. With a view of finding out something of our dispositions he made a strong reconnaissance towards Karm, employing in the venture a couple of regiments of cavalry, some guns, and about three battalions of infantry. This force managed to mop up a couple of Yeomanry outposts, though it cost them very dear. Then the Welsh Division swung into action and the Turks bolted back to their trenches on the Gaza-Beersheba Road.

At the second Battle of Gaza, the British commander had presumed that the Turkish left-flank trenches and works put any encircling movement by our cavalry out of the question. So the infantry were given the almost impossible task of capturing by frontal attack a series of redoubts bristling with machine guns. General Allenby's appreciation of the situation was different. He realised the cost of a frontal attack and the advantages of a flank attack. So he just chopped Beersheba off the left of the Turkish line. This left their flank exposed. He then hurled his cavalry and camelry on to the exposed left flank of the enemy, crumpled it up, and disorganised the Turks' whole plan of defence. Gaza fell.

The first phase, then, was the capture of Beersheba. Strategy dictated this, as well as the urgent necessity for supplementing the water supply. All through the campaign the water problem was acute. Besides the army there were 30,000 camels and thousands of horses and mules to be watered.

It was vitally important that the enemy should not guess from which direction the main attack was coming. The artillery therefore opened a three days' bombardment of the whole Turkish position, and on the third day the warships under Rear-Admiral Jackson joined in the chorus and directed destructive salvos at the works round Gaza. Under cover of night the Light Horse, Camel Corps, Artillery, and London and Welsh Infantry congregated at the rendezvous within striking distance of Beersheba.

The Beersheba battle began with the Londoners dashing forward at dawn and seizing the Turks' advanced position. Incidentally they killed a goodly number of the enemy and captured a hundred more. This enabled the guns to push forward and tear the wire entanglements to smithereens. All the preliminaries being satisfactorily accomplished, the Camels attacked the defences to northward. Cavalry threatened the south and east, while the main advance from the west by British infantry resulted in the capture of the positions between the Khalusa Road and the Wadi Saba. This took till midday; the enemy artillery, being exceptionally active, did some execution among the troops advancing in the open. A force encircling the town attacked the strongly fortified Tel el Saba and Bir es Sakaty, but met with a stout resistance. Meanwhile the Australian Light Horse, having ridden 35 miles during the night, swung in towards Beersheba from the east. The steady advance by platoons of infantry over the open was too slow for their liking, so with a wild yell they charged straight for the town.

It was quite unorthodox, considering the force holding the defences, but it was eminently successful. It was a surprise packet. It decided the day. Like steeplechasers the Anzacs cleared two lines of deep trenches and galloped right into the town. Turks surrendered wholesale. This happened just about seven in the morning, so the demoralised Turks never knew how many foemen were amongst them. The Yeomanry and Londoners charging from the west gave the garrison no chance to recover from their panic. The ancient city of Abraham, with its wells and precious water supply, was captured with comparatively slight loss to the British. At least 500 Turks were killed and 2000 captured. A dozen cannon and a vast quantity of ammunition and stores were gathered as spoils to the victors. This was Allenby's first step on the road to Jerusalem.

The following tribute to the Light Horsemen—in the *Melbourne Herald*—is worth quoting:

These Light Horsemen that night carried through by endurance, grit, and fine horsemanship, one of the great feats of the war . . . a brilliant feat of arms. No better cavalry have existed. The great ride of the Australians and New Zealanders to Beersheba outdid Stewart's long dashes in the American Civil War and French's rounding-up work in South Africa.

It was round Beersheba that 'Tibbie' Cotter the cricketer was killed, with many more Light Horsemen and Cameliers. There are rough wooden crosses dotting the land of the Philistines. Some bear the names of comrades; some are nameless.

Comrade of knapsack or bandolier,
Tread light, we pray, when you pass this way;
For sake of the brave one slumbering here.
Nameless in death till the Judgment Day:
Tread light, lest the tramp of your martial host
Or the rattle of rifle or bayonet blade
Should ring down the night to their silent post.
And rouse them too soon for the Grand Parade.

CHAPTER 20

Allenby—2

Our army was now in great heart. The optimism of October had developed into an absolute certainty of victory. Beersheba had been bitten off. The Turks' left flank lay exposed, and they were feverishly hastening the supplementary defences round Khuweilfeh and Sheria.

It was, however, still essential that they should remain in ignorance of the next move. The scene of operations was therefore suddenly shifted from their extreme left at Beersheba to their extreme right at Sheikh Hasan and Umbrella Hill. These two works are only about 2000 to 2500 yards from the town, so their capture would be a distinct menace to Gaza itself. It was also hoped that an assault here would pin the Turkish reserves to the town and prevent them reinforcing the threatened left flank.

Umbrella Hill was first essayed. The Lowland Scotties moved out over the heavy sandhills at night on 1st November. It was heavy going and stiff fighting on arrival, but there was no doubt of the result. To show their anger at the loss of the 'Gamp,' the Turks opened a violent two hours' bombardment of our line, and also plastered Umbrella Hill. Then at three o'clock on 2nd November the attack was hurled at the enemy's right. After a heavy preliminary bombardment the British infantry moved out, and in splendid style captured the 5000 yards of trenches comprising the Sheikh Hasan position. Our left was now firmly settled on the seashore. The bombardment had caused many casualties among the Gaza garrison, while the infantry landed 450 prisoners, apart from killed and wounded. What .was more important, the Turkish commander had not dared to deplete his reserves to reinforce his exposed left flank.

Out here—the Turks' left—the Welsh and Irish infantry, with the cavalry and camelry on their wing, were threatening Sheria and beginning the work of crumpling up the line. It was no easy task. The whole line had been strongly fortified, while trenches, pits, and barbed wire provided obstacles against the cavalry. The Irish Division moved up and captured Abu Irgey. The Welsh pushed on through the hills north of Beersheba and attacked Sheria on the flank. The Cameliers on the right of the Welsh pushed on to Khuweilfeh. The Anzac Mounteds moved north along the Hebron Road towards Dhaheriyeh. By 3rd November a concerted movement by Irish, Welsh, and Colonials, north and west towards Sheria and Khuweilfeh, made plain the British strategy. The path was strenuously contested by the Turkish garrison, and strong reserves were hurried from Gaza to save the left flank. Here some of the hottest fighting of the campaign took place. Time and again for three days the Turks counter-attacked the Cameliers and Light Horse and the Welsh. Here it was that Lieut. Dixon of the Anzac Camelry won his D.S.O. and his Captaincy, by rallying some scattered infantry and I.C.C., and with a mere handful of men barring the road. against repeated charges of the enemy.

Fighting in this sector was fierce and indecisive for a couple of days. The Welsh by a brilliant charge captured Khuweilfeh, but a counter-attack drove them off. They came again with undiminished ardour, retook the hill, and went on. Then on the 6th the main attack on the Turkish left centre was driven home. Yeomanry, Irish, Londoners, Welsh, Australians, and New Zealanders converged from the south and east on Abu Hareira, Wadi Sheria, Kanwukah, Khuweilfeh, and Rijin el Dhib. Behind them the artillery thundered away at the redoubts and the Turkish batteries.

On the left of this sector the Yeomanry charged the hills and stormed the redoubt with magnificent valour, taking several lines of trenches and reaching the Sheria Station, with a bag of 600 Turks to their credit. On the right the Welsh had another strenuous day's fighting, from which they emerged victorious, having captured several hundred more prisoners. For four days the Camel Corps had sustained the shock of successive battalions of Turkish reinforcements, holding the ground manfully, and by using up the army's resources made possible the victory in the centre. But their casualties had been heavy. Hardly a company could put fifty men in the firing line. Sections had dwindled to about a dozen men. But they stuck it.

The commander-in-chief had wisely refrained from frittering away his reserves, trusting to the right sector to carry out its own job. Thus, on the night of 6-7th November he was able to concentrate for the final blow at Outpost Hill, Middlesex Hill, and Turtle Hill, immediately in front of Gaza. The artillery once more pounded away at the defences, and the infantry started out to finish the job. But Abdul didn't wait. With Beersheba captured, Gaza itself threatened, his left flank turned, and his line crumbling up, he made a second get-away. Gaza had fallen at last!

CHAPTER 21

Allenby—3

The third Battle of Gaza made ample amends for the failures of 26th March and 19th April. All the energies of the 'C.-in-C.' were now concentrated on driving home the victory, and preventing the enemy taking up further defensive positions farther north.

When the main defences of Gaza had been occupied, a force was immediately pushed on to the mouth of the Wadi Hesi. Here the Turkish rear-guard temporarily held up pursuit. Away on the right, round Sheria, the enemy held on daring the 7th, but that night they joined the great trek northwards. Our airmen, during the 7th and 8th, made good practice with bombs and machine guns amongst the retreating enemy. The whole British Army, from Beersheba to the sea, moved on. Every now and then the pursuing columns were checked for a brief time by small parties of Turks with machine guns fighting scattered rear-guard actions. Hareira and Sheria were captured at the point of the bayonet, and the Mounteds pushed on towards Jemaminah and Huj. At the latter place a more determined stand was made by the rear-guard, but the Warwick and Worcester Yeomanry made a fine spectacular charge, routing the enemy and capturing amongst the booty 12 field guns.

But for the lack of water and the difficulty of bringing up supplies, the retreat would have developed into an absolute rout. As it was, the cavalry pushed on relentlessly, driving the foe before them. Prisoners were surrendering wholesale all along the line. There had been only nine days of fierce fighting, yet a modern army nearly a quarter of a million strong had been driven from an almost impregnable fortress and was in full retreat. It was surely a nine days' wonder.

There was, however, no easing up and resting on the laurels already won. An ordinary soldier may win a battle, but it takes a military genius to reap the full fruits of victory. And this is what General Allenby was bent on doing. The mounted troops were assembled, and with scarcely a pause pushed on after the enemy. "The main Turkish army had retreated north along the plain towards Jaffa, while the considerable force that had held Sheria and the Hareira positions had made a more leisurely get-away towards Menshiye. In fact, at one time the position of this force constituted a menace to the right wing of the main pursuing British army. An undefeated army well in hand might have caused considerable trouble by a determined attack westward along the Wadi Hesi, behind our advancing troops.

But all the fight had been taken out of Abdul. He was useless for any strategical move. The most he could do was to fight spasmodic rear-guard actions. It would have needed Marshal Ney at his best to hold up the British advance. But in case any flank attack did come from the hills, the Camel Corps was pushed on towards Nijile, while the Anzac Mounted Division hung pitilessly on the right rear, hustling the rear-guards, cutting in on detached bodies, capturing hundreds of prisoners, and transforming the retreat into a rout.

By 11th November the main Turkish Army was moving on Junction Station. By strenuous labours the German Staff had been able to rally about 20,000 men. The main army on the plain had outdistanced the force retreating through the Judean hills, so the line of resistance stretched in a general south-east direction from Wadi Sukereir on the coast *via* El Kustineh towards Beit Jebrin. So for a brief space the pursuing British had perforce to halt while the men and horses rested, and to enable supplies to come forward.

It had been terribly strenuous work. Although nominally winter, it was very warm during the day. Hot wind and dust inflicted severe thirst on the troops, and water was very scarce. At night in the hills it was bitterly cold.

There had been intermittent fighting on nth and 12th November. On the right of our line the Australians and New Zealanders, giving the hapless Turks no rest, had pushed on and driven the rear-guards back to Balin and Tel es Safi. On the other flank the cavalry and Lowlanders had pushed the enemy back towards Nahr Sukereir and Burkah. So on the 13th the Turks had taken up a very strong semi-circular position defending the all-important Junction Station, whence the line runs east to Jerusalem and north to Ramleh.

Once more the victorious army got ready for attack. Supplies were brought up and a few guns ranged in support. Then once again Allenby hurled his troops at the enemy. Round Katrah and El Mughar the strong natural position had been strengthened by the defenders, and there was stiff fighting before the Scotties won home. The Anzacs on the right drove back the Turkish left, while the cavalry, by a magnificent charge from the north-west, broke through the last defences, sabring all who disputed their path. Falkenhayne's proud army was cut in two, half fleeing north towards the coast and the remainder making all haste east to Jerusalem.

CHAPTER 22

Allenby—4

Someday the full story will be written of Allenby's Palestine Campaign—one of the most brilliant and decisive campaigns in history. Historians will do justice to the English, Scots, Irish, Welsh, Indian, Australian, and New Zealand Divisions engaged in the great enterprise.[1] These few chapters, written near the banks of the old Jordan River, provide a very sketchy and imperfect resume of the victorious progress of Allenby's army.

Nor does it profess to present more than occasional vignettes of that truly imperial force, the Imperial Camel Corps. In the fighting which began at Beersheba and ended at Jerusalem on 9th December, the Cameliers claim—not very seriously—that they fasted for forty days and forty nights. Which, of course, is an exaggeration; yet it gives an inkling of the hardships which the whole army must have suffered, for the Cameliers are the last to go short of tucker. Ordinarily we marched out with five days' rations and water aboard, and time and again this supply had to be shared with the less fortunate cavalry and infantry. Out on the western desert, during the fighting with the Senussi, Light Horsemen and infantry often besieged the Camel Corps, offering pound notes for bottles of water, but no matter how long the trek or how distant the next supply, the Cameliers always gladly placed their *fantasses* at the disposal of their comrades.

During the campaign under review, the Camel brigade, under Brigadier-General Smith, V.C, M.C., was represented by one Australian battalion, one Anzac battalion, one British battalion, two Indian batteries, besides Engineers, Army Medical Corps, and details. This

---

1. An excellent trilogy of the Great War in the Middle East by W.T. Massey in two volumes, *The Great War in the Middle East:* 1 and 2 is also published by Leonaur.

Imperial brigade, working mostly on the right of the line, formed the connecting link between the infantry and the mounted troops, and the pivot upon which the cavalry swung when attacking the flank of the enemy. Some of the hottest fighting round Khuweilfeh fell to their lot, and throughout the entire forty days they co-operated loyally with the Welsh and other infantry with whom they were associated. It will be remembered that by 13th November the demoralised Turkish Army had been defeated near Junction Station, and cut in two, the main force still retreating north towards Jaffa, and the remainder making along the line to Jerusalem.

Once more the British pushed on in pursuit. The successive though sacrificial rear-guard actions had indeed enabled the main army to effect a get-away, but it was a demoralised and beaten force. As they neared Jaffa, however, a last effort was made to hold up the pursuit. A strong line was chosen south of Ramleh, the right resting on Ayun Kara, and the left lining the ridge at Ancient Gezer, which covers the main Ramleh-Jerusalem Road. Without hesitation this defence was attacked on 15th November. The cavalry swinging up from the south charged the Gezer heights and brilliantly carried the position, capturing several hundred prisoners and a field gun. On the Mediterranean wing the New Zealand Mounted Rifles found the Turks strongly entrenched, but the irresistible dash of the Colonials carried the heights. The Turks came again with a determined counter-attack, driving the New Zealanders back.

Once again the New Zealanders scaled the hill with fixed bayonets. The Turks met them fair and square—one of the few occasions when Abdul has dared to meet the Anzac in the open with the cold steel. A wild *melee* ensued, the cries of the Turks mingling with the wild yells of the Maorilanders. But in spite of their numerical superiority and the frenzied exhortations of the German officers, the Turks were no match for the Anzacs at close quarters. They broke and fled, leaving many killed behind, and Ayun Kara in possession of the New Zealanders.

Throughout the whole Sinai and Palestine Campaigns, from Romani onwards, the New Zealanders had been conspicuously successful. They had suffered the most intense privations with the utmost cheerfulness. Their charge was always irresistible. The Australian Light Horsemen, who had shared the rigours of the campaign with them, were supposed to be rather jealous of their own reputation. Yet I heard at Jericho an English staff officer, who ought to know, exclaim, "The New Zealanders are absolutely the pick of the whole Palestine army," and the

Australians, without hesitation or dissentient voice, heartily agreed.

After the victory at Ayun Kara and Abu Shusheh the army pushed on, and the mounted troops and Cameliers occupied Ramleh and Ludd. Next day they pushed on, and without hindrance entered Jaffa. Towards Jerusalem there was some fierce fighting round the Judean Hills. Infantry with Australian Light Horse on their flank rooted guerrilla fighters out from amongst the *wadis* and defiles. But the German machine gunners now made some amends for their long retreat. They seized all the vantage-posts on the hills. They commanded all the approaches, even the goat-tracks. The British, storming the heights, suffered considerable casualties, but after a brief spell for relief on 4th December pushed on to the north of Jerusalem. Round Nebi Samwil and El Burg and El Toka there were fierce fighting and repeated counter-attacks by the Turks, but all to no avail.

On the coast round Jaffa most determined counter-attacks were made by the enemy from 25th November to 1st December. Time and again they charged our lines. For eleven days the Cameliers dared not take the saddles off their unfortunate camels. Hardly any grain or fodder had come up to feed them. The Light Horsemen were almost continuously in the saddle. Fighting was fierce and incessant. On 29th November the Turks charged in force, and 150 were promptly surrounded and mopped up by the Australians. Again, at El Burge on the extreme right a mass attack resulted in a serious break through, but here again the Australian Light Horse counterattacked with brilliant success, killing many Turks, driving the wedge back, restoring the line, and capturing over 200 prisoners.

Then came the final move on Jerusalem. Roads were constructed, guns were brought up, water supplies were developed, and troops set in motion. Then came the rain. The roads became impassable for wheeled transport and camels. Difficulties of transport and manoeuvre and signalling were increased tenfold. But through the mud and slush and mire the troops pushed on. Camels slithered over the slippery hill-track and broke their legs. Motors could not move. But the army moved on. Rations failed to arrive. But the infantry went on without them. The Australians raided the orchards, paying whatever was asked so long as they got tucker. And an unlimited supply of oranges saved the situation. In due course Jerusalem was surrounded and the Turks retreated northwards.

On 9th December, without a shot being fired at its walls, the ancient city surrendered.

CHAPTER 23

Allenby—5

Allenby has entered Jerusalem. Another conqueror has passed through the walls of the ancient city.

But the glory has departed from the city of David. Gone are its pristine splendour, its prosperous days, its thriving commerce, its gorgeous bazaars, its thronging pilgrims. War and misrule have sorely tried the Holy City; famine and disease have cowed the unfortunate citizens.

It has been said that where the Red Sultan merely lashed the Jews with whips, the young Turks had flayed them with scorpions. Commerce was only possible when the merchants heavily bribed the Turkish officials. Being a non-producing city, the citizens lived an artificial life, based on the gold left in the wake of the constant stream of pilgrims. But when war came the pilgrimage ceased. The main source of supply was cut off. The sole industry—that of manufacturing and selling souvenirs and relics and curios—languished and died. Soon shops and eating-houses became fewer and fewer. Famine and pestilence were rife. The young men were conscripted for military service. All over the city, shops and houses were shut and deserted. The evil days had come upon the city.

Remittances from abroad kept many of the Jews from starvation. But the iniquitous Turkish officials received the full value, American and British, and paid out the depreciated Turkish note, thus robbing the unfortunate inhabitants of 75 *per cent*, of their remittances. Then came the sound of guns, and hope fluttered in the breasts of the sorely-tried citizens. Anon the streams of Turkish fugitives passed through and on to Nablus. The German staff in haste gathered their treasure and fled, and to the relief of all, and the joy of most, the British came; and after four centuries of tyranny and misrule the Ottoman dominion came to an end. Many times has the city of David seen the conflict of armies and the invasion of conquerors, but there was none like the present. Though the Turkish guns fired from the Mount of Olives and the sacred hills round the city, no British bullet or shell was turned in its direction.

On 9th December the city was surrendered, what time the diminishing firing showed that the Turks were being driven north and east from its walls. Next day General Allenby entered the city. But he came not with pomp and panoply and egotistic ceremonial, like the Hun pseudo-conqueror twenty years before. With a small staff and representative units of the Imperial Army, he formally entered the city. He came on foot, not by the Joppa Gate, nor by the presumptuous breach made by the Hun, but by the ancient gate known as 'The Friend,' and the citizens welcomed the deliverer with tears of joy.

The ceremony was brief but impressive. The procession marched from Mount Zion to the citadel, and at the base of the Tower of David the proclamation was read. It promised liberty to all to carry on legitimate commerce and industry. It assured the protection of every shrine, mosque, and sacred building, according to its own religious customs and practices, and the freedom of worship to all. After this simple ceremony General Allenby formally received the city notables, the patriarchs of the various religious denominations, and the leading *sheikhs*.

The spectacular victories of General Allenby, followed by his simple yet dignified entry into Jerusalem, have appealed to the imagination of the Arabs. Scarcely less potent a factor in securing the loyalty of the Arabs is the General's name. The Arabic *Alla-nebi* means 'The prophet of God.' Scholars have translated All-en-by as meaning ' God lodges with us,' while read backwards, as in the Arabic, the name implies 'The servant of *Allah*.' And coming into the city on foot as he did, the Arabs have called him ' The Pilgrim.'

So a new era has dawned for the Holy City. Trade is livening up. Stores and bazaars and eating-houses are opening. There are life and movement in the air. The blight of the Turk and the menace of the Hun are now things of the past. The German staff never thought the big British push had sufficient momentum to carry the invaders much farther north than the neighbourhood of Gaza. But they, came on and on and on, and the Turks and their masters went back and back and back. Still the Huns believed that General Allenby could not hold Jerusalem. To show their confidence, they entered into a big wheat deal, the grain to be available a fortnight from date, by which time the British would certainly be driven back from Jerusalem. Reinforcements were hurried down from Damascus, and the big counterattack launched against the tired British Army. But, contrary to Hun expectations, the hated English had not lost their punch. They stood firm, while the Turks spent their fury in wild but hopeless charges. Then Allenby pushed on again, and the only effect of the attempted recapture of Jerusalem was to lose more Turkish territory.

And so the old war-scarred year ended with Southern Palestine freed from the Turkish yoke, and antipodean Colonials walking proudly through the streets of the Holy City. Colonel Todd and his Westralians were the first in, and surely their splendid record from Gallipoli to Jerusalem entitled them to the honour.

The Jews in the city looked thin and half starved; so much so, that a casual sand-groper, remembering his Old Testament, exclaimed, "No wonder it took two of them to carry a bunch of grapes." And his comrade in the same strain remarked, "Old Moses was wise all right. He had one good look at this country, then pegged out."

There was, however, no doubt of the satisfaction of the populace at the British occupation. With tears of joy they welcomed "The Deliverer." Some months before—after the second Battle of Gaza—when British prisoners were taken through Jerusalem, the people cheered the captives, and for this demonstration were punished vindictively by the Germans. But now German prisoners were marched through, and the people came out to feast their eyes on the spectacle and revile their old-time persecutors.

British Colonial statesmanship is constructive, in striking contrast to the destructive incidence of Turkish misrule. So it was not long before British Engineers were busily engaged laying water-pipe lines to Jerusalem. And when the citizens found the ever-flowing stream at their doors, instead of relying on the old-time cisterns, they marvelled. One Armenian priest with tears in his eyes exclaimed:

> The Turks held Jerusalem for hundreds of years and gave us nothing; the English have been here a few months and they have given us a permanent water supply. Long live England!

Somehow, I think, that prayer finds an echo in the hearts of all the peoples of Palestine.

CHAPTER 24

Red Triangle

Among the various institutions which have catered for the army of Egypt, not a single one in any way compares in excellence with the Y.M.C.A. The maps of Egypt, Sinai, Sudan, and Palestine are dotted with Red Triangle huts, scores of them, each one a boon and a blessing to the soldiers, a home of healthful recreation and a needful centre of social and spiritual activities.

These Y.M.C.A. huts, tents, and canteens are so much an integral part of the army organisation that one shudders to think what the E.E.F. would have been without them. The regimental *padres* have done noble work, yet I dare maintain that without the inspiring influence of the Y.M.C.A. the morale of the army would have sagged, the communications with home would have been much more precarious, and the vitiating influences of camp life, unchecked, would have seriously affected the efficiency of the troops.

Once freed from the irksome restraints of camp routine the average soldier is only too glad to throw himself down in his bivvy and smoke or play cards. It is quite an effort to write home. Besides, paper and envelopes are scarce. And it is so easy, to procrastinate. So the thoughtless soldier goes on day after day, and week after week—always intending to write home, but always putting it off. Then he saunters into the Y.M.C.A. tent, and staring him -in the face is the imperative injunction: "Write Home Now." Paper and envelopes and pen and ink lie invitingly on the table. The careless soldier is filled with remorse. He did not mean to be cruel to the old folks at home. He was only thoughtless and tired and fed-up with the war. So he sits down and writes and writes and writes. Then in a month or so, way back in the Hunter River Valley, or in the Riverina, or in the Darling Downs, or out in the Never-Never Country, some mother or sister or sweetheart is gladdened by a letter from the wanderer. In one month in one camp alone 80,000 sheets of paper and 70,000 envelopes were used by the soldiers.

Owing to the exigencies of the military situation large bodies of men are transferred from time to time from one camp to another. Someone in Cairo or Rafa or Kantara writes a few orders, then, with the rapidity of the prophet's gourd, a canvas town springs up, maybe in the wilderness. Thousands of men are congregated together. It is necessary that someone should cater for their physical, social, mental, and spiritual needs. So in due course a Y.M.C.A. hut or tent is erected. A canteen is started, and the crowds of patrons testify to the need. Then someone else in authority writes more orders, and the battalion or brigade moves out to the front line. The camp is deserted. So the Y.M.C.A. packs up its impedimenta and follows the army. Tel el Kebir was once a great camp with tens of thousands of Anzacs. Six months later a few tired soldiers gazed on a beggarly array of empty huts. Mena at the end of 1914 was the home of the immortal 1st Australian Division. A year or so later the Sphinx and the Pyramids stood sentinel over a deserted landscape.

So the Y.M.C.A. is ever on the move. When the Sinai Campaign developed and a big army moved along the old caravan route from Kantara to Gaza, no fewer than 59 new Y.M.C.A. centres were 'opened in one year. The army pushed on, and 44 of these centres had to be abandoned. There was no one left to cater for. So in the course of three years 120 different Y.M.C.A. centres were established. Many of these were short-lived. A few are permanent, most of them moved on. As I write there are about 70 in active operation, extending from Khartoum to Jaffa and Jericho.

The work centres in Cairo, and it is good for the moral and physical welfare of the soldiers that this is so. It is difficult to estimate the value to the army of the Anzac Hostel, but its space is limited to about 550. It is always well patronised and often crowded. In March 1916 the Y.M.C.A. took over the hostel, and it has been a godsend. The concerts there are crowded with grateful soldiers down from the front line. When one remembers the many distractions and temptations of Cairo, the work of the hostel is beyond all praise.

Right in the centre of Cairo are the Esbekiyeh Gardens—a cool and refreshing haven from the dust and heat of the city. Here among the trees and flowers and purling fountains the soldier finds recreation and rest. Last year the daily average attendance at the Esbekiyeh

Y.M.C.A. was over 1500. There is an open-air concert stage, buffet, reading- and writing-room, roller-skating rink, and an inquiry bureau. This centre has been about three years in operation and deserves well of the army and of the Empire.

All over Sinai and Palestine I have encountered the Red Triangle; its ramifications are extraordinary. The canteen work alone is a great business enterprise. In Cairo and Alexandria tens of thousands of convalescents have been entertained at concerts, sports, and sight-seeing, and with refreshments. And the little Y.M.C.A. tents and marquees follow the men right up to the firing line, where they are most needed, where the everlasting bully beef and biscuits are hated cordially, and where a change of diet, got from the canteen, is thrice welcome. Once, out near the Wadi Ghuzzie, after the second battle of Gaza, I stumbled across a heap of stores, dumped unceremoniously on the plain, and near by was the Y.M.C.A. secretary selling his stock to clamorous Cameliers and hungry Light Horsemen.

Do battle and the imminence of death make men more religious? The question has often been asked. It is difficult to gauge the thoughts of others and presumptuous to pretend to portray the soul of the soldier. Yet I dare affirm that battle makes no noticeable difference to the average Australian soldier. He goes laughing or singing or swearing into battle just as he goes about his ordinary work. So I am inclined to answer the question in the negative. After battle there is an obvious sense of relief and gratitude for coming out scathless, but it is rarely expressed. Still one *feels it*.

Does camp life tend to improve men, or the reverse? This question also is often asked. Admittedly war brings out the best and the worst in men. The one great act of patriotism and self-sacrifice would seem to more than compensate for all minor faults and failings. So when the Australian soldier—purely a volunteer—first goes into camp, he has made the great decision and offered his life for his country and freedom. It is his great hour of self-sacrifice; he is at that hour probably a better man than ever before.

Then come the weeks and months and years of soldiering far removed from home and restraining moral force. For many weary months—as in the Sinai Campaign—there is never the sight of a woman's face, never a softening or uplifting influence. Is it to be wondered that men grow coarse, that their manners and their language deteriorate? Almost the only relaxation they find is in gambling. Home folks will never believe to what an extent the gambling craze has captured the army in Egypt. It has been said that the first thing the Australians did in the Holy Land was to start a 'Two-up School.' Old hands on the transports and hospital ships make hundreds of pounds at the expense of soldiers coming to and from the war. Bookmakers and others at Tel el Kebir made thousands of pounds at 'Crown and Anchor' and 'Two-up' and other games out of the Australian soldiers.

Many of these spielers boasted of the amounts they had cabled home to Australia to supplement their banking accounts Every payday in Palestine or Sinai or Egypt every camp was the signal for 'Two-up Schools' to start working, and thoughtless youths time and again lost the money that should have kept them in little luxuries to vary the bully-beef diet. It would be interesting to compute how many thousands of pounds changed hands in this way in the A.I.F. "Stop it?" As well attempt to stop the flow of the Nile.

If a hundred soldiers taken at random were asked the question, "What effect has soldiering had on your character?" I think the majority would honestly say it had not improved them. They would probably claim a wider knowledge of countries and men and life generally, and a broader charity and forbearance for the actions and opinions and beliefs of others. But I fear they would acknowledge a loss of ideals once held sacred, a too generous toleration of evil, a want of sympathy with strict rules of conduct and duty, and a cynical indifference to religion. This, of course, is only a phase. It will pass. But it is right here that the spiritual side of the Y.M.C.A. activities have been most valuable. It hag, against great odds, fought all along the line for clean living and clean thinking and clean speech, for noble ideals, and a maintenance of the standards which soldiering inevitably undermines. It is a helpful sign to see how readily the soldiers respond to the Y.M.C.A. appeal. Out in the front line the spiritual side of their nature became deadened; they sagged morally. And the measure in which the Y.M.C.A. combats this influence and inspires the soldiers with spiritual ideals is the measure of its success in this department of its work.

In his delightful story, *Barlasch of the Guard*, Henry Seton Merriman says that war leaves no man as it found him: it either hardens his heart or the reverse. I wonder what will be the final verdict with regard to the war's effect on the Cameliers. They have known the solitude of Sinai, the excitement of Egypt, the appeal of Palestine, and the lust of battle as probably no other troops have. If these distracting influences in the final phase leave them better men than when they were mere civilians, then the credit will be largely due to the Y.M.C.A.

So the Y.M.C.A. followed the army on into Palestine, to Jerusalem, and Jaffa, and the Jordan, as near the front line as they were allowed. When we were in the Wadi Ghuzzie there were a dozen Y.M.C.A. dugouts scattered along the line. Some were within a few hundred yards of the front line trenches. Here the boys came to write their home letters and see the home papers. During the heat of summer, lime-juice was served out *gratis* by day. As the nights grew cold, hot cocoa was given to the men at night. One little dugout would give out as many as a thousand cups of cocoa in one night.

The Y.M.C.A. now runs the Jerusalem Hotel in Jaffa, a splendid up-to-date soldiers' club in Jerusalem, a fine swimming-bath in the Esbekiyeh Gardens in Cairo, and scores of other propositions all calculated to help the soldiers. I wish all those public-spirited, wealthy folk back home, who give so generously to the Y.M.C.A., could realise how grateful the boys are for all these good things. We know it all costs millions sterling, and we know somebodies are footing the bill. And we're grateful.

CHAPTER 25

Camel Races

"War is Hell."
So said the American general. Perhaps he is right.
Still, war is not all Hell. Some phases of war are quite the reverse. So in the dim and distant future, when the boys go marching home, they will tell tall travellers' tales of the strange cities they have seen, and in these peaceful times to be, the Cameliers will forgather and talk about the sports they held in Egypt and Sinai and Palestine.

Mange and sore backs and debility, and the other ills camelflesh is heir to, were specially preordained by a beneficent Providence in order to periodically withdraw the Camel Brigade from active warfare, so as to enable the Cameliers to satisfy their lust for sport. Hence the Camel Brigade sports have become an institution. The first big meeting was held at El Arish in February 1917, what time the Hun airmen proved themselves the only decent sports in the whole German Army by paying a friendly visit. The second combined sports were held at Rafa in September the same year, when the Pennant was first made a bone of contention, and was carried off in triumph by the 2nd Battalion. Other minor gatherings have been staged by isolated companies at Assiut and Kubri, while the Reds retained pleasant recollections of the Ismailian sports, attended and witnessed by a galaxy of youthful beauty from that famous seaside resort.

With such a sporting record emblazoned on their A.F.B. 122 it was only to be expected that the Camel Brigade, having fixed up such minor details as the capture of Jerusalem and Jaffa and Beersheba and Gaza, should in the spring let its fancy lightly turn to thoughts of sport. A date was fixed. But Jupiter Pluvius proved unkind. It rained for fourteen days and fourteen nights. Then the medical officer, instead of concentrating his attention on fleas, accidentally held a Sick Parade and banished a couple of companies to the wilderness. However, all obstacles were eventually surmounted, and in the fullness of time—to wit, February 1918—the Third Great Sports Meeting of the Camel Brigade eventuated, and, lest we forget to mention it later on—was an unqualified success.

If this prosaic record of events were compiled for circulation amongst the uninitiated, it would have to suffer numberless explanatory interpolations. For the stranger cannot understand the wiles of the camel or the woes of the Camelier. For instance, should a stranger or a soldier chance to scan these lines he might ask why 'Kabrit,' *alias* 'Mange Dressing,' *alias* 'Onward,' *alias* 'The Galoot,' *alias* '*Murphy*,' could only scramble home a bad second in his heat in the Camel Trot, yet could show a clean pair of heels to the whole field in the final. Macaulay's schoolboy knows who won the Melbourne Cup, and why Bill Adams won the Battle of Waterloo, but even a university degree is useless when picking the winner of a Camel Scurry. So outsiders will not appreciate the situation, and since the Cameliers all know what happened, this serves merely to refresh their memory, and to remind their children what Daddy did in the Great War.

Well, the 1st Battalion won the pennant, won it handsomely, and, in the threatening language of the chief of the Red Flashes, they will fight mighty hard before they will release their grip of it. They fought hard for it, and well deserved their victory. But every dog must have his day, and as the Black Pyramids handed over the symbol of their former glory, the Blues with one accord cried, "Our turn next! "The final points which decided the fate of the Pennant Championship for the ensuing period were:

1st Battalion	23½ points.
4th Battalion	13½ points.
2nd Battalion	11 points.

There must always be one battalion minding the shop and cooeeing as the steamers pass, homeward bound, through the Suez Canal, so the gallant 'Thirds' were missing from the tourney. Still, they were well represented by their burly quartermaster, who assisted in the judging, and went back home fairly bristling with points for the edification of the Green Triangles.

Let not the judges, stewards, and committee say that theirs was a thankless task, for they are hereby thanked heartily and gratefully by the whole brigade for the unselfish labours which made the sports such a pronounced success. It was invidious to particularise: from the time the engineers started laying out the ground till the man with the megaphone yelled "Out!" all went well; and anyhow virtue is its own reward. Alas for poor old Newson! He was clerk of the course, and his cry of "Out!" as each successive competitor failed to clear the high jump quite tickled the crowd. Yet within a few weeks he himself was out, killed by a treacherous foe at Amman, after the Turks had surrendered.

One would like to place on record some appreciation of the splendid enthusiasm and painstaking efforts which were concentrated on the best turned-out section. Practically all the competitors were turned out fit for a King's Review. The ensemble, as the sections were lined up prior to judging, was brilliant. Right gladly will C.O's fork out the *'feluce'* (from regimental funds) for Kiwi and Blanco and paint and polish.

Once again the 2nd Battalion proved preeminent in this department. Seven and Nine being bracketed top, with Seventeen and One fighting for second place, and Four next in order of merit.

The tables were turned in the next event, for the Reds secured the first five places in the Midday Halt—the 1st Battalion H.Q. leading the four companies home.

The fickle goddess Fortune having first favoured the Seconds and Firsts, now smiled on the Fourths. The Wrestling on Camels now proved a most popular event, stubbornly contested. The 'Eighteens,' with Avard in the van, finally managed to unhorse Hamilton's bunch, leaving number Nine to fill third place. In the Indian section some strenuous scruffling resulted in 'B' section of the Bing Boys downing the 'A's.' In the Gun Competition also the same section carried off the honours, mounting their gun and dismounting with commendable celerity.

Considerable interest centred in the High Jump, but on account of the sandy nature of the ground no records were broken. Fielder finally won home, with Newman next in the list, and the Indian Singh quartet some distance back. Pretty much the same field assembled for the Hop, Step, and Jump, which Footner won with 36 feet 5½ inches, next in order being Stevens, 36 feet 4 inches, and Dunstan 35 feet 7½ inches.

With Sully and Cochrane out of the hunt, it was hard to pick the winner of the 100-yards championship. The heat winners were Shaha Khan, Bayley, M'Namara, with Hamilton and Ash running a dead heat in the last prelim. The final, however, went to Footner, who had been beaten by Bayley in the second heat. Second and third places were filled by M'Namara and Shana Khan. This event showed the battalions how to pick their relay teams, and an excising run followed. A dropped flag at a critical moment blighted many hopes. Eventually the Blues scored a splendid win, with Reds second, and the Field Ambulance third.

The outside world—lacking the advantages enjoyed by the Cameliers—has no idea how fast a camel can trot or gallop. For the first few times one sees a camel galloping nothing is more ludicrous and mirth-provoking. But much water has passed under the bridge at El Arish since first we saw camels fully extended. So we just forgot how funny it used to look, and focused our attention on their pace. The Trot was run in four heats and a final, the finalists being 'The Quack' and 'Kabrit,' 'Jamestown' and 'John Lobban,' 'Starlight' and 'Scotch Mist,' 'Strychnine' and 'Cyanide.' Most fancied were 'Strychnine,' 'Starlight,' 'Kabrit,' and 'The Quack.' The last named had beaten 'Kabrit' in the first heat, but in a subsequent try-out 'Kabrit' had shown such a clean pair of heels to 'The Quack' that the latter fell from grace. 'Strychnine' was known to be very fast, but very erratic on the post. So followers of form sent the camels to the post with 'Kabrit' and 'Starlight' favourites. Their judgment was vindicated, for amid intense excitement and the hilarious yells of successful punters, 'Kabrit' cantered home a length ahead of 'Cyanide,' with 'Starlight' third.

There were several 'Unknowns' in the Camel Scurry, and possibly some 'dark horses.' However, the cognoscenti of the Reds, remembering how 'Horace' had mopped up the opposition down on the Canal, stuck to their favourite. 'Bedouin Chief,' 'Joe,' 'Gaza,' and 'Tom Thumb' were also in request. The preliminary heats sent the following to the post for the final: 'Horace' and 'Tom Thumb,' 'Bedouin Chief' and 'Sappy,' 'Francis' and 'Poppy,' 'Bluey' and 'Gaza.' The field got away to a good start, and old 'Horace' at once showed prominently. He galloped like a champion and never looked like being beaten, finally passing the post over a length ahead of 'Tom Thumb,' 'Gaza' coming with a rush into third position.

As a mirth-provoker the Egg and Spoon Race on camels was *some* stunt. Maybe it was the pained expression on the face of the riders, or perhaps the supercilious indifference of the camels. Anyhow, the crowd yelled with delight. The winner turned up in Sergeant Floyd, with Rur Singh second.

No less diverting was the Musical Chairs. Here again the camels hardly entered into the spirit of the chase. If camels *do* think, then they must wonder why *Allah* ever permitted these Cameliers to cross the seas and make merry at the expense of the erstwhile dignified dromedaries. From the medley of shouts and music and halters and camels and sand-bags, Hargreaves captured the prize, with Connors and Foyle also securing a few *piastres*, and thirty others in the 'also ran' department.

In the Bayonet Fighting Competition some excellent teams lost many points through not appearing in full Marching Order. The prize went to No. 2 Company, with No. 9 second, and the Machine Gunners third. Considerable interest centred in the Section Area Bivouac, though the suggestion that the keenness of the contestants was due to the prize being a barrel of beer is staunchly repudiated. After carefully considering the *pros* and *cons*, the judges decided for Nos. 10, 17, and 3. If the thirst of the competitors had been taken into consideration, the result would have been far different.

From the time the idea of holding a Sports Meeting was first mooted, the hefty men of the Reds, Blues, and Blacks have been asking themselves the question, "Can we beat the Bing Boys in the tug-of-war?" The Indians thought not. However, the battalions had a very hard try to down the gunners, but failed. The final between the Blues and the Battery was witnessed by a great crowd of cheering spectators. It was a strenuous tussle, but resulted, as all previous similar contests, in victory for the Hong-Kong and Singapore Battery. The battalions have the requisite strength for the job; next time it is hoped they will settle down and train their teams solidly, and then in all probability—the Bing Boys will win again.

There was much speculation over the horse events, and considerable uncertainty. Several days before the race, fancy prices were taken about some of the hacks. In the Arab section there was a division of opinion which was settled, to the surprise of some, by 'Bint' romping home ahead of 'Mahamidiya' and 'O'Bee.' For the others. Class I., 'Asquith,' was mostly favoured, with 'Touch and Go,' 'First In,' ' Blue Spec,' and 'Chester' in some demand. Long odds had been given about 'Buster Brown,' and a well-informed clique of Red Flashes risked good *piastres* on him. Had 'Asquith' been more tractable he might have landed the prize, but just when the crowd began to yell, "Asquith, Asquith!" the doc cried, "Wait and see!" and Holland came with a fine rush and got 'Buster Brown' first past the box.

Naturally the main witticism over the Class II. event was to the effect that 'Fleas' had been scratched. But this was only a rumour. Lieut. Holland carried off the double by steering Dr. de Boer's 'Fleas' to the front, to the surprise of almost everybody.

A big field faced the starter for the 'All Comers' Officers' Pony Race, but despite the stable rumours anent the invincibility of 'Ginger,' Major Buxton's 'Mahogany' streaked home an easy winner. There were two concerts in the evening to top off the day's sport.

As a wind-up to the meeting, the G.O.C., Brigadier-General C. L. Smith, V.C., M.C., presented the prizes to the successful competitors, and congratulated them all on their prowess. The pennant, with cheers, was handed to Lieut.-Colonel G. F. Langley, and now flutters proudly in the breeze before the *wigwam* of the Chief of the Red Flashes. It will probably be presented to the Australian War Museum.

The victory of the many-named 'Kabrit' in the Camel Cup was celebrated in the following lines:

WHAT'S IN A NAME?

There was a gallant Camelier, whose name was Patsy Murphy,
And every time he told a tale, the boys said, "It's a furfy."
Now, Murphy found a camel, and he thought it was a trier;
But when he tried its paces, sure, it proved to be a flier.
So he christened it with whisky, and he called it 'The Galoot,'
And entered it to win the Camel Cup down at Assiut.
The boys were in no hurry
To back it for the scurry,
But Murphy didn't worry, for Murphy bagged the loot.

The Camel Corps swung eastward to the wilds of El Arish,
But Murphy, sure, was stony broke—all his felouce mafish.
So when the sports came round again, Pat Murphy saw his chance.
He called his camel 'Onward,' and he led the books a dance;
They'd never heard of 'Onward,' so they gave him ten to one.
But Murphy had them thinking, at the setting of the sun.
For 'Onward' proved a winner.
For the books it was a skinner;
Pat had whisky with his dinner, sure, the world was made for fun.

In course of time the 'Fighting First' went down to Ferry Post;
The boys all started training with the hacks they fancied most,
But to the sports a camel came which set the old hands guessing.
They seemed to know the animal, but not the name 'Mange Dressing.'

But Murphy wasn't far away, he risked his last piastre,
And still the camel stood to him and saved him from disaster.
It was just as he intended,
For when the day was ended,
Some camels were just splendid, but 'Mange Dressing' travelled faster.
Now, every dog must have his day, but Murphy's day lasts years.
He seems to have the luck of half a dozen Cameliers;
For when the I.C.C. camped' in the Land of Milk and Honey,
Pat Murphy and his camel won another pot of money.
We all had speedy camels that we fancied for the trot;
The 'Quack' was fast, 'Starlight' was fine, and 'Strychnine' was redhot.
But Murphy made a hit.
With his mount—now called Kabrit,'
For the wretch was simply IT; it's time the brute was shot.

CHAPTER 26

Over the Jordan

There is a well-known and stirring battle-poem beloved of the Irish, which, quoting from memory, begins like this:

Thrice at the heights of Fontenoy the English column failed,
And twice the lines of St. Antoine the Dutch in vain assailed.

This couplet has been parodied for the benefit of the Turkish *communiqué*, which claims:

Thrice at the heights of Amman the English column failed,
And twice the Hedjaz Railway, Anzacs in vain assailed.

However, the Turkish *communiqué* is not absolutely correct. Thrice indeed the right wing of Allenby's army crossed the Jordan and moved up through the mountains towards the railway. On the first occasion a flying column of Light Horse and Cameliers, supported by London infantry, was sent out to capture Es Salt, threaten Amman, and blow up the Hedjaz Railway. All this was accomplished, yet, as shall be explained, the venture was not an absolute success. The second stunt was purely a demonstration, a kind of Jeb Stewart cavalry dash, for the Anzacs had express orders not to go beyond Es Salt, not even to enter that town, for fear the Turks would make reprisals on any of the Christians there who welcomed the British. This stunt was quite successful. The third venture was rather unlucky. Shunet Nimrin—captured in the first stunt and abandoned—happened to have a double garrison, for the Turks were changing over when the British attacked. However, the splendid work of the Anzacs in the mountains, and the capture of several hundred Turks and Germans, more than neutralised this setback. The loss of nine guns is admittedly one to Abdul. 233

The Cameliers participated in the first venture only. So I leave to other and abler chroniclers the task of telling how splendidly the New Zealand Mounted Rifles and the Australian Light Horse and the London Tommies fought in the subsequent frays into the land of Gilead.

When the Turks retired north and east after the capture of Jericho, they blew to smithereens the concrete bridge over the Jordan at Ghoraniyeh. It thus became necessary to secure new crossings and establish bridgeheads before the army could move over preparatory to advancing against Amman. Perhaps some of the Anzac Engineers will tell how, in face of snipers and machine guns and big guns and a raging torrent, they swam the Jordan, threw ropes across, then made a pontoon-bridge, and finally established a safe bridgehead. Anyhow, when the Camel Brigade reached the Makhadet Ford, just north of the Dead Sea, the Engineers—what was left of them—were sitting down and smoking contentedly. So, with some persuasion, the camels crossed the swaying pontoons, fearful of the yellow current surging below, and we moved out over the Jordan, even as did the two and a half tribes of the Children of Israel many years before.

On 22nd March the crossing was forced, and the Anzacs, spreading fanwise, east and northwards, cleared out the Turks on the eastern bank; after them came the London infantry, Camel Brigade, artillery. Field Ambulances, demolition parties, and supplies. Shunet Nimrin had first to be captured, as it barred the main road up to Es Salt and Amman. So with splendid gallantry the Cockneys advanced to the assault. Behind them the artillery thundered, while the Anzac Mounted Division swung wide on the flanks, threatening the rear. Kabr Mujahid was occupied, and the road from Madeba blocked on the south. On the north the Mounteds pushed on *via* the Wadi Meidan road. The position of Nimrin was now precarious, and the garrison, fearful for their rear, soon succumbed to the attacking Londoners.

Three roads now lay invitingly before the British, and along these the army pushed towards Amman. Then the weather—which had been fine—swung round all in favour of Abdul. It rained day after day. The rough mountain tracks became almost impassable. The Walers ploughed through. Infantry struggled on up to their knees in mud, frequently fording *wadis* in spate three feet deep. Camels slithered and slid all over the place. Pack animals laden with explosives gave their drivers hair-raising thrills every minute. The Cameliers dismounted and led their mounts all the night—a night they will long remember. It is on record that one patch of mountain track was so precarious that in twelve hours the column covered less than 200 yards. Now and then a pack camel, top-heavy with explosives or ammunition, would lose its footing and topple over a precipice. Once a beast slipped and fell over the cliff, turned numerous somersaults, then to the surprise of all landed on its feet and started grazing contentedly. Then on they went in the mud, mud, mud.

In due—or overdue—course the Flying Column reached their objective. The Anzacs, with impetuous dash, charged at Es Salt, and captured the garrison amid the plaudits and thanks of the populace. Then they swept on to Amman. But the German 'planes flying over the Plains of Jericho had seen the league-long columns of horse, foot, camelry, and artillery crossing the Jordan. Reinforcements were hurriedly entrained and sent down from Damascus. If the rain had held off another day or two, all would have gone swimmingly; but the Turkish reinforcements reached Amman in time to be thrown into the firing line. Our information was that the town was garrisoned only by a few hundreds. But when our attack developed Abdul had several thousands to oppose us, and more on the way.

The demolition project was, however, persisted in. The Cameliers swung round on to the Hedjaz Railway, blew up Kissir Station, some culverts, and five miles of the permanent way. The Light Horse brushed aside all opposition, and, reaching the line, blew up the main arches of the railway bridge over the *wadi*. Unfortunately the damage done here was not beyond repair. But the stiff defence put up opposite Amman itself prevented the blowing up of the railway tunnel.

Opposed to the strong force of Turks now in Amman the Flying Column only had two companies of London Irish and a portion of the Camel Brigade, with Light Horse and New Zealand Mounted Rifles, and the Bing Boys' battery of mountain guns operating on either flank. The Turks, with a dozen guns skilfully concealed, were posted on a commanding eminence, Hill 3039, and this had to be taken. At three in the morning, in the midst of a cold, misty rain, the Cameliers—English, Scotties, and Anzacs—attacked. Creeping up under cover of darkness, they were upon the Turkish trenches before the alarm could be given. Then with a wild yell the Cameliers threw themselves upon the dazed defenders. There was fierce bayonet work, scores of Turks were killed, and the remainder threw up their hands. The first line having surrendered, the Cameliers pushed on to the second trench.

But this left unguarded a number of Turks and Germans in the front line who had yelled for quarter. With Teutonic treachery several of these grabbed the rifles they had thrown down and fired on the backs of the men who had spared their lives. In this way was Lieut. Newson killed, one of the most popular officers in the Camel Brigade. Some of the Cameliers, with 'Matt' in the van, charged right on till they reached Amman itself. But their ranks had been thinned, and Turkish reinforcements were still coming up. So they retired to the hill, dug in, and awaited developments. Then came the get-away.

CHAPTER 27

Back to the Jordan

The Indians working the Camel battery of mountain guns did splendid execution till their ammunition gave out. They swore and tore their hair, as excellent targets presented themselves and not a shell left. The O.C., however, managed to borrow a few rounds from a British battery which came up, and they resumed their work. But the German guns behind the town knew the range to a nicety, and did considerable execution among our ranks. The firing line—New Zealanders, Irish, Scots, English, Indians, and Australians—hung on to the ground they had gained till the demolition parties had finished their job. Then word came for the retirement.

Several hundred prisoners and much munitions had already been sent back to Ghoraniyeh, and the task of evacuating the wounded was proceeding apace. Now if Abdul had been really alive to the situation he might have so harried and hurried our retreat as to make it a ticklish business; but he evidently had not the slightest idea of our movements. Anticipating another attack, he was feverishly improving his defences, what time our infantry and artillery were quietly tripping back to the Jordan. Without a hitch the army meandered along the mountain tracks in long, snake-like columns, leaving the Anzac Light Horse and the Cameliers to bring up the rear.

For a day or two the Hun 'planes swarmed over Jericho and the Jordan and Shunet Nimrin, reconnoitring our movements, and at times their bombing squadrons heavily bombed our Hues. The exact damage done need not be mentioned here, but—as illustrating the luck of the game—it may be told that one bomb landed fair in a bivvy occupied by four officers. Two were killed outright, the one next them escaped scathless, the fourth had his leg blown off.

So in due course the Flying Column returned to the Plains of

Jericho. Our casualties, considering the nature of the expedition, were not numerous. The enemy, in killed, wounded, and prisoners, lost far more heavily. But the Cameliers mourn the loss of Saunderson from Westralia, Newson from England, Adolf, the brilliant footballer, from New Zealand, and several more officers and men who a week before had so light-heartedly crossed the ancient rivef.

Then it suddenly dawned on Jacko that the army which had the temerity to push so far into his territory had quietly melted away. All unmolested now, the Turk came along the same mountain roads, expecting an ambush at every boulder. Reaching the foot-hills he was finally convinced of the getaway. So he gathered his forces, and on nth April made a very determined onslaught on our bridgehead at Ghoraniyeh. But Fighting Charlie Cox's Light Horsemen, with some London infantry and machine gunners, had been just itching for Jacko to do this very thing. They lay doggo till the Turks had definitely committed themselves to the attack.

Then our artillery blazed away at known ranges and plumped unceasing salvos of shrapnel on the crowded ranks of the enemy. Machine guns in carefully chosen possies opened a devastating fusillade, while the infantry amongst the scrub added their quota. As Cromwell would have said, "*The Lord had delivered them into our hands.*" As the careless Anzacs put it, "It was a shame to take the money." The Turks halted and wavered and then turned in full retreat. This was the signal for the Light Horsemen, who raced their horses out of the *wadi* tributaries, and charged the fleeing foe.

In the attack on Nimrin and Amman the Turks, besides killed and wounded, lost over 700 prisoners and 4 pieces of artillery. In this abortive counter-attack they had nearly 400 killed alone, many wounded, and nearly 100 prisoners, while our casualties were insignificant. So said the official *communiqué*. But for every lone grave on the Jordan side or on Amman Ridge there's a broken-hearted woman way back in Australia.

As Brentomnan puts it:

There's a church bell rings down the Hawkesbury
When the night hush hovers near;
And an old boat swings on the Hawkesbury,
Longside an old worn pier.
There's an old wife dreams o'er the Hawkesbury,
By the pier and the swaying spar,

While prayer-ships swim out o'er the Hawkesbury,
To seas and strange lands afar.

There's an old camp down by the Jordan-side,
And an old bloke a-weary there
For a mate gone over the Jordan-side,
And a bivvy-sheet to spare;
For a task that films all the Jordan-side
In a mistiness of tears,
And a tale far-flung from the Jordan-side
To the Hawkesbury's listening ears.

There's a new-made grave on the Amman Ridge,
Where no limelights staked a claim,
Though some brave blood crimsoned the Amman Ridge
With the 'red' that knows the game.
But the Hawkesbury to the Amman Ridge
Is a forlorn cry and wide,
And the Bedouin prowls o'er the Amman Ridge
With the dead that the mountains hide.

An incident not unworthy of note was the exodus of Christians and others from Es Salt and the neighbourhood when our troops entered. These seized the opportunity to flee to Jericho and on to Judaea, and so place themselves under the protection of the British flag. Many leading citizens of Es Salt welcomed joyfully the advent of the British, but when they found it was only a raid on a big scale, with a return to the Jordan in a few days, they knew the Turks would deal harshly with them for their manifestation of sympathy with Britain. So they too packed up their treasures and bolted to Jericho. One disappointed citizen speaking excellent English remarked, "It took the English four years to get to Es Salt. It took them only four days to get away."

There are few things more pitiful than a people fleeing from their homes in the face of an army. Here, however, the exodus was accompanied by none of those heart-rending scenes which marked the Serbian debacle. These were mostly well-to-do people. Scores of them had horses and donkeys. Many of them, however, had just taken up their beds and walked. Long lines of refugees, carrying huge bundles on their backs, trudged steadily westward to the Jordan and on to Jericho.

Soon the ancient city was filled to overflowing. In the streets and gardens and houses were thousands of homeless, mostly women and children and old men.

The quixotic chivalry of some Cameliers was exemplified by an incident at Mujahid. A party of Bedouins, heavily laden, was making for the Jordan. But while seven or eight women of assorted ages were carrying huge bundles, about a dozen men were striding along unhampered. So the Cameliers stopped the procession, and made the poor old women drop their bundles. Several of the heftiest young men were selected, and ordered to pick up the *impedimenta*. But this was contrary to all their traditions. It was a unique experience. They demurred. But the Australians sent the women on ahead, and gently applied the boot till the astounded males grasped the situation—and the bundles. Amid derisive cheers of the Cameliers the party moved off, the scowling Bedouins labouring under the unaccustomed burdens...

Of course when they had gone on a' mile or so and were out of range of the interfering Cameliers, they promptly dropped their loads, the women resumed their proper role in the Bedouin business, and became beasts of burden again.

CHAPTER 28

Kantara

Kantara has changed. In the old days, before Romani, it was a dreary caravanserai. It is now a delight to pass through Kantara. Light Horsemen and Cameliers coming in from the never-never country in Sinai find in Kantara a refreshing oasis.

The reason for this? Simply that two Australian ladies came to Kantara. Now there are thousands of Australian ladies doing splendid war work back home, or in England, or France, or Egypt. But when the Light Horsemen start heaving bouquets about, they think first of these two ladies at Kantara. Tired troopers trekking to town, sick of the scorching sands of Sinai, find their first feed at Kantara. Dirty and travel-stained, with a week's whiskers on their sunburnt faces, they find rest and comfort and a cheery Australian welcome. There are flowers (real flowers), butter (real butter, on ice), fruit salad, and nice soft fresh bread. It's just like a breath of Australia.

Kantara is "the bridge" joining Asia and Africa. It is on the old caravan route from the East. For thousands of years the shambling camel trains from Palestine have passed through here and on to Cairo. Then, when war awakened Sinai to life and activity, Kantara began to assume the importance and dimensions of a port. The army of Egypt marched through. Then came the rebound. Sick and wounded soldiers came back through Kantara to the Cairo hospitals. When the scrapping eased up, men came through on leave. But they had to sleep on the Canal side. There was nothing to eat except the bully beef they brought with them. Men were only too glad to shake the dust of Kantara off their feet, and train for Cairo.

The need for some halfway house was early felt. Many folk thought of it, and many more spoke of it. Then on Anniversary Day, 26th January 1917, the Soldiers' Rest was opened by Mrs. William Chisholm and Miss Rainey M'Phillamy. There was one little marquee, one small spirit stove, one mule, one water-cart, one big table—quite a modest beginning, was it not? Yet already over 250,000 men have passed through. As many as 4000 soldiers have been fed and cheered in a single day, and 5000 eggs have been sacrificed between dawn and midnight. The Soldiers' Home has increased and prospered. There are now several big tents and a substantial hut. There are huge ovens and ice-chests, and bread bins and cake baskets and boilers, and about twenty-five big tables. The original staff of two has increased until now there are 30 assistants—all 'B' class men from Moascar.

Though the two cheerful pioneers do not mention it, one can readily guess at the strenuous times they had in the beginning. Trains arrived at all hours, and soldiers sauntered into the canteen for a snack. The 'Open all night' notice was not up, but men came along just the same. Sometimes for two or three days on end the ladies never had a chance to get to bed. A couple of times the tent was blown down, and dust storms made life miserable. Then came torrential rains. There were millions of mosquitoes. Water was scarce. Eggs went bad. A rush of hungry soldiers time and again cleared out the larder. But the indefatigable workers just smiled and carried on.

All the officials on the line of communication were most kind. But officialdom was as usual fairly apathetic. Miles of red tape had to be cut through. A rest hut, something more substantial than a tent, was urgently required, and there were scores and scores of empty huts laying idle at Tel el Kebir and other deserted camps. But no one would give the ladies the necessary timber. So £150 had to be paid for a little bit of timber for a hut. Wood is very dear in Egypt. Tanks were needed badly. All recognised how much they were required; but no one could give or sell them. So a couple of enterprising young Australians just sauntered off and 'found' a couple of empty tanks.

The main object of the canteen is to give a rest and a welcome and a cheap meal to all soldiers passing through Kantara. It is not confined to Australians. The men get the same food as the officers, only the men pay seven *piastres* and the officers ten. All the profits go back to the boys in the shape of more food and luxuries, and better accommodation. On one occasion word came that a whole division of Territorials was to detrain at Kantara. Mrs. Chisholm promptly wired to Cairo and Port Said for a huge stock of bread, cakes, eggs, and fruit, and the Tommies had a glorious and most unexpected feast.

Another time a perspiring orderly rushed in to say that 80 officers would be in to lunch, and could they be accommodated? The ladies smiled and said "Yes." Five minutes later another excited Tommy bolted in to say that the officers would not be in to lunch. The ladies sat down and breathed a sigh of relief. Three minutes after the 80 officers arrived. An hour later they went away well fed and happy, wondering withal why the army could not feed them as satisfactorily and graciously as these Australian ladies.

Many an Australian mother, could she see this Kantara canteen at night, would bless the motherly care of Mrs. Chisholm; and many a trooper, returning to the dangers and privations of the desert campaign, thinks gratefully of the smiling greeting and kindly welcome of the little Australian girl at Kantara.

At first officialdom was sceptical, then tolerant, then relieved, and finally enthusiastic. Nowadays when the boys are sent in from Palestine to a school at Zietoun or a rest camp at Port Said, arrangements are made for them to breakfast at Mrs. Chisholm's. And going back to the firing line, they write home paying generous tribute to the Kantara canteen. In the fullness of time this chorus of praise reached the ears of the powers that be, and the whole A.I.F. was delighted beyond measure when the official announcement was made that Mrs. Chisholm and Miss M'Phillamy had been decorated with the Order of the British Empire.

Time came when the theatre of war was shifted from Sinai to Palestine. The army moved on beyond Jerusalem and over the Jordan. And always there were men coming and going. Some were on duty, some sick, some on leave. And they all had to wait an hour or a day or a night at Jerusalem. But there was no accommodation for them. The need for a rest camp at Jerusalem was as badly felt as had been the need for one at Kantara.

So Miss M'Phillamy got busy. Once again there was the initial trouble with rules and regulations, but several generals, knowing the good work done at Kantara, put their influence into the scale. All the officers concerned were courteous and sympathetic. Only officialdom was apathetic. But in course of time the Empire Soldiers' Club was established on the outskirts of the Holy City. Miss M'Phillamy soon had everything running smoothly, and all the boys coming up from the Jordan side found a home from home and a cheery welcome. There were troubles and worries at first on account of the lack of accommodation. A dignified senior supply officer was nonplussed one hot morning when an orderly handed him an urgent message from the young lady in charge of the Soldiers' Club. It ran:

I have half a bullock and a ton of onions in my bedroom. *Please* send wood for a storeroom.

Chapter 29

Valley of the Jordan

This is the story of Musellabeh—at least one little chapter of its eventful history, for Musellabeh is as old as the ages. When the trumpets of the Israelites sounded round ancient Jericho, Musellabeh heard the clarion note echoing and re-echoing from the hills. But of its previous record the Cameliers knew nothing and cared less.

Up on the heights of Bethlehem spring had only just awakened the wild flowers to beauty. Hill and dale were clothed in a carpet of splendour. The *wadis* were ablaze with scarlet poppies. The wind that played over the Judean hills was cool and bracing, and at night it was cold enough to make the Cameliers snuggle close under their three or four blankets.

Then, skirting the walls of Jerusalem, we went by Bethany into Jericho. And down by the Dead Sea it seemed that we had dropped from winter into the cauldron of midsummer. And down in the valley by the ford where John the Baptist preached and baptized, the Camel Brigade crossed the Jordan and, climbing the Anti Lebanon range, smote the men of Amman, hip and thigh.

Coming back from their adventure—the Turkish *communiqué* called it a misadventure—in the land of Gilead, the Camel Brigade left their mounts grazing contentedly on the Plains of Jericho—not too contentedly, for the Hun 'planes bombed the area repeatedly, and did some damage now and then. On foot we therefore went forward and took over the line, stretching from the Jordan to the mountains. And there we stayed for some weeks while the summer sun scorched and blistered our faces, while enemy artillery splattered shrapnel over our lines, while flies by the million made day a misery, while venomous mosquitoes at night made us forget all about the flies, and while snakes and scorpions at all hours reminded us that there are worse things than war.

Where the foot-hills settle down on to the plain, Musellabeh rises imposingly up, the last protest of the disappearing mountains against the levelling hand of time. It was the strongest point in our line—probably that was why Jacko was so anxious to secure it. Anyhow, he made half a dozen attacks before he was finally convinced that the game was not worth the candle. He had made a few abortive attempts while the British infantry held the hill, but when the Cameliers came along early in April, the Huns reckoned it was high time the position was captured. They began—on 8th April—by subjecting the old hill to a furious bombardment. To be sure, Jacko was, during the whole month, most lavish with his shells. And because the hill was mostly rock and our fire possies were rather shallow, we had a few casualties.

Some glimpse at the topography of the place is necessary to appreciate the situation. Our trenches on the hill faced north. Running north past our right flank and on to Damascus was the old Romani Road. Right in front of the hill was a deep ravine, and from this rose the steep sides of a hill, half a mile long, known as Green Hill. Farther north and a little bit west was Brown Hill, or Beghalet. To westward rose the mountains like bastions, and here the enemy guns were nicely hidden, while their observation officers could see a man if he so much as moved a yard from his funk-hole on Musellabeh. From the mountains a dozen shallow *wadis* meandered towards the three hills, giving excellent opportunities for Jacko to sneak up and congregate in the ravine between Musellabeh and Green Hill. Away east, the plain gently subsided into the Wadi Mellahah and the River Jordan.

So it was over Green Hill and the little *wadis* that the Turks first advanced to the attack, about .a battalion strong. But the British artillery was posted in likely spots some distance behind Musellabeh, and when the first wave of the attack, about 200 strong, moved forward, our barrage swooped down and cut them off from the supports, who remained impotent behind Green Hill. Coming on, the Turks came under a well-directed rifle fire from our trenches, to which their response was feeble and ineffective. Then our barrage, shortening, poured shrapnel on to them and took all the sting out of their attack. The German guns meanwhile made excellent practice, landing salvos all along the hill in advance of the attack. Eventually the move was brought to a standstill, with the Turks in the ravine and under the brow of Musellabeh. Our guns continued to play on them, and when darkness shielded them from observation they slunk back over Green

Hill, whence they came.

When next Jacko advanced, he surely never meant to take the place. His raiders managed to effect a lodgement in our unoccupied possies low on the north-east corner of the hill. From this spot they were summarily ejected. For their venture they showed nothing but their casualties.

A subsequent demonstration, productive of no result whatever, preceded their main attack on nth April. A violent bombardment at dawn presaged the coming storm, and after a reckless expenditure of shrapnel and high explosives they came on. German officers and non-commissioned officers urged on the attackers, while German machine gunners, from vantage posts on Green Hill, concentrated a fusillade on our trenches.

Under cover of this barrage the enemy managed to negotiate Green Hill without much opposition, and got into the ravine. The telephone wires connecting our front line with our artillery were severed by the hail of shells, so our guns were silent. All unmolested, Jacko prepared for the final assault.

A company crept up the steep front of the hill, while a couple of platoons swung westward and enveloped our left wing. Here also, they enjoyed the shelter of the hillside, and were able to heave grenades, effectually attacking our left rear. M'Kenzie's section was then taken from the centre of the line to block this threatening move, and then for an hour or two there ensued a bombing duel. At first our bombs fell harmlessly over the Turks' heads, till the bombers lobbed them gently on the brow of the hill and the momentum caused them to roll nicely on Jacko ere they exploded.

Meanwhile the frontal attack developed. The Turks crept up the hill, but just as they were in position to fire at our centre they came under well-directed rifle and machine-gun fire from our right. This checked the onslaught, so the affair resolved itself into a battle of grenades at close range, each side for the most part being out of sight of the other; but our thin line of Anzacs had only a limited supply of bombs, and in places these gave out, so for luck the defenders heaved big boulders over the brow of the hill on to the hidden enemy.

There were some splendid deeds of derring do performed on Musellabeh that day. Signallers ran out and joined up the wire under a heavy hail of shrapnel. From battalion headquarters the 'soft job' men staggered laden with bombs, which, under heavy fire, they carried to the front line. Orderlies time and again ran the gauntlet carrying orders and messages to and from the firing line. Dozens of men were wounded and several were killed. Reinforcements were hurried up from the supports, and the sorely tried front line had a well-earned respite. But for hours Jacko hung round the base of Musellabeh and in the ravine. Rifle grenades let him see that we were still ready for the 'Call of Stoush,' but in dribs and drabs, risking the rifle fire from the hill, he melted away, leaving the Cameliers undisputed masters of Musellabeh.

A never-failing theme for discussion is the luck of the game. Old originals of Gallipoli and Romani and Gaza were killed on this ancient hill. During the day one solitary shell landed in the spot where battalion headquarters were camped, and it killed young Signaller W. E. Smith, who had run the gauntlet of the hill 3, dozen times, and had a score of times escaped death by a hairbreadth, only to meet his fate in a dugout far from the firing line. Lieut. A. R. Nield, known and loved as 'Ranji' by the whole Camel Corps, was killed, and every other officer on the hill at the time was wounded.

When the relief came in, we dug in deeper. At night the lads we lost were buried, the casualties were hurried off, and the old 'Doc' worked overtime. Next, morning we again awaited the onslaught, but Jacko sulked behind Brown Hill, and let his artillery vent its wrath on Musellabeh. Then for a week Abdul hardly showed his face. An odd sniper or two let fly occasionally, and a few tired Turks were seen going to and from Brown Hill and Green Hill. Out on the plain their cavalry patrols moved hither and yon. And we dug and dug and dug, and wired our front, and linked up our line, till Musellabeh was like unto Achi Baba. Of course the enemy guns blazed away at all hours of the day and night. But we never worried much; Abdul had had enough. The only things we worried about were the snakes and scorpions and spiders and the mosquitoes. But by day the swarms of flies made us forget our other ills.

Anon General Allenby came along and congratulated the Cameliers on their performance. Captain Mills, who was in command of the hill during the main attack, got a bar to his M.C., and Military Crosses were awarded to Lieuts. M'Kenzie and Holland. Several decorations were awarded to the rank and file, and the C.-in-C. proclaimed in orders that to commemorate the defence, Musellabeh would in future be known as "The Camel's Hump."

The following verses essay to portray the stunt in more picturesque language than the above account:

The Camel's Hump

They called it Musellabeh in the days of long ago.
When old Joshua and the Israelites were there;
When caravans from East and West meandered to and fro.
And the war cry of the Hebrews filled the air.
It's a bold and rugged mountain, rising sheer above the plain
Like a camel to its belly bogged in mud;
And the hill was red with poppies in the Springtime after rain.
But today the hill is redder far—with blood.

Oh! the new crusading Anzacs crossed the Jordan's flowing tide, And they smote the men of Ammon hip and thigh;
They cantered into Jericho, and took it in their stride,
And charged the Hun with murder in their eye.
Then the little English Tommies, trudging gamely through the heat,
Took the foot-hills of the Lebanon and stayed;
They camped on Musellabeh, with the Turk in full retreat.
And they shelled him—lest his going be delayed.

Oh! the Camel Corps swung northward with the Dead Sea far behind,
Left the camels grazing happy in the rear;
They took over Musellabeh, which the Tommies said was kind,
For it wasn't very healthy living there.
Then 'Jacko' came in thousands, Musellabeh to regain,
With his horsemen, footmen, airmen, and his guns.
And the battle raged with fury as he charged across the plain.
Food for slaughter, at the bidding of the Huns.

German gunners in the highlands loosed their wrath upon the hill.
The ground was rent and shattered with their shells;
And the thinning Camel phalanx yelled a fierce defiance till
Their dying groans were mingled with their yells.
They blazed away unceasing, gasping hard and gritting teeth,
They bombed till all their bombs had given out;
Then they heaved big mountain boulders on the enemy beneath.
And still retained their grip on the redoubt.

Oh! the British guns came roaring up the valley to the fight.
And their barrage fire caught 'Jacko' in the neck;
And the gunners toiled like Trojans all the day and half the night.
Till 'Abdul' quit, and handed in his check.
Then the Camels took a breather, and they gathered up the slain,

Tho' they wished that every Turk had been a Hun;
For they rather like old 'Jacko,' and they hate to give him pain.
But war is war—and battles must be won.
Oh! Allenby came smiling o'er the hills of Palestine,
And victory came hot upon his track.
He sent congratulations to the Camels—said 'twas fine;
Said he knew that we could keep the blighters back.
And to celebrate the battle, lest the world forget the deed,
And the day we gave the foeman such a bump.
Now and henceforth and for ever, he solemnly decreed,
Musellabeh should be called "The Camel's Hump."

The report in the official *communiqué*, however, was much more concise. It was as follows:

An attack on our right was repulsed with loss.

CHAPTER 30

Sister and Soldier

Summer swooped down with scorching wings on the valley of the Jordan. It was too hot to eat—let alone fight. So the armies marked time. Now and then a gun loosed off apologetically. No one seemed to care what happened. Someone had a spasm and cracked a joke—to wit:

Owing to the severity of the summer in and around Jericho, all *white* troops are to be withdrawn, and only the Indians and *Australians* left there.

But the Anzacs were too tired to laugh.

Up on the hills of Judaea things were not too bad; life was quite bearable. Soldiers from the line came up to Jerusalem and Bethlehem for a day's spell. Occasionally a few nurses from the Advanced Hospital motored across to see the historic and sacred places. Thus it chanced that one day Robert Blaine—now a lieutenant with a Military Cross Ribbon on his breast—jogged in on his favourite camel to Bethlehem. Perhaps it was destiny, but that very day was the one chosen by Sister Livingstone to go with a party of nurses to see the Church of the Nativity.

Now it would have been quite easy for Flora to have gone in the morning and Bob in the afternoon, or *vice versa*; and they would have escaped or at any rate postponed what happened. But Cupid had been busily watching the pair since the first big Camelier had been carried wounded into sister's ward at the 14th Australian General Hospital. And Cupid took a hand in shaping their destiny.

Bob had just handed the camel over to his orderly when he noticed the motorcar swing round the corner. And as there were nurses in the car he very naturally waited, and watched them alight. Then he caught sight of Flora, and in a few giant strides was across the road, squeezing her little hands, and rather disconcerting her by the warmth of his welcome. "Sister," he cried; "it's three whole years since I've seen you."

"Three months," she corrected demurely.

"I suppose," he replied, "that you'd say it's too obvious if I said it seemed like three centuries."

"No; I'd say you have been learning pretty speeches from the bints of Palestine."

Having disclaimed such a source of inspiration, Bob was introduced to the two nurses who accompanied Sister, and the old medical officer who accompanied them. But somehow, as they wandered through the ancient Church of the Nativity, the pair became separated from the others. And as the passages down into the crypt were narrow and ill-lighted, he instinctively took her hand in his, and so, hand in hand, humbly and solemnly like two children, they stood before the shrine where, for nearly twenty centuries, pilgrims from all over the world have bent the knee in homage to the Babe of Bethlehem.

Here, according to tradition, stood the stables hewn out of the rock, and used by travellers who stayed at the ancient Khan which, according to trustworthy evidence, did stand hereabouts in the second century. In a recess on the floor is a silver star with the inscription: "*Hic de Virgine Maria Jesus Christus Natus est*" (Here Christ was born of the Virgin Mary).

This is believed to mark the spot of the Nativity. In a manger opposite is the traditional spot where Mary and the Babe received the offerings of the adoration of the Magi. This sacred grotto contains many ancient paintings, and quaint old lamps perpetually burning.

Near by is the tomb of St. Jerome, and in a niche of the wall are little oil lamps always burning. Here an incident occurred which shocked many folk and certainly showed one Australian's absolute lack of reverence and propriety. A guide had been descanting on the various historic sites, and telling wonderful and impossible stories about each. When he came to the tomb of St. Jerome he exclaimed, pointing to a little lamp, "This light has been burning for five hundred years." And one of the listening Anzacs cried, "Well, it's high time it had a spell," and promptly blew out the light. Was it sacrilege, I wonder, or a contempt for and protest against hypocrisy and sham and commercialism that have been superimposed on the simple teachings of the lowly Nazarene?

The nurse and the soldier wandered over the famous Convent of the Nativity, which rears its castle walls high above the surrounding houses. It was built in the year 327 by the Empress Helena or the Emperor Constantine, and has suffered varying fortunes, still remaining one of the chief holy places of the world.

It is probably the oldest Christian church in the world. There are portions of the church assigned to and used for services by the Greek and Armenian Churches, while in the adjoining Church of St. Katharine, the Roman Catholic Church holds its services. Today there was a special service in the Greek Church, and the visitors congregated in the back of the church listening to the beautiful organ, and the children's voices singing the anthem. Somehow the anthem in this spot seemed more inspiring than away at the other end of the world.

The others were not in sight as the sister and the soldier emerged from the church, so they strolled round the ancient town, visiting the shops where were made the crucifixes and rosaries and various objects of mother-of-pearl and olive wood. Having selected a few souvenirs, they wandered on through the town and out to the Field of the Shepherds. Here, so tradition hath it, the angels appeared to the shepherds and told them of the birth of Jesus. There is a grotto in the field, converted into a chapel, which some devout believers have beautified with pictures of Biblical stories. There was once a mosaic on the floor of the chapel, but it has almost disappeared.

"Here it was," said Blaine, as he emerged into the open air, "that the shepherds watched their flocks, and there"—pointing above—"was the doubtless star of Bethlehem that led the wise men of the East to . . ."

For some seconds the soldier gazed with unbelieving eyes into the heavens, his sentence dying away on his lips. Sister watched him in astonishment.

"What ails you?"

"Say, honey," he demanded, "I haven't been drinking, have I?"

"No; why?" she replied.

"Well, can you see a star right overhead?"

"People don't ordinarily see stars at midday."

"So I was thinking," he concurred. "But just you look there."

Flora looked as he pointed above, and then gave a queer little cry of surprise. "Oh, I can see it plainly as anything!"

"That means I'm sober anyhow," said Bob, with a grin. Then for a while they stood silent, gazing at the phenomenon.

"Well, I'm . . ." began Bob, and finished lamely, "nonplussed. I've never seen a star before at this hour of the day. Have you?"

"Never," declared Flora.

"Oh well, that's something to talk of when we go back home; but I doubt if people will believe us. I wonder if, by any other chance, that is *the* Star of Bethlehem."

Anon they visited the Tomb of Rachel, where very probably Rachel was not buried at all, and the famous Cave of Adullam, where—possibly—David hid from the wrath of his enemies. Here it was that when David expressed a wish for a drink of water from the well where he had so often slaked his thirst when a shepherd lad, that three mighty men of valour from his bodyguard broke through the Philistine ranks and brought him the water. King David was evidently a soldier who inspired his followers with chivalrous devotion.

Here they met again the rest of the party, and proceeded by car to Solomon's Pools for luncheon. These three wonderful reservoirs are a few miles out of Bethlehem, and tradition hath it that they were built by King Solomon to supply Jerusalem with water. Archaeologists, however, ascribe the building to Pontius Pilate. However, the party enjoyed a quiet lunch there, and during the heat of the day rested in the shade of the trees on the terraces. They were gathered together, the men smoking, the girls lazily turning the pages of a guidebook, when Blaine turned to Flora and said, "There's the most beautiful sight in the world to be seen from that hill yonder. Will you come?" And Flora rose and followed him.

Hand in hand they climbed the steep ascent, he pausing now and then that she might not be fatigued overmuch. Reaching the summit they saw, below, the white houses of Bethlehem, the placid pools of Solomon, the terraced gardens and vineyards of the Judean hills, and, afar off, the spires and domes and minarets of old Jerusalem.

"Oh, but this is fine," exclaimed sister.

"Yes," he admitted, "but that is not what I came to see, I came here hoping to see the love-light in a woman's eyes, for that's the most beautiful sight in all the wide world. I'm just an ordinary Australian soldier—but I love you. I have not done anything startling or heroic in this old war—but I love you. I'll never set the Thames afire—but I love you. I've kissed girls before—you're not the first, but you are the last, and I've never before said to any girl, 'I love you.' All that is left of life I place at your disposal, for I love you. To you I shall be more loyal than to any king; more faithful than to any god, for I love you. Tell me.

Flora; do I go back to the front tomorrow just a devil-may-care Anzac, or shall I be the happiest soldier in the whole Empire?"

He took her unresisting hands in his. For a brief second she lifted her love-lit eyes to his. He caught a glimpse of the most beautiful sight in the world. Then he caught her in his arms. . . .

Away down under the trees the genial old medical officer, who had been idly scanning the hills through his binoculars, suddenly exclaimed, "Goodness gracious me!"—and promptly put his binoculars back into the case again.

L'Envoi

THE ANZAC'S FAREWELL TO HIS 'STEED.'

In the days when I was younger, when I never knew your worth;
When I thought a prancing palfrey was the finest thing on earth;
When a ride upon a camel seemed a punishment for sin,
And made a man feel fed up with the land we're living in:
It was then my errant fancy lightly turned to thoughts of verse.
And I libelled you, old Hoosta, in a wild iambic curse.
I know you now for better; but for you I might be dead.
 So I recant, old Hoosta; I take back all I said.

You have borne me late and early o'er the sands of Sinai,
When the khamseen lashed our faces and our water-bags were dry;
And in the long night marches, when I dozed and dropped the rein.
You somehow found the pathway, and you lobbed in camp again.
All through the mud and slush and mire of rain-soaked Palestine
You struggled like a hero. Now all gratitude is mine.
I once hurled maledictions at your supercilious head—
 I'm sorry now, old Hoosta; I take back all I said.

When winter nights were freezing on the hills of old Judaea,
You humped my load of blankets and a ton of surplus gear;
When summer's sun was scorching and my head seemed like to burst.
You bore a full fantassie, and quenched my raging thirst.
I have never yet gone hungry, I have never yet gone dry;
That's something to your credit in a place like Sinai.
You have been my board and lodging, you even humped my bed—
 Honest Injun! Oont, I'm grateful; I take back all I've said.

Once more I'll feel the thrill that only horses give to man.
As I canter gaily onward from Beersheba unto Dan;
I'll sense the dawn-wind's message and the mystery of the stars,

And hear again the music of the bit and snafflebars.
So it's farewell now, old Hoosta, our paths diverge from here;
I have got to be a Horseman now, and not a Camelier.
You were smellful, you were ugly. Now I've got a horse instead.
Still, you had the camel virtues, so I take back all I've said.

ALSO FROM LEONAUR
AVAILABLE IN SOFTCOVER OR HARDCOVER WITH DUST JACKET

THE 9TH—THE KING'S (LIVERPOOL REGIMENT) IN THE GREAT WAR 1914 - 1918 *by Enos H. G. Roberts*—Mersey to mud—war and Liverpool men.

THE GAMBARDIER *by Mark Severn*—The experiences of a battery of Heavy artillery on the Western Front during the First World War.

FROM MESSINES TO THIRD YPRES *by Thomas Floyd*—A personal account of the First World War on the Western front by a 2/5th Lancashire Fusilier.

THE IRISH GUARDS IN THE GREAT WAR - VOLUME 1 *by Rudyard Kipling*—Edited and Compiled from Their Diaries and Papers—The First Battalion.

THE IRISH GUARDS IN THE GREAT WAR - VOLUME 1 *by Rudyard Kipling*—Edited and Compiled from Their Diaries and Papers—The Second Battalion.

ARMOURED CARS IN EDEN *by K. Roosevelt*—An American President's son serving in Rolls Royce armoured cars with the British in Mesopatamia & with the American Artillery in France during the First World War.

CHASSEUR OF 1914 *by Marcel Dupont*—Experiences of the twilight of the French Light Cavalry by a young officer during the early battles of the great war in Europe.

TROOP HORSE & TRENCH *by R.A. Lloyd*—The experiences of a British Lifeguardsman of the household cavalry fighting on the western front during the First World War 1914-18.

THE EAST AFRICAN MOUNTED RIFLES *by C.J. Wilson*—Experiences of the campaign in the East African bush during the First World War.

THE LONG PATROL *by George Berrie*—A Novel of Light Horsemen from Gallipoli to the Palestine campaign of the First World War.

THE FIGHTING CAMELIERS *by Frank Reid*—The exploits of the Imperial Camel Corps in the desert and Palestine campaigns of the First World War.

STEEL CHARIOTS IN THE DESERT *by S. C. Rolls*—The first world war experiences of a Rolls Royce armoured car driver with the Duke of Westminster in Libya and in Arabia with T.E. Lawrence.

WITH THE IMPERIAL CAMEL CORPS IN THE GREAT WAR *by Geoffrey Inchbald*—The story of a serving officer with the British 2nd battalion against the Senussi and during the Palestine campaign.

AVAILABLE ONLINE AT **www.leonaur.com**
AND FROM ALL GOOD BOOK STORES

www.ingramcontent.com/pod-product-compliance
Lightning Source LLC
Chambersburg PA
CBHW031617160426
43196CB00006B/172